DRAMA/THEATRE/PERFORMANCE

What is implied when we refer to the study of performing arts as 'drama', 'theatre' or 'performance'? Each term identifies a different tradition of thought and offers different possibilities to the student or practitioner. This book examines the history and use of the terms and investigates the different philosophies, politics, languages and institutions with which they are associated.

Simon Shepherd and Mick Wallis:

- analyse attitudes to drama, theatre and performance at different historical junctures
- trace a range of political interventions into the field(s)
- explore and contextualise the institutionalisation of drama and theatre as university subjects, then the emergence of 'performance' as practice, theory and academic discipline
- guide readers through major approaches to drama, theatre and performance, from theatre history and sociology, through theories of ritual and play, to the idea of performance as paradigm for a post-modern age
- discuss crucial terms such as action, alienation, catharsis, character, empathy, interculturalism, mimesis, presence and representation in a substantial 'keywords' section.

Continually linking their analysis to wider cultural concerns, the authors here offer the most wide-ranging and authoritative guide available to a vibrant, fast-moving field and vigorous debates about its nature, purpose and place in the academy.

Simon Shepherd is Director of Programmes at Central School of Speech and Drama in London. **Mick Wallis** is Professor of Performance and Culture at the University of Leeds.

THE NEW CRITICAL IDIOM

SERIES EDITOR: JOHN DRAKAKIS, UNIVERSITY OF STIRLING

The New Critical Idiom is an invaluable series of introductory guides to today's critical terminology. Each book:

- provides a handy, explanatory guide to the use (and abuse) of the term
- offers an original and distinctive overview by a leading literary and cultural critic
- relates the term to the larger field of cultural representation.

With a strong emphasis on clarity, lively debate and the widest possible breadth of examples, *The New Critical Idiom* is an indispensable approach to key topics in literary studies.

Also available in this series:

DRAMA/THEATRE/ PERFORMANCE

Simon Shepherd and Mick Wallis

Routledge
Taylor & Francis Group

LONDON AND NEW YORK

First published 2004
by Routledge
2 Park Square, Milton Park, Abingdon,
Oxfordshire, OX14 4RN

Simultaneously published in the USA and Canada
by Routledge
270 Madison Ave, New York, NY 10016

Routledge is an imprint of the Taylor & Francis Group

Reprinted 2009

© 2004 Simon Shepherd and Mick Wallis

Typeset in Adobe Garamond and Scala Sans by
Keystroke, Jacaranda Lodge, Wolverhampton
Printed and bound in Great Britain by
CPI Antony Rowe, Chippenham, Wiltshire

British Library Cataloguing in Publication Data
A catalogue record for this book is available from the British Library

Library of Congress Cataloging in Publication Data
A catalog record for this book has been requested

ISBN 978-0-415-23493-1 (hbk)
ISBN 978-0-415-23494-8 (pbk)

Contents

SERIES EDITOR'S PREFACE

The New Critical Idiom is a series of introductory books which seeks to extend the lexicon of literary terms, in order to address the radical changes which have taken place in the study of literature during the last decades of the twentieth century. The aim is to provide clear, well-illustrated accounts of the full range of terminology currently in use, and to evolve histories of its changing usage.

The current state of the discipline of literary studies is one where there is considerable debate concerning basic questions of terminology. This involves, among other things, the boundaries which distinguish the literary from the non-literary; the position of literature within the larger sphere of culture; the relationship between literatures of different cultures; and questions concerning the relation of literary to other cultural forms within the context of interdisciplinary studies.

It is clear that the field of literary criticism and theory is a dynamic and heterogeneous one. The present need is for individual volumes on terms which combine clarity of exposition with an adventurousness of perspective and a breadth of application. Each volume will contain as part of its apparatus some indication of the direction in which the definition of particular terms is likely to move, as well as expanding the disciplinary boundaries within which some of these terms have been traditionally contained. This will involve some re-situation of terms within the larger field of cultural representation, and will introduce examples from the area of film and the modern media in addition to examples from a variety of literary texts.

INTRODUCTION

'Drama', 'theatre' and 'performance' all have long-established common usages. A recent insurance commercial on UK television promises that the firm will not 'make a drama out of a crisis'. We speak of 'theatres of war'. Performance, especially, shifts between areas of meaning. A child might be warned not to 'make a performance' out of a disappointment; cars are promoted and people sacked according to their claimed 'performance'; and we 'perform responsibilities'.

Through history there have been attempts to define the words. Aristotle distinguished between 'drama' and 'epic' and argued that 'drama' is the form proper to the stage. Brecht inverted that binary. Also through history people have found productive relationships between different aspects of the same word. 'Performance' now is an inclusive term covering: performance genres such as music, dance, theatre and performance art; the specific genre of 'performance art'; and a paradigm for the investigation of culture at large.

Models of drama, theatre and performance have also been deployed at different junctures by other disciplines, notably the social sciences. Dramatic shapes, especially around crisis and resolution, have provided models for the ways in which societies behave, or perform; cultures represent themselves to themselves in 'cultural performances' such as rites and ceremonies; and individual social behaviour and then identity have been thought of in terms of theatre and performance. Especially since the mid-twentieth century, there has been productive feedback between these deployments and the disciplinary field of drama, theatre and performance. And in the same period, the supposed fundamental cultural shift into postmodernity has been theorised in terms of performance and performativity.

Both the etymology of a word and its various usages can be suggestive. 'Theatre' derives from the Greek *theatron*, part of a cluster of words associated both with looking and with 'theory'. And 'theatre' designates an activity, a building and a cultural institution.

We can map the words structurally in relation to one another. In traditional Western theatre, the written drama scripts the theatrical event. And we can map them sequentially. Performance, in the sense of live art, emerged out of fine art and experimental theatre; some claim that Performance now displaces drama/theatre.

This brings us to the shape of this book. It falls into two parts, the first divided into chapters. Their sequence roughly traces the successive emergence of Drama, Theatre and Performance as academic paradigms: from the study of plays as dramatic literature; through the emergence of departments specifically committed to the study of drama and theatre; to the challenge of performance as a proposed new paradigm. The first part, then, maps the genealogy of a disciplinary field. (We should note that a similar mapping has been done specifically for the US by Shannon Jackson, whose *Professing Performance* appeared while this book was in press. She invokes Foucault to track the complex history of the various 'legitimating discourses' (p. 21) by which drama, theatre and performance have been designated areas of academic enquiry (Jackson 2004: 1–39).)

Chapter 1 looks at the establishment of Drama and Theatre as a university subject; Chapter 2 explores the place of drama within the English literary tradition, and how this influenced the study of it. Chapter 3 traces the relationship between drama and theatre and the study of history and society. Chapter 4 then deals with the concept of drama as an autonomous genre, with a definable essence and a special relationship to human nature and origins.

Chapter 5 begins the turn into our present situation. While dominant assumptions within the academy have been challenged from many directions, feminism has had the most institutional impact thus far; chapter 5 reviews some feminist arguments about both theatre and universities. Chapter 6 considers accounts of the links between contemporary Performance and the historical avant garde, and traces the emergence of poststructuralist thinking in the 1960s. Chapter 7 reviews arguments for and against regarding 'performance' as a new paradigm to displace 'theatre', as Performance Studies became established as a subject. Chapter 9 maps some of the key concepts that the new discipline has brought into play. And chapter 9 considers the complex relationships between postmodernism and performance. Chapter 10 then looks at some of the most recent ways in which the terms 'drama', 'theatre' and 'performance' have been mapped in relation to one another.

The second part, Keywords, offers genealogies of and/or debates around some key concepts. This is not intended as a comprehensive list; we have selected words that we think are most pertinent, or provocative, to an explication of the three terms that give the book its title. The invitation is to dip in and out of this part; as indeed with the book as a whole. While its first half is arranged roughly chronologically, it is not an unfolding argument. Each chapter can be read as a free-standing entity; or as part of an interlocking web of arguments.

The book offers no definitions; rather, it sets out maps and narratives. A major part of its work is to investigate what definitions, maps and narratives others have made, to what effect, and in what circumstances. Thus it is in many ways a genealogy of terms as well as of a disciplinary field. Sometimes we work with a very close focus; at others with a wider view. But we do not attempt to take a juridical overview. Rather, we pull at threads, to unravel discourses, institutional practices, and especially problematics.

The book was originally conceived by the publisher as two: *Drama and Theatre* and *Performance and Performativity*. But we argued that this would work to shore up a hierarchised binary division that needs deconstruction, and is indeed beginning to crumble. The division tends to relegate 'theatre' to literary models and the Aristotelian tradition; and to suggest a necessary coincidence between new forms of aesthetic performance, concerns with the performativity of everyday life and the theorisation of culture through the frame of performance. But the story is not as simple as this, as we hope we demonstrate. Our own position is not locked into either side of that vanishing binary, for our purpose is to set the three terms in play, rubbing against one another within specific historical circumstances.

Every book has to define its limits. Our chief narrative focus and frame mean that we have not, for instance, considered Performance in the East; tracked those other discourses beyond feminism that have challenged the exclusions of dominant Western categories, or attended much to dance. And we have not discovered sufficient material to warrant keyword entries on, say, Process or Documentation. Neverthless, we hope that the book will be of use not only in the study of drama, theatre and performance, but in all those disciplines that now use the word 'performance'.

Most words are slippery, and performance words as slippery as any. Practices too go under different names. For the sake of consistency within this book, we have adopted Nöel Carroll's suggested convention of capitalising 'Performance' to designate what might also be called 'live art', 'performance art' or 'art performance' (see p. 183).

We are especially grateful to our editors, Liz Thompson and Talia Rodgers at Routledge for their guidance, patience and persistence; to series editor John Drakakis; and to Sophie Nield for her stimulating advice.

PART ONE

A GENEALOGY

1

DRAMA AND THEATRE AS UNIVERSITY SUBJECTS

The first drama degree programme in the United States was established in 1914. The first English university drama department was founded in 1947. Why was there such a long gap? In exploring the answer to that question, we shall encounter not only different attitudes to university drama as an institution, but also different conceptions of the subject itself. This will begin our book-length process of mapping out a range of understandings of drama and theatre.

Let us start with the founding moment in England, and then return to the United States. That first department was established at Bristol. It had two main aims: 'to study drama as a living projection of a text and to tackle social problems created by rapid developments in popular dramatic entertainment'. There was no intention to train students for the theatre. They were, however, to study the subject 'not only as literature but also in terms of the arts, architecture and social conditions, of the theatre' (Wickham in James 1952: 106–7).

In large part these aims followed from the conditions which made possible the formation of the department. Internally Bristol already had enthusiasts and experts in drama in its departments of modern and ancient languages. Externally there was the presence in the city both of the Old Vic, at the Theatre Royal, with its theatre school, and the BBC;

Bristol's Vice-Chancellor was involved with both organisations. The focus on text was a development from the sort of work done in language departments; the interest in developments in 'dramatic entertainment' was more the province of the BBC. But it went beyond that. Looking back from the moment of his inauguration in 1961 as the first professor, Glynne Wickham said that, in bringing the department into existence, Bristol 'happened to give form and substance to something which in a multitude of vague, unexplored, and unexpressed ways was becoming of interest to people too numerous and too widespread to count' (1962: 44). There was a sense that, in the mid-1940s, drama was something on a larger social agenda, and the formation of a university department was meeting a social need.

As the first such department, however, there was nevertheless uncertainty about its role and remit. It had to define itself, and did so by positioning itself in relation to three points of reference. We shall look at each of these, and argue that university drama's habitual range of concerns and debates flows from its institutional positioning and history, much as the curriculum aims of the Bristol department more locally flowed from the interests of those who supported it.

The first point of reference for British university drama in the late 1940s and early 1950s was the USA (see Jackson (2004) for an account of the emergence of Theatre Studies in the context of the changing social mission of the universities). In 1912 George Pierce Baker had introduced playwriting into his English class at Harvard, and established a venue in which to perform the plays. The first drama programme leading to a degree was, however, established at the Carnegie Institute of Technology in 1914. In 1926 the first professional graduate programme was started at Yale. But although it was longer established American university drama was perceived as being rather different from what the British were trying. It was seen as more practice-oriented.

The matter had come up at a Colston symposium at the University of Bristol in April 1951. The topic was 'the Responsibility of the Universities to the Theatre', significantly explained as 'less a venture in pure scholarship than the previous symposia' (James 1952: v). One of the contributors, Sawyer Falk, described the American system. He stressed that drama was regarded as a respectable academic subject and that American departments were concerned with educating 'complete men and women' rather than producing graduates 'merely fitted for jobs'. But, while a theatre vocation was not the principal aim, he argued that it is 'no more unreasonable for drama departments to turn out practising theatre artists than for a medical school to turn out practising doctors'. Where curricula contained courses in both 'content' and 'performance', he noted a snobbery with respect to the latter. At the same time he was careful to define which crafts are proper to university study and which are not: stage design and costume but not carpentry and make-up (in James 1952: 8–11).

Now although in Falk's statement the principle of a humane education was uppermost, Tyrone Guthrie, in his introduction to the volume of seminar papers, says 'some of us were loud in disapproval of what was considered Falk's over-emphasis on practical work. . . . Dramatic technique, we maintained, is a specialist occupational study and such a study belongs not to the university, but in its elementary stages to a technical school, or, in more specialised form, to the dramatic academics.' After further discussion of the relationship of university drama to professional practice, which mainly consists of students watching it, Guthrie concludes: 'The function of the university in relation to drama, then, seems to me to be to supply a theory of drama. . . . We want from the universities a theoretic, philosophic basis to which practical activity may be related' (in James 1952: 2). Here, four years after its establishment as a university discipline, the subject is displaying the anxieties around the proper role of practice which were to remain with it. The 'loud' disapproval of Falk seems to suggest a nervousness, in the context of text-based university humanities departments, about both craft and vocational training.

Those humanities departments themselves provided a second point of reference for the newly emerging university drama. At Bristol, as we have noted, they played a part in the forming of the new department, but the link was also more generally acknowledged. One of those at the Colston seminar in 1951 was Neville Coghill, who taught English at Oxford University and was active in student theatrical production (Bentley 1948: preface). He suggested university drama could be compared both with History and with the more recently established Modern Languages and English Language and Literature. In making this comparison Coghill was trying to define the quality of mind necessary for, and developed by, study of drama at university.

He contrasts the proportions of 'rational knowledge' with 'intuitive perception' in different disciplines. In historical studies the intuitive is subordinated to the rational, which 'gives toughness and teaches accuracy and patience to the student'. The balance differs in English Literature where the proper object of study is the imaginative work of the poet rather than historical fact. Nonetheless, the study of literatures encourages 'the pursuit of an exact and detailed factual knowledge'. The meaning of a play, however, can only be discovered in rehearsal and production. Thus, 'unless a reader is endowed with a faultless three-dimensional imagination he cannot read the real style of a play off a printed page'. When he uses the word 'style' Coghill is trying to put his finger on something that marks the difference between arts and sciences. It is a slippery word, and its definition depends on something equally slippery. Style is primarily concerned with 'quality', thus 'To understand style . . . is to perceive the quality of a proposition over and above the proposition itself.' Coghill is suggesting something that is separate from the division between the factual and the imaginative: 'style' (in James 1952: 41–3).

He concludes that the study of drama must 'involve a greater number of subjective judgements not amenable to the discipline of thought in any convincing way'. It provides 'a less rigorous training than literature'. At Oxford, for example, the teaching of Medieval and Old English literatures is partly designed to guarantee 'toughness'. What detracts from this is 'pleasure', and pleasure is especially associated with drama, which is 'aimed at entertainment more whole-heartedly than non-dramatic literature'. That said, drama has 'a *particular* contribution to make within the field of literature' and needs to be understood in production. While literature in general reflects the 'perpetual flow' of human thought and history, however, dramatic literature of any excellence is 'discontinuous'. Its students can only attain 'a very patchy acquaintance with human development' (in James 1952: 45–7).

The intellectual distinctions identified by Coghill seemed to be institutionalised in the early years of the Bristol department. Looking back on those years from 1961, Wickham described how the department's syllabus moved from the study of plays and dramatists to places, scenes and machines, and then to audiences. Those who were hostile said that their objects of enquiry belonged more properly with architects, scientists, economists and social historians. 'Drama, in short, was not a subject;

simply a collection of fragments, more or less interesting', but all 'peripheral' to already existing disciplines (Wickham 1962: 46). In a later account of the development of the discipline Rose suggests that this attitude to drama led into another area of worry, namely that the more 'intuitive' engagement with performed drama was not properly academically assessable, which in turn led to imbalances in the teaching (1979: 13). Just as we observed, in the references to American departments, the apparent formation of a persisting anxiety in the discipline around practice, so again we need to observe the roots of another persisting feature. This is not so much Rose's point about assessment, though that remains important: it is instead the fixation on an apparently clear distinction between facts (textual, historical) and feeling (intuited, subjective). This connects with the idea that drama, when it is trying to be intellectually 'respectable' (Wickham's word), ceases to be a discipline. It borrows from the domains of literature, architecture, sociology, etc. without observing their intellectual protocols. It is a 'collection of fragments'. Although it has been flipped on its head, this sort of observation has persisted into the 1990s: some proponents of Performance Studies argue that the discipline's strength lies precisely in its eclectic nature.

Wickham, back in 1961, had a different answer. Describing the hostility of other disciplines he said: 'we were meeting face to face that fragmentation of knowledge, that artificial divorcing of one aspect of a subject from another, implicit in specialization, that division of a society against itself that results in anarchy'. Specialisation ignores everything a student should be interested in: 'instead of preparing himself to understand his own society, its traditions and its prospects, he is systematically isolated from it, insidiously dragooned into becoming, as a graduate, part of a governing class . . . and cut off from the larger part of society whose dreams and struggles propelled him into a university in the first place' (Wickham 1962: 48). One of the reasons for having drama on an undergraduate curriculum is that it escapes this damaging specialisation. In fact it can do, but even better, everything Coghill had claimed for literature ten years before: 'drama can treat of Western civilization as a single homogeneous tradition, not like English literature beginning more than halfway through, not artificially divided on a geographical basis like modern languages, not split in two like the self-contained worlds of modern and ancient history' (p. 50). This homogeneity, this access to wholeness through study, has a beneficial effect on the person doing the studying: 'within an arts discipline the hands can be reunited with the heart and with the head; the whole human personality working as a coordinated entity. It is no coincidence that modern psychiatry has discovered a therapeutic value in dramatic activity' (p. 51). And there is another value attached to drama study at university which is even more important – for this is welfare-state Britain in post-war reconstruction: drama 'offers a forum for the study and discussion of moral values – one of the few surviving forums left to us where the duke's interest and the dustman's can be discussed, not individually and separately, but as mutually related within the framework of society – a commonweal' (p. 53).

There is, however, more in what Wickham was saying than the enthusiasm of welfare-state democracy. There was the third of our points of reference against which new university drama was positioning itself. Wickham's argument for a curriculum that makes a psychically whole person who then recognises their social duty is an argument derived from pre-war educationalists.

In 1921, the Board of Education had set up an Adult Education Committee. Adult Education had grown from the 1880s university 'extension' movement, which sought to extend the benefits of university education to, for instance, those members of the working class interested in their self-improvement. From the Committee it commissioned a report on *The Drama in Adult Education* (1926). Representing the Board in these discussions was the amateur theatre historian, Sir Edmund Chambers. One of the witnesses, playwright and director Harley Granville Barker, said he believed the present interest was 'an endeavour not merely after self-expression, but after the far more complex co-operative expression that drama provides'. Other witnesses said that 'class work only develops one faculty, the intellectual, while the production of a play necessitates the training of the whole man' (in Rose 1979: 5). The Committee recommended to universities and local education authorities 'the promotion of classes in the literature of the drama': 'In the union of serious study under class conditions with the subsequent production of the plays studied we find drama at its highest as an instrument of education' (in Rose 1979: 5). While welcoming the School of Dramatic Study and Research at East London College (where Allardyce Nicoll worked) and the University of London Diploma in Dramatic Art, its main recommendation was that lectureships in the Art of the Theatre be established in the extra-mural departments of universities (Rose 1979: 5).

The strange status of drama – official but always external – is demonstrated at Oxford. The University had contained within itself, since the 1880s, a strong tradition of student drama (as had Cambridge), for which there was support from lecturers. But this work was, crucially, extra-curricular. Like much of the drama work nationally, the driving force came from, and was associated with, amateurs. When the University explored the viability of introducing theatre studies into the undergraduate curriculum, the *Report of the Oxford Drama Commission* (1945) concluded that it was unsuitable (Granville Barker had given the cue, by distinguishing between actors who immerse themselves and students who remain 'detached' and 'critical'). On the other hand, Oxford was very happy for drama to remain a part of its Adult Education work.

While training of the 'whole man' was the province of Adult Education, the defining qualities of undergraduate education were a focus on critical ability and specialism. The assumption about drama's suitability for the first but not the second was precisely what Wickham felt he was facing at Bristol. His move, in his inaugural address in 1961, was to turn this on its head. As we have seen he caught the spirit of his times by arguing that university education in a civilised 'commonweal' should actually be about wholeness, and the vehicle for that was drama. It set the path for departments to come. The programme for the Manchester department, founded in 1961, said that 'the drama student's education is pursued as much through the heart and the body as it is through the head'; and similarly the Hull department, 1963, said that their formal teaching was reinforced by practical work, so that 'head, heart, and hand are engaged at one and the same time' (in Rose 1979: 20, 21).

For the drama departments the Adult Education focus on the 'whole man' may have been a useful way of defining themselves within university culture. Adult Education itself still remained an outsider, however. At Leeds University there was, again, a strong amateur tradition of drama, but the initiative towards a drama department came in 1960 from George Hauger from Adult Education and Arthur Wise from Education. Their proposed syllabus put alongside work on performer, audience and genres consideration of sociology, psychology and philosophy. The University decided the time was not right for a separate department, though it compromised by funding a new fellowship in Drama. Significantly the unashamedly unliterary department envisaged by Hauger and Wise never came into being; Leeds drama became part of the English department (Kane nd: 8–12).

The Leeds case brings back to the surface something which was neatly masked by Wickham's hands-and-head rhetoric. It is the anxiety around the place within university drama of education and social commitment versus analysis of drama's art. This anxiety can manifest itself in arguments as to what the institutional place of history and textual analysis should be; and whether or not the proper study of drama should be focused on that which is both contemporary and of social 'relevance' (to use a favoured word).

The re-uniting of hands and head, the experience of wholeness, has a major attraction within the discourses of drama, because it offers to reconcile with one another the other potential oppositions we have noted: theory versus practice, distinction between facts and feeling, drama as both eclectic and collection of fragments. Yet not long after it appeared on the scene, the grounds for its credibility began to crumble. The rhetoric of wholeness came out of a long liberal Adult Education tradition, reaching back to the mission of 1880s reformist Anglicanism and its ideology of the 'whole' person. It gathered urgency to itself in the days of post-war reconstruction of a new democratic Britain. But by the early 1970s such ideas appeared to be sentiment. By the early 1980s there was in place a prime minister who declared there was no such thing as society. And one of her government's earliest acts, in 1981, was the closing down of a range of drama departments.

2

DRAMA AND THE LITERARY
TRADITION

This section surveys the contributions to dramatic theory by what is regarded as traditional literary criticism. It argues that the production of drama unsettles critical activity. Its method is to describe some of the key ideas of a series of canonical authors, while at the same time noting drama's assumed relationship, on one hand, to poetry and, on the other, to conditions of live performance. From these interrelations emerges a criticism which is not so much literary as cultural.

MINGLING KINGS AND CLOWNS: SIDNEY

One of the earliest attempts in English to account for the functioning of drama is that of the Elizabethan writer and theorist Philip Sidney (1554–86) in his *Defence of Poetry* (c.1579). The remarks on drama come as part of a general account of poetry's importance in the nation. Using an argument that derives most famously from Horace, Sidney says that poetry is an effective medium of instruction because, in contrast to philosophy, it also delights its reader or listener. The demonstration of poetry's distinctive quality, its capacity for emotional engagement, leads into reflections on the relationship between audience and artwork: 'Who readeth Aeneas carrying old Anchises on his back, that wisheth not it were his fortune to perform so excellent an act?' (1975: 41). This form of empathy is generated from the activity of reading. For a watching audience, however, the experience is rather different: tragedy 'maketh kings fear to be tyrants, and tyrants manifest their tyrannical humours; that, with stirring the affects of admiration and commiseration, teacheth the uncertainty of this world' (p. 45). Although commiseration has a place, Sidney's formula tends to suggest the dominant response to tragedy is moral.

As media for stirring admiration and commiseration, the actual plays Sidney has seen fall short of the ideal. They do so because they do not respect place and time, 'the two necessary companions of all corporal actions' (1975: 65). Audiences are being expected to accept that Asia is one side of the stage and Africa the other, or that within two hours a child is born, grows up and has a child of his own. Sidney tells us that his views on place and time accord not only with Aristotle but also with 'common reason' (1975: 65). Actually these 'unities' of place and time had been attributed to Aristotle by the sixteenth-century Italian theorist Castelvetro. For Sidney, writing in England in 1579–80, the full flourishing of late Elizabethan drama had not yet happened; his work is less a commentary on actual theatrical practices than a synthesis of major European theories. In doing the job of importing those theories into English culture, the *Defence* has a key status. But its outlook is not completely unaffected by domestic artistic practices.

For as it moves closer towards consideration of 'corporal actions', the model of poetry which effectively instructs through delight gets complicated. This becomes apparent when, having noted the failure with place and time, he argues that plays have no respect for generic boundaries: 'mingling kings and clowns . . . so as neither admiration and commiseration, nor the right sportfulness, is by their mongrel tragi-comedy obtained' (1975: 67) (only a culture that prides itself on its pedigree dogs will have problems with mongrels). The comical parts of tragedy show 'nothing but scurrility, unworthy of any chaste ears, or some extreme show of doltishness, indeed fit to lift up a loud laughter, and nothing else' (p. 67).

The actual, all too 'corporal', practice of drama, with a real audience present, takes it far away from the ideal world which is poetry, with its offer of unalloyed empathy. Poetry, the medium of reporting and describing, can avoid the impropriety and muddle which result from drama's attempts to show what cannot – or, rather, should not – be represented.

NATURE AT A HIGHER PITCH: DRYDEN

Eighty-five years later it is poetry again which figures in the title of the work on drama by the Restoration poet John Dryden (1631–1700). 'Of Dramatic Poesy: An Essay' was written in 1665–6, and, once again, it predates a major dramatic flourishing, that of the Restoration. And like Sidney's work the Essay is a synthesis of European ideas. But whereas the native drama embarrassed Sidney the bias of Dryden's work is towards the national and the contemporary. The Essay is written as a dialogue that moves through sets of oppositions: the ancient against the modern, in favour of the second, and then the French against the English, in favour of the second. Once arrived at a preference for the immediately contemporary, Dryden sets up a debate on the naturalness of language, in order to promote the value of rhymed verse. The ideal drama is, then, that which is modern, English and artistically heightened.

Rhymed verse has a specialised relationship to 'nature'. The discussion of this takes Dryden into perhaps his most interesting territory. Early on the Essay makes appropriate 'Aristotelian' noises, famously naming the Unities as such, for the first time in English. The version of Aristotle is that of Sidney, where pity and fear are replaced by compassion, concernment and a new third element 'admiration' (which Sidney took from the Italian poet and critic Minturno). But while Sidney disliked the mingle-mangle of contemporary practice, for Dryden that practice is to be valued for its own sake. In Jonson's drama he locates a concept of 'humour' not present in French drama but characteristically English. Indeed Dryden's spokesman claims the English have borrowed nothing dramatically from the French: 'our plots are weaved in English looms' (1968: 65).

The job done by this image of looms is not primarily to assert that everything they produce is good because they are English. Rather the suggestion is that what English looms produce is something which will, indeed, be English. In other words, the form of the artefact has something to do with the society in which it is produced. This idea is articulated most fully where Dryden offers the reasons why the French prefer tragedy to comedy; 'as we, who are a more sullen people, come to be diverted at our plays; they, who are of an airy and gay temper, come thither to make themselves more serious' (p. 60). The debate over the merits of the English as against the French has relativised Sidney's discussion of dramatic form, making form inseparable from the conditions of its production (even if these conditions depend on a generalised notion of national character).

While the relativising thrust implicitly departs from Aristotle's theory, the discussion of verse explicitly refutes it. Aristotle, Dryden notes, had argued that it was best to write tragedy in the sort of verse that comes nearest to prose. Dryden himself, however, says that tragedy should be written in rhymed verse, on the grounds that while comedy imitates 'common persons and ordinary speaking' tragedy is 'the representation of nature, but 'tis nature wrought up to a higher pitch' (p. 87). As he takes the argument forward, Dryden reverses Sidney's relation of poetry to drama, seeing tragedy as superior to epic poetry. And, like epic, a play 'to be like nature, is to be set above it; as statues which are placed on high are made greater than the life, that they may descend to the sight in their just proportion' (p. 88).

This paradoxical formulation – being like nature by being set above it – at a stroke makes more complex the idea of drama imitating life. It is concerned with the activity whereby imitation is seen and recognised. As Dryden well knew, the process of looking has a range of distortions in it, produced, for example, by perspective. The statue will not look like nature from below if you make it like nature. The mechanisms of watching and hearing thus play a crucial part. From here Dryden moves towards a joyously sensual account of the desiring relations between listener and dramatic form. In repartee, he says, 'the quick and poignant brevity . . . joined with the cadency and sweetness of the rhyme, leaves nothing in the soul of the listener to desire'. Like the 'shadowings' in painting it is an art which appears in order to disappear. While the roundedness of the painted object is contemplated one forgets how it comes to look round: 'while we attend to the other beauties of the matter, the care and labour of the rhyme is carried from us, or at least drowned in its own sweetness, as bees are sometimes buried in their honey' (p. 89).

THE STAGE IS ONLY A STAGE: JOHNSON

Eighty years later, however, Dryden's delight in drowning in sweetness was seen somewhat differently: 'The wits of Charles found easier ways to fame, / Nor wished for Jonson's art or Shakespeare's flame.' This assertion, although incorrect, was characteristic of an English culture which now saw the Restoration as a time of sensual abandon that needed sternly to be ended by the Glorious Revolution of 1688 in which the political initiative was taken by gentlemen of property: they invited the Dutch William of Orange to take the throne, ushered in the moral rule of Protestantism and founded the Bank of England (1694). The sensuality of the Restoration was followed by a backlash. So tragedy, that began life as something above nature itself, declined, 'crush'd by Rules, and weaken'd as refin'd' (Johnson 1971: 81). All became empty, formalist, philosophical – not passionate or natural.

This particular history of drama, which was to imprint itself on the next two centuries, was spoken from the stage on the opening night of the new theatre at Drury Lane in 1747. The speaker was the actor, and theatre manager, David Garrick (1717–79). It was in both capacities that he spoke when he shifted the responsibility for the shape of this history onto the audience:

> The Stage but echoes back the publick Voice.
> The Drama's Laws the Drama's Patrons give,
> For we that live to please, must please to live.

Pleasure now has become a matter not of individually drowning in honey but of corporately defining that which is deemed to please. And it is the job of the audience to insist that drama returns to being an imitation of nature.

Sidney's radical puritanism had deplored a form of drama that sold out to the base tastes of its audience. Dryden, writing a few years after the collapsed puritan Commonwealth, viewed the connections between form and temperament with a sort of agnostic relativism. For Garrick, however, London in the 1740s saw itself as a 'civil' society. The audience referred to itself as the 'Town', a gathering of those who had wealth and influence, but were urban gentry rather than country aristocrats. By exercising their independence of taste and judgement they were proclaiming their freedom from absolutism, tyranny and decadent artifice. The responses of this audience, the supporters of Nature's return, were of major interest to the man who wrote Garrick's script for him that opening night, Samuel Johnson (1709–84).

Johnson thought about drama and its audience mainly in connection with the work he was doing on Shakespeare's plays, of which he was preparing an edition, published in 1765. In his preface, he develops a theory about audience response. The key to Shakespeare's quality, he suggested, is that it is based in generalisation: 'His persons act and speak by the influence of those general passions and principles by which all minds are agitated and the whole system of life is continued in motion' (1969: 59). By laying this foundation, Johnson will later enable himself to explain how drama can move its audience. His argument comes from what some would see as an Aristotelian tradition. It suggests that audiences are never expected to believe in the worlds of plays: 'the spectators are always in their senses and know, from the first act to the last, that the stage is only a stage, and that the players are only players' (p. 70). How then, asks Johnson, does a play move its audience? It does so through being generalised: it represents to 'the auditor what he himself would feel if he were to do or suffer what is there feigned to be supposed or to be done. The reflection that strikes the heart is not that the evils before us are real evils, but that they are evils to which we ourselves may be exposed.' Johnson then ties these observations into a neat formulation. His suggestion is that we the audience 'rather lament the possibility than suppose the presence of misery' (p. 71).

DRAMA AND ORDER: SIDNEY, DRYDEN, JOHNSON

This scepticism about both belief and presence enables Johnson to return with renewed force to that obsessive topic in literature's theory of drama: the relationship of the staged to the written, the play and/as the poem. Sidney's version of this relationship makes clear why it is fraught with anxiety: the written text is that which is fixed. In front of an audience and their immediate demands other bits get added in, the thing becomes unfixed, fluid. And that anxiety characterises almost all theorists of drama whose milieu is writing and books. In societies where literacy is an obvious class characteristic, the vulnerability of the written draws to itself fears which are as much social as aesthetic. Thus even for Dryden drama needs to be kept in place by rhymed verse, which is 'a rule and line by which it [judgement] keeps his building compact and even, which otherwise lawless imagination would raise either irregularly or loosely' (Dryden 1968: 91).

In each case the written dramatic text emerges as a site of negotiation between constructed orderliness and forces which would challenge it. Next to no other artform analysed by the literary writer faces a similar negotiation. The problem with the dramatic text is that in most societies the point of initial publication and consumption of that text is social, the filled theatre. Not only is this not the solitary engagement between reader and written text, but the evidence of how the text is received is materially present. Sidney's contemplation of orderly dramatic form is, as it were, broken in upon by audience voices: instead of 'right comedy' there is 'some extreme show of doltishness . . . fit to lift up a loud laughter' (Sidney 1975: 67).

Laughter, a nonverbal noise, is Sidney's name for the force that destroys proportion or orderliness. The namings of this opponent of order change as do the societies of each writer. Sidney's London had seen the openings of the first commercial theatres, where the low entry price allowed in artisans and apprentices. Playgoing offered a place where people could gather without the disciplines of respect or reverence. Laughter marks that impropriety. By contrast laughter mattered less when London, after 1660, had only two licensed theatres playing to an audience that was principally drawn from the same elite group. The threat to orderly form got a different name. When Dryden discusses multiple plots he says they should be arranged hierarchically. The opposite of an organisation governed by rank and subordination is one where everything is 'coordinated': thus, for multiple plots, 'coordination in a play is as dangerous and unnatural as in a State' (Dryden 1968: 59).

Drama is the medium in which 'coordination' (or equality) in form connects with the form of the State. Thus Johnson explains that Shakespeare's plays were designed for people who 'had more skill in pomps or processions than in poetical language' (Johnson 1969: 75). A preference for the visual over the aural is a symptom of educational level: 'As knowledge advances, pleasure passes from the eye to the ear, but returns, as it declines, from the ear to the eye' (p. 75). This is a familiar literary theme, with roots going deep into the protestant culture of England, where the visual is seen as idolatrous and treacherous. It also has a class basis to it, where the upper classes are distinguished by their ability to read. At this point, despite their theoretical differences, a similarity of positions emerges: from Sidney to Johnson, the literary defenders of drama were members of a literate class. And they aimed to preserve drama's dignity by separating it from bodily spectacle. Whereas comedy can be aided by the facial grimaces of the actor, 'what voice or gesture can hope to add dignity to the soliloquy of Cato?' (p. 72). Just as Sidney's *Defence* became more panicked as he thought more closely about 'corporal' actions, so for Johnson Cato's soliloquy is at its most forceful and dignified when it has no trace of the corporal about it.

CONFUSION OF THE NATURAL ORDER OF THINGS: COLERIDGE

This tense relationship between dramatic text and its bodily performance also created problems for the poet and philosopher Samuel Taylor Coleridge (1772–1834). Earlier dramatists of England and France, like Shakespeare, he says, 'neither sought in comedy to make us laugh merely, much less to make us laugh by wry faces, accidents of jargon, slang phrases from the day, or the clothing of commonplace morals in metaphors drawn from the shops or mechanic occupations of their characters'. In tragedy the scenes were meant to affect us, 'but within the bounds of pleasure, and in union with the activity both of our understanding and imagination' (Coleridge 1985: 437). This quotation contains in it the whole of Coleridge's problem.

As an artform, Coleridge thought, drama had more potential than poetry precisely because its performance made it actual, like 'a species of actual experience' (Coleridge 1930: 1. 209). Drama can thus be a powerful mechanism for educating and reforming the mental faculties of audiences, which will in turn lead to political reform, so long as it is the right sort of drama.

When Coleridge went to see a contemporary melodrama called *Bertram*, by Charles Maturin, he watched the opening of the fourth act with horror and disgust. When Bertram entered after having committed adultery, Coleridge was horrified by the audience's enthusiastic applause.

His project of using drama to reform the public mind found itself confronted by a couple of problems: first, the plays are wrong. But second, a direct appeal to experience is not appropriate for all audiences. In a discussion of the 'moral and intellectual Jacobinism' (Jacobinism implies egalitarian and revolutionary ideals) of German drama (and melodramas such as *Bertram*) he says that 'the whole secret of dramatic popularity . . . consists in the confusion and subversion of the natural order of things', which includes 'representing the qualities of liberality, refined feeling, and a nice sense of honour . . . in persons and in classes of life where experience teaches us least to expect them' (1985: 440).

Coleridge's relationship with drama is, then, screwed up by some familiar features. Although he is committed, notionally, to the power of live performance he consistently refers to 'the reader' in his accounts of plays, and his system of analysis and evaluation depends on the sort of close verbal analysis which would be impossible as the play passes in performance. And while live performance is powerful, its audiences are the wrong class of people. In London in the early decades of the nineteenth century they came mainly from the artisan class, whose tastes and politics tended to be precisely what drama should have been reforming.

In Coleridge's case, as in that of Sidney and Dryden, literary criticism's theory of drama seems partly to be shaped, whatever its ideals, by the activities of real audiences. It is their class base, their cultural positioning, which exert different degrees of pressure on the dramatic text at its point of entering a social existence through being performed. These material circumstances of drama's practice, the real performers and audience, then make themselves felt in the fundamental definitions of what drama is. Dryden, for example, says it is 'the lively imitation of nature' (Dryden 1968: 56).

IMITATION: AN INTERLUDE

Let us pause over this formula, and gather up some of the ideas about both imitation and nature. The act of imitating (see also Keyword: Mimesis) is often supposed to encourage belief in its audience, or rather, in Coleridge's famous phrase, 'that willing suspension of disbelief for a moment, that constitutes poetic faith' (Coleridge 1985: 314). The context of this remark is, symptomatically, the act of reading: Coleridge is talking about the effect of the poems he was to contribute to the *Lyrical Ballads*. But it was a model he also applied to dramatic text. In the case of Shakespeare's characters the poet 'solicits us only to yield ourselves to a dream; and this too with our eyes open, and with our judgement *perdue* [lost] behind the curtain, ready to awaken us at the first motion of our will: and meantime, only, not to *dis*believe' (p. 459). The metaphoric language seems to indicate a private space – the curtained bed – rather than a public auditorium. And it is perhaps only that which makes Coleridge's model distinctive. For the notion of suspended disbelief has been a regular feature of dramatic theory from Sidney onwards. 'For a play is still an imitation of nature' says Dryden, 'we know we are to be deceived, and we desire to be so' (Dryden 1968: 79). Even Johnson concedes: 'In contemplation we easily contract the time of real actions and therefore willingly permit it to be contracted when we only see their imitation' (Johnson 1969: 70–1).

We may note the difference between desiring to be deceived and permitting deception to happen, but in either case it is the audience that allows the play to do its work. And that work turns out to be production rather than simple reflection. Dryden says 'nature' is imitated. But when he spoke of nature at a higher pitch he implied that this was something inside, rather than outside, the play. Through such devices as its rhymed verse the play does not so much imitate nature as produce it. Coleridge, influenced by the German philosopher Kant, puts it this way: 'the French tragedies are consistent works of art. . . . Preserving a fitness in the parts, and a harmony in the whole, they form a nature of their own, though a false nature' (Coleridge 1985: 436). This idea has the potential to disentangle drama from a persistent assumption, namely that it is subservient to a world outside it which it is trying to imitate, represent or reflect.

If drama has a nature of its own, it can be free-standing. It need have no reference to a reality outside it. It may not even need performance. It is at this juncture in the history of literary criticism that drama is most firmly commandeered for the practice of private reading. Coleridge, as we have seen, approaches the play as a reader. His contemporary, the critic Charles Lamb (1775–1834), recommended that plays be read rather than acted: 'What we see upon the stage is body and bodily action; what we are conscious of in reading is almost exclusively the mind and its movements.' The materiality gets in the way. Thus Shakespeare's plays are not really 'calculated for performance on a stage' (Lamb 1903: 99).

Most notoriously, Lamb and (mainly) his sister reduced the works of Shakespeare to a series of prose tales.

Almost as notorious are the accounts of Shakespeare's characters written by the critic William Hazlitt (1778–1830). He, too, shared the preference for reading plays. But when Hazlitt criticised the contemporary stage it was on the basis that performance could actually have a valuable effect. Drama's key quality, as he saw it, is that it deals with the individual and the concrete. This enables it to engage the imagination of audiences: 'The objects of dramatic poetry affect us by sympathy' (Hazlitt 1991: 330). Because it is sympathetically engaged, the audience is taken out of itself, beyond its normal prejudices (see also the earlier views of Holcroft, in Keyword: Empathy). For the political Hazlitt, this had value in a conservative society. But the effect was blocked by the limitations of contemporary acting and staging, which were not adequate to, say, the witches in *Macbeth*. While drama's power lay in dealing with the concrete, the very concreteness of staged embodiment was clumsy and distracting. This threat of stage to word is a familiar notion, but Hazlitt modified it. He saw it as historically local. It is caused not so much by general technical inadequacy; indeed Hazlitt suggested different ways of playing tragic character, such as not always facing out to the audience. The real problem was the urge of the contemporary stage and its dramatists, including Coleridge, towards that enemy of good drama, abstraction. This urge they shared with 'the public mind and manners of the age' (p. 112). While Macbeth's character gains power from its context of superstition and primitiveness, such things, embodied in witches, look ridiculous on the modern stage. Thus the decline in effectiveness of live performance has to do with social evolution: 'The progress of manners and knowledge . . . will in time perhaps destroy both tragedy and comedy' (p. 345).

MODERN TRAGEDY: BRADLEY

Romanticism's character-centred approach to drama received its first significant modification towards the end of the nineteenth century. Through the work of the literary critic A.C. Bradley (1851–1935) the tragic hero gained importance as a site of the key conflict of a play. In doing this, Bradley opened the way towards a more psychologised reading of the dramatic person.

Bradley's standpoint grew out of a study of the theory of tragedy proposed by the German philosopher Georg Wilhelm Friedrich Hegel (1770–1831). In Bradley's 1901 lecture on this subject he identifies in Hegel a preference for the ancient tragedy of the Greeks and then starts to modify the theory so that it can address modern drama.

In Hegel's view modern tragedy replaces universal concerns with those which are merely personal. Bradley, writing near the emergence of high modernism, summarises: 'The importance given to subjectivity – that is the distinctive mark of modern sentiment, and so of modern art; and such tragedies bear its impress' (Bradley 1911: 77). Our interest in Orestes, the hero of Aeschylus' play *Libation Bearers*, derives from our sense that Orestes is identical with the ethical position or power he represents. What engages us with Hamlet, by contrast, is his conflict 'not with an opposing spiritual power, but with circumstances and, still more, with difficulties in his own nature' (p. 77). The person of modern – that is, Shakespearean – tragedy is conceived by Bradley as complex, as internally divided and shaped by 'circumstances'. An intellectual culture formed by the theories of Karl Marx and then Sigmund Freud might recognise this account of the modern person.

Bradley's correction of the value Hegel put on the personal leads to the need for 'supplements' to Hegel's theory. According to Bradley, attention to suffering was omitted. This allowed an emphasis on reconciliation at the end of tragedy which was inappropriate, for 'the very existence of the conflict . . . remains a painful fact, and, in large measure, a fact not understood. For, though we may be said to see, in one sense, how the opposition of spiritual powers arises, something in us, and that the best, still cries out against it' (Bradley 1911: 83). From here Bradley goes on to re-write Hegel's theory by arguing that the essential 'division of spirit', the tragic conflict, in which there is spiritual value on both sides, can be found in a variety of situations. As illustration, he argues that Macbeth has good, even if not morally good, qualities, which can be admired and sympathised with. What is tragic is that 'the elements in the man's nature are so inextricably blended that the good in him, that which we admire, instead of simply opposing the evil, reinforces it' (pp. 88–9). In the central tragic conflict the two opposed elements are linked together, dialectically: both in opposition yet neither worse than the other. Famously, Antigone in Sophocles' play has to choose between duty to husband and duty to brother. Bradley says this conflict is not so much in the circumstances of the tragedy as within the character, who then has to be interpreted dialectically. The conflicted character produces, in its turn, an engaged but similarly conflicted audience.

Bradley is not arguing with Hegel alone. Another figure is in the background, and is perhaps controlling the reading of Hegel. In *Shakespearean Tragedy* (1904) Bradley says Hegel's theory of drama was the most important since Aristotle. By re-writing that theory to make it appropriate to modern tragedy, Bradley seems to be positioning himself as Aristotle's successor in the modern age. And indeed, after his summary of Hegel's omissions, he notes: 'If Aristotle did not in some lost part of the *Poetics* discuss ideas like this, he failed to give a complete rationale for Greek tragedy' (Bradley 1911: 85). The modern Aristotelian notes that, while action is of course central to tragedy, in Shakespeare's greater plays 'action is essentially the expression of character' (Bradley 1983: 13).

Whereas in the Hegel lecture this character was clearly conflicted, the characters as described in *Shakespearean Tragedy* have, however, become almost tragically singular. They have a special status because of an 'intensification': 'a fatal tendency to identify the whole being with one intent, object, passion, or habit of mind. This, it would seem, is, for Shakespeare, the fundamental tragic spirit' (p. 13). What is happening here is a movement away from the conflicted, or dialectical, version of character to a concentration on a single 'tragic trait'. The similarity of this to Aristotle's 'hamartia' is pronounced; both, however, became flattened out into the simplistic idea of 'fatal flaw'. In making his move Bradley stepped aside from an interpretation that operated dialectically and encouraged a form of analysis that simply hunts down the key tragic trait: 'What then were the real moving forces of Iago's action?' (p. 185).

For many students of English Literature courses this sort of question became the stock format of college, and sometimes university, examinations. But alongside it there often appeared a different sort of question, one which emerged out of an attack on Bradley.

DRAMATIC POEMS: KNIGHTS AND NEW CRITICISM

The title of L.C. Knights' essay 'How Many Children had Lady Macbeth?' (1933) prompts readers to see Bradley's forensic psychological method as a departure from the text of the play (even though it may have been an appropriate question for a contemporary Stanislavskian performer). Knights argues for a return to what is concretely there, the words: 'Read with attention, the plays themselves will tell us how they should be read' (Knights 1946: 5). But this return to the concrete also works to close down the play's potential as a play. Although a Shakespeare play uses action and gesture, 'its end is to communicate a rich and controlled experience by means of words'. It is, in short, 'a dramatic poem' (p. 4).

That thing which has haunted literary criticism's discussion of drama, the poem, returns, and subsumes the play within itself. Knights' essay was followed a couple of years later by another influential work, Caroline Spurgeon's *Shakespeare's Imagery*. Here Spurgeon shows how it is possible to identify the major concerns of a play by attentive reading of its patterns of images. These are conceived as the verbal images of poems rather than the scenic or bodied images of the stage. Offering an accessible route into the essential meaning of a Shakespearean play, this mode of analysis privileged the verbal text and the act of reading.

In that form it spread from Shakespeare's work to all drama. Thus, for example, in Cleanth Brooks and Robert Heilman's student textbook of 1945, *Understanding Drama*, the authors argue that what distinguishes drama from mere verbal exchanges is 'not just action' but 'meaningful action'. Meaning is provided by dialogue, for 'language is perhaps our richest and most subtle means of significant expression' (1966: 11). This leads the authors to a basic definition:

> the legitimate drama is primarily an auditory art, and . . . the dialogue is its primary element. For drama, therefore, costumes, setting, and even acting itself are, finally, secondary. It is the word which is primary here; and this fact may explain why a good play retains so much of its dramatic power even when merely read in the study or the classroom.
>
> (p. 12)

The year 1945 was the heyday of a forcefully influential mode of criticism, New Criticism; Cleanth Brooks (1906–94) was one of its major practitioners. The mode is predicated on the idea that reading that is accurate enough can lead into the vision of the poet, which expresses itself in the free-standing poem, ironically distanced from the world, under no obligation to mean anything. The central importance of both this reading relationship and the non-referential artwork meant that the poem was the preferred object of attention. So when it applies itself to drama, Brooks' approach sidesteps the social event of a dramatic performance, its negotiation with a real, and multiple, audience. While Bradley was concerned with what an audience desired, Brooks and Heilman give pride of place to the quest to define the essence of the form. While Bradleianism so far enters the world of the characters that analysis can forget the precise shape of the artefact, New Criticism can be so concerned with the precise shape of the artefact that it forgets the actuality of the audience. Both approaches came to be highly influential in English literary criticism for several decades.

Marginalised by the ascendancy of these approaches are two positions which attended closely to the dramatic artefact while not ignoring its embodiedness. The first of these pre-dates Knights' attack on Bradley.

HUMAN NEEDS AND SATISFACTIONS: ELIOT

The poet T. S. Eliot's (1888–1965) first essays on drama date from 1919. In them he consciously takes issue with the literary tradition's view of the dramatic, and in particular its view of Shakespeare and his contemporaries. In the 1919 essay on Ben Jonson Eliot challenges the criteria underpinning the common assumption that Shakespeare's characters are real while Jonson's are schematic. He conceives them as not so much acting upon as fitting in with one another, as parts of a whole. In a play such as *Volpone*, there is something larger than the characters; it is not the plot that holds the play together but 'a unity of inspiration' (Eliot 1999: 155). Eliot is heading towards a position that he reiterates elsewhere, namely that the great play creates a world of its own, which has its own rules and is not to be measured according to an external reality: 'Jonson's characters conform to the logic of the emotions of their world' (p. 156).

This New Critical – or indeed Coleridgean – concept of the autonomous artwork enables Eliot in a later essay, 'Four Elizabethan Dramatists' ([1924] 1999), to dispense with the quarrel between ancient and modern drama, but on grounds very different from Bradley. What ruins modern drama, says Eliot, is an assumed distinction between drama and literature. In saying this he is not, however, anticipating Knights and the New Critics. The crucial difference is that for Eliot the text is more than words: 'Below the dialogue of Greek drama we are always conscious of a concrete visual actuality, and behind that of a specific emotional actuality. Behind the drama of words is the drama of action, the timbre of voice and voice, the uplifted hand or tense muscle, and the particular emotion' (p. 68). The poetry is embodied and it works on bodies: 'The human soul, in intense emotion, strives to express itself in verse. It is not for me, but for the neurologists, to discover why this is so, and why and how feeling and rhythm are related' (p. 46). When that interconnection of feeling and rhythm is applied to the spectator, it assumes a form of watching that is more like participation. So Eliot's idea about the way great drama works on its audience invokes not only the play's separate world but also a power that is both bodily and beyond thought. There is in Jonson's work 'a kind of power . . . which comes from below the intellect' (p. 157).

While Eliot insists on seeing the body behind Greek verse, his thinking, however, is detaching itself from the actual bodies around him. The modern world's technological accomplishments, he says, dull the responses of the working man. That same world interposes itself between Eliot and the drama he watches: 'I want a direct relationship between the work of art and myself, and I want the performance to be such as will not interrupt or alter this relationship' (pp. 114–15). The problem with 'realistic' – which is to say, for Eliot, modern – drama is that 'you become more and more dependent upon the actor' (p. 115). Somehow great drama, with its power from below the intellect, has to be prised away from the materiality of the actor.

Once again, the physical practice of performance seems to be at odds with its poetical effectiveness. Thus, in a paradoxical move, Eliot insists on the visceral quality of the dramatic text but his alienation from modernity takes him for his examples to Greek drama, the greater Elizabethan plays and the High Mass. All the examples, apart from the last, are from past societies. And High Mass is not to be watched as drama but participated in by believers. The believer does not think about it as an art. The bodily reality in Mass is conceptually necessary, as the body of Christ, which is of course at the same time physically absent as a body.

Although High Mass is not drama, there is a connection. One of Eliot's speakers in his 'Dialogue on Dramatic Poetry' puts it this way: 'drama represents a relation of the human needs and satisfactions to the religious needs and satisfactions which the age provides. When the age has a set religious practice and belief, then the drama can and should tend towards realism' (p. 49). In an age of 'fluid' and 'chaotic' beliefs, drama has to tend in 'the direction of liturgy', towards 'form' (p. 49). Eliot was writing this a year or so after the General Strike in 1926 had tested the fluidity of class relations. Dryden, five or six years after the Commonwealth, espoused a drama of rhymed verse as a way of imaging the higher nature that was the restored monarchy. Each disavowal of realism has within it a sense of the autonomous, and physical, power of dramatic worlds; and, at the same time, a need to make orderliness in the face of democratic fluidity. Each conservative standpoint has a sense of the relations between form and cultural moment. In these relations a particular need, say for orderliness, is being satisfied by the form. From this something new emerges: once you suggest that drama mediates particular historical needs you start to develop a theory of cultural production that thinks in terms of what is relative rather than absolute.

EMBODYING HISTORY AND PRESENCE: WILLIAMS

Thus it was that in the development of his influential theories of cultural production the critic and theorist Raymond Williams (1921–88) found drama such an enabling medium for his argument. We have noticed how from Sidney onwards the literary consideration of drama has been shadowed, and vexed, by drama's concrete materiality, testing its form in front of a real and multiple audience. It is precisely this quality of drama which facilitates a movement from literary criticism into what, after Williams, had to be called cultural studies.

For Williams drama differs from other literary forms. This is made clear in his thinking about tragedy. He notes a separation between tragedy as a particular kind of art and 'tragedy' as the name given to experiences of loss and death in ordinary life. He then traces the development of the artform in relation to the experience of real life. Thus of ancient Greek tragedy he says:

> Much of the creative vigour and tension of the tragedies is in this unique process of remaking the myths as particular and presently experienced

dramatic actions, yet within the organic character of the festivals, with inescapable general connections to contemporary experience and its social institutions.

(Williams 1966: 18)

The particular art always – inescapably – has its general connections. But these themselves have a specific shape. The art is 'deeply rooted in a precise structure of feeling' (ibid.).

'Structure of feeling' was a key, though regularly modified, concept. One definition of it is that

It is as firm and definite as 'structure' suggests, yet it is based in the deepest and least tangible elements of our experience. It is a way of responding to a particular world which in practice is not . . . a 'conscious' way – but is, in experience, the only way possible. Its means, its elements are not propositions or techniques; they are embodied, related feelings.

(Williams 1973: 10)

Thus for Williams what is important is not the proposition or argument posed by the artwork so much as its shape, its rhythm.

The analysis struggles not just to explain, but almost to inhabit, particularities. Thus in his work on naturalist drama Williams focuses in on the naturalist room. In the closing chapter of *Drama from Ibsen to Brecht* (1973) he argues that any precise analysis of the relationship between structure of feeling and its dramatic conventions will look at assumptions which are made about the relations 'between men and their environment': 'If we see, in its detail, the environment men have created, we shall learn the truth about them' (p. 386). Commenting on the rooms Ibsen and Chekhov require, he suggests that such settings are felt to be necessary and articulate within a specific phase of bourgeois society

in which the decisive action is elsewhere, and what is lived out, in these traps of rooms, are the human consequences. . . . To stare from a window at where one's life is being decided: that consciousness is specific, in this great early phase.

(p. 387)

The sort of room relates precisely to the historical era. But the crucial element Williams is trying to map is more slippery than this. In his essay on monologue he argues that the speech mode of soliloquy, as it is used on the Renaissance stage, is particular to its period: 'the representation of mental *process* . . . as distinct from the articulation of mental *product*' (Williams 1983: 54). In Renaissance soliloquy, 'The degrees of address . . . control much more variable and complex relations, which the modern private/public dichotomy cannot construe; indeed often literally cannot read' (p. 55). Human experience is, by implication, shaped by its own cultural moment. And part of what is doing the shaping, moving between the inherited and the new, the 'residual' and 'emergent', is drama:

> The drama of any period, including our own, is an intricate set of practices of which some are incorporated – the known rhythms or movements of a residual but still active system – and some are exploratory – the difficult rhythms and movements of an emergent representation.
>
> (p. 16)

So whether he is dealing with soliloquy, the naturalist room or tragic form in general, Williams feels able to map cultural and social change through the particular shapes and embodiments of the drama: 'I learned something from analyzing drama which seemed to me effective . . . as a way of getting through to some of the fundamental conventions which we group as society itself.' But here, just as drama seems to be positioned as a tool for doing social analysis, he qualifies the method by adding that the social analysis leads in turn to a new appraisal of the specificities of the drama – 'by looking both ways, at a stage and a text, and at a society active, enacted in them' he saw the significance of the enclosed room 'as at once a dramatic and a social fact' (p. 20).

By seeing dramatic fact as simultaneously social fact he made a major intervention. It led to the shift in critical method which he announced in that year of rebellion, 1968 (although it took another decade or so to take hold):

> A theory of kinds, which still haunts dramatic criticism, is now obviously null. Its inherent notions – of hierarchy, separation, fixed rules for each

kind – belong to a social and philosophical order built on exactly those principles. The order and the theory have fallen together. The terms that succeeded, in art as in society, were of movements.

(Williams 1973: 381)

A theory of kinds cannot properly account for the necessarily social operation of drama. To focus on that operation is to develop a consciousness of movements, of the making and re-making of social and cultural formations. Thus literary criticism is turned, via that social practice which is drama, into cultural studies.

3

HISTORY, THEATRE, SOCIETY

DRAMA, THEATRE AND HISTORY

In his ten-volume edition of the plays and poems of Shakespeare, which came out in 1790, Edmond Malone (1741–1812) included 'An Historical Account of the English Stage'. He explained that this account was necessary in order for readers to understand better both the context within which Shakespeare was writing and his distinctive achievement. In 1790 a history of the stage assumes that it is dealing with a continuous development away from barbarity towards civilization: as Malone's full title has it, its 'Rise and Progress'.

Origins

The relationship between drama, theatre and history mainly takes two forms: an 'internal' history of the theatre and its practices or an 'external' account of theatre's – or more often drama's – engagement with a larger cultural history. The internal history is divided by the value it places on literary text, as against non-literary data. Indeed, in every case the values informing the history are a part of what must be analysed.

Thus it has been argued that Malone's account is part of the process whereby properly serious theatre history was defined by the value placed on literariness. The account is an adjunct to an edition of Shakespeare. The primary business is to focus on the work of an author who by then had become pre-eminent, and to write a history which confirmed that eminence. Effaced by this strategy was an older tradition of writing theatre history.

That tradition is described in Jacky Bratton's authoritative overview, which begins with works published by James Wright in 1699 and John Downes in 1708 (to which might be added Gerard Langbaine's *Account of the English Dramatick Poets* of 1691). From these she traces two main elements – the 'playlist' giving information on play, author, date of performance, etc. and the 'annals' of theatrical doings. The authors of such works tended to be already connected with the theatre, as minor actors or prompters, and their books reflected this in their display of minute detail and re-telling of gossip and anecdote. As Bratton notes, oral as well as written tradition informs this work.

Malone fits into this story as part of the late eighteenth-century process which discriminated 'serious' bibliographical from 'trivial' theatrical information. Malone replaced anecdotes with scholarly facts. This then paved the way for the publication in 1831 of John Payne Collier's *History of English Dramatic Poetry*. For Bratton this is a key turning-point, not on its own but because of the use that was made of it. Collier was a crucial witness before the Select Committee which in 1832 looked into the state of drama. This committee, Bratton shows, was a vehicle whereby the reforming, and literary, middle class could take possession of the theatre. In doing so they discriminated high culture from low, written text from the non-written. This class manoeuvre in the early 1830s gave birth, says Bratton, to the modern approach to theatre history.

Literariness and social practices

While Malone may have dispensed with theatrical anecdote, he also did something else. His 'Historical Account' has a second part to its title: 'and of the Economy and Usages of Our Ancient Theatres'. As the account probes back to the origins, it finds not texts but a set of practices. Malone quotes Thomas Warton's observation that in the eighth century fairs played a key role for traders: 'The merchants who frequented these fairs . . . employed every art to draw the people together. They were therefore accompanied by jugglers, minstrels, and buffoons' (in Malone 1790: 5). For Malone and others the progress towards civilisation was marked by the transformation of non-verbal juggling into the poetic texts of Shakespeare. Nevertheless their histories have a sense that an account of the stage is also partly a history of social practices, of economy and usages. While the newly elevated Shakespeare text became the central reference point, lesser 'literary' texts had the status of, and fell into place alongside, documents of social history. Thus one of the earliest records, after 1600, of the playing of medieval mysteries, comes in John Stevens' *History of the Antient Abbeys* (1722). More famously William Hone described and quoted mystery plays and folk customs in his *Ancient Mysteries Described* (1823).

For Hone (1780–1842), author, publisher and political polemicist, the publication of folk customs and mysteries was a retrieval of a people's art. The texts and accounts of their entertainments offered a stark contrast to the oppressive, censoring regime of Regency England. What Hone was doing here is important for three reasons. First, he was clearly refusing the 'rise and progress' model of English culture. His medieval texts suggested a society more free than the present. Second, his work was not constrained by assumptions about literary value. Rather than aiming to tell a history of an already established canon, he treated the texts as documents of social practices. And, third, his historical activity had a conscious, explicit, purpose in relation to the present. His medieval documents challenged dominant contemporary assumptions.

These features of Hone's work inhabit an important strand of dramatic historiography. For example, the work on Restoration drama in the 1820s, the Mermaid editions of Renaissance plays in the 1880s, and, say, Montague Summers' engagement with the Restoration in the 1920s all seem to be using a previous dramatic mode in order to stretch, if not taunt, the constraints of the present. Most noticeably under pressure were ideas about sexuality and sexual practices: the general editor of the Mermaid series, Havelock Ellis, was most famous for his publications on sexuality; Summers' interest in sado-masochism was explicit (see Shepherd and Womack 1996 for all details here).

At the time the Mermaid texts were appearing a rather different form of scholarship was engaging with Renaissance drama. Very soon after graduating from Oxford, where he studied classics, E.K. Chambers (1866–1954) was giving lectures on Elizabethan literature for the

Association for the Education of Women in Oxford. In 1892 he edited Shakespeare's *Richard II* and in the same year got a job as a civil servant with the Education Board. In his spare time he was editing English classics, especially Shakespeare, for use in schools and simultaneously beginning work which would grow into the multi-volume series *The Medieval Stage* (1903), *The Elizabethan Stage* (1923) and, in 1930, two volumes on Shakespeare. In *The Medieval Stage* Chambers' concern to describe the 'dramatic' conditions led to a lengthy volume on folk drama, shifting the balance of the whole work away from the usual concentration on religious plays. Indeed Chambers seemed, as Wilson and Wilson (1956) say, to leave out the religion when he wrote about religious plays. Influenced by Frazer, and *before* the Cambridge School (see p. 58), he developed a theory of the seasonal basis to dramatic performance.

His biographers claim that Chambers was the first to describe the social and economic 'facts', 'insofar as they affect the English stage', with the opening two volumes of *The Medieval Stage* being 'the first consecutive histories we have' (Wilson and Wilson 1956: 277). His 'amateur' literary studies, beginning before English was established as a subject for study at Oxford University, seemed motivated by a drive to understand drama as the social and economic practices of a period, rather than simply being a collection of actors' anecdotes or a set of playtexts. So Chambers' historical approach took him to legal documents, letters, accounts of audiences. The object of scrutiny is dramatic practice, both as a localised deployment of techniques of the stage and as the larger customs and behaviour of a society. As a founder member of the Malone Society in 1906, and its president until 1939, Chambers presided over the publication of social documents as well as playtexts.

This was a literary approach only insofar as it worked with written documents. It was not governed by the assumptions and values associated with 'literariness', the superiority of the fictional written text, the focus on reading as opposed to doing. In part this movement from elite texts into the culture as a whole may be a reflection of Chambers' own embrace of liberal values. Later work on drama would continue not only the tradition of recovering and analysing documents of all sorts but also the proposition that drama is a key mode for understanding, and maintaining, the shared values of a society. As we shall see, however, these two elements became separated as the discipline developed and became institutionalised.

A professionalised history of facts

We approach that institutionalisation by picking up again with the sorts of history ostracised by literariness.

Roughly contemporary with Malone, the playwright Charles Dibdin the elder's (1745–1814) *Complete History of the Stage* appeared between 1797 and 1800. It continues the annals tradition in presenting detailed accounts of the business affairs of theatres and notes on performers; but it also aspires to an overarching historical narrative, beginning with ancient Greeks, and cultural relativism, comparing French and English theatre. The journalist T.J. Wooler (?1786–1853) would build substantially on this when he attempted to introduce a new mode of writing about theatre in *The Stage* (1814–17). He incorporated reviews of plays alongside historical accounts of drama and commentaries on the social milieu of contemporary theatre.

Dibdin's son, Charles Dibdin, Jr., also a playwright, produced his own theatre history. His 'Account of the Origins and Progess of the Drama in England' was part of a larger work, just as it was for Malone. But, whereas Malone's larger work was an edition of Shakespeare, Dibdin's was a survey of buildings, a *History and Illustrations of the London Theatres* (1826). He described spaces and furnishings, illustrated with plans and drawings. Growing out of the annalist's passion for detail, this was to become a specific area of focus.

In 1927 Allardyce Nicoll claimed that his overview, *The Development of the Theatre*, was the first book in English to attempt 'a summary of theatrical art from the beginnings' (p. 5). This claim alerts us to the emergence of a discrete interest in theatrical art and technique. An example of such is Richard Southern's *The Georgian Playhouse* (1948), commissioned not as a theatre history book but as part of a series of illustrated monographs on 'aspects of Georgian Architecture and Decoration'. Its author had been writing books on the technical aspects of staging plays, such as making scenery, since the late 1930s. In *The Georgian Playhouse* Southern explored the building specifically as an engine for putting on plays, describing its technical possibilities and the relationship with the audience produced by the shape and dimensions of the stage. From here flowed a series of studies of specific physical aspects of theatres, which included such works as Southern's *The Open Stage and the Modern Theatre in Research and Practice* in 1953 and Terence Rees' *Theatre Lighting in the Age of Gas* (1978).

Southern's *Open Stage* originated as a series of lectures delivered for the Bristol University Drama Department. In a self-defining gesture the new department invited a professional practitioner to lecture. But it was a move that also helped to confirm the institutional place and value of theatre history.

In the early years of the twentieth century, the growth of 'English' consolidated a focus on the literary text, which thus excluded Chambers' various searches through the documents of the Office of Revels or wherever. When drama later emerged as a university subject, it was in tension both with the textual analysis that was then fashionable in English departments and with the training done in acting schools. In terms of historiography, accounts of plays and histories of practices were poised to go down separate routes. Theatre history, maintaining its distinctness from the literary, becomes associated with the collection of documents, with archiving and description rather than with analysis and interpretation. The most famous, or notorious, example of this tendency is the work of scholars working on the Records of Early English Drama, who lift bits out of medieval written texts and offer them, neutrally, as the facts of dramatic activities (Shepherd and Womack 1996: 44; Bratton 2003: 4).

The separation between accounts of plays and histories of practices is stated early on, and fairly polemically, in the argument of A.M. Nagler's introduction to his *Source Book in Theatrical History*. Writing in 1952, he notes how the discipline of theatre history was only fifty years old. He dates it from the first lectures given by Max Hermann in the University of Berlin in 1901 (Hermann later founded *Theaterwissenschaft*, an institute for the historical study of theatre practice, in 1923). For Nagler the early initiatives were made in Germany and France. English theatre history only became institutionally conscious of itself with the founding of the Society for Theatre Research in 1948 and its publication, *Theatre Notebook*, a slim volume compared to the theatre encyclopedias of German and French scholars. The US in 1952 had, according to Nagler, no theatre history publication at all. Yet, as we have already suggested in this section, Nagler's picture of English scholarship may not look entirely correct. For instance Chambers' work on medieval drama postdates only slightly Hermann's first lecture. So too, while the French Société d'Histoire du Théâtre was founded in 1932, in 1928 the communist novelist and dramatist Montagu Slater was recovering, and writing about, the playbills and texts of English melodrama.

Insofar as Chambers and Slater were 'amateurs', Nagler was certainly right about the lack of institutional base for theatre history written in English. The insistence derives from his academic mission. He was writing in the United States, where the division between literary analysis and vocationalism still obtained. Underpinning his position is a desire very firmly to separate analysis of dramatic texts from what may more properly be regarded as theatrical history, the facts about buildings, scenic elements, censorship, etc. This insistence on the factual was, and remains, an argument for the seriousness of theatre history as a discipline, making it worthy of a formal university base.

In a different relationship between institution and social practice, however, the value of facts may derive from their application in rather than separation from social practices. Contemporary with Nagler, in postwar Britain the movement to democratise and decentralise the arts led to the planning of new theatres outside London. The new theatre architecture was to reflect the democratic accessibility of the art form. Accessibility included a re-valuing of the 'amateur'. This is demonstrated in the career of Richard Leacroft, which encompassed work both as scenic artist and as Principal Lecturer in Architecture at Leicester Polytechnic. One of his earliest works was a Special Pamphlet, *The Theatre and You* (1946), followed in 1947 by *The Theatre Royal: A plan for the drama in Leicester,* and in 1949 by a Penguin pamphlet, *Building a House.* These were works addressed to new, 'provincial' and amateur audiences. In 1958, in a short book written with Helen Leacroft, *The Theatre,* they again addressed a non-academic audience: after their survey of theatre history they note that 'much experimental work in the 1920's was carried out by groups of amateurs who built their own theatres' and they celebrate the new Questors theatre in Ealing, which will be able to break free of the limitations that had constrained theatre buildings. Amateurism connected to both democracy and innovation. The history of theatre that grew out of 1950s Britain was, then, less about the industry and its stars than about communities and experiments. In its focus on spaces in relation to real people this work clearly is very different from the abstracted, desocialised, computer modelling of theatre buildings that emerged a few decades later, in a more technocratised academy.

Remaking the discipline

By 1989 theatre history had become a 'proper' discipline. In the opening chapter to Postlewait and McConachie's *Interpreting the Theatrical Past* (1989), R.W. Vince recounts the story of institutionalisation and then identifies a 'crisis' in the discipline. He suggests there are four areas of 'concern':

> 1. the relationship of theatre history to the study of dramatic literature, 2. the relationship of theatre history to theatre practice, 3. the nature and scope of theatre history as an academic discipline, and 4. the relationship of data and historian.
>
> (1989: 8–9)

In his exposition of these areas he notes that the study of literature and theatre may be completely separate activities, though possibly overlapping in study of drama; that theatre historians are concerned with past performances rather than contemporary drama; that theatre history remains of uncertain remit as a university discipline, hovering between extremes of being central to liberal education and too subjective to be a proper discipline; and that it is improper to privilege collection of data over their interpretation.

Another thing wrong in 1989 was that it had barely caught up with feminism. Either side of the Atlantic Tracy Davis (1989) and Susan Bassnett (1989) set out prospectuses for feminist theatre history which would attend to the wider context of women's theatre work and use new types of evidence. While their impatience was very proper, however, feminist work on drama and theatre was actually going on, but institutional 'theatre history' was separate from it. By 1989 in English literature departments feminist analysis was re-writing cultural history. An approach made to the theatrical via close attention to the dramatic text established the ground for an engagement with the imagined and the felt; with ideological and fictive shapes in a culture; with desires and pleasures in their theatrical specificity (as seen, for example, in Kate Belsey's *The Subject of Tragedy* 1985). Underpinned by cultural materialism as much of this work was, it recognised the concreteness of evidential facts, about buildings, audiences, acting modes, laws. The relationship between facts and the felt was not offered as a choice, however, but a dialectic.

But the effect of institutionalisation bit another way. By 1989 it was known that puritan women led prayer meetings, women publicly cross-dressed, they engaged in pamphlet gender controversy, they prophesied and witnessed in public. If feminist cultural analysis had known more of the emergent discipline of Performance Studies it would have been able to propose what it was revealing as the basis for a re-definition of the practice of women's performance in early-modern society. But an invocation of Performance Studies itself does little to help theatre history (perhaps, indeed, the reverse). The binary between literariness and facts remains.

As a new way forward, Jacky Bratton has developed the concept of 'intertheatricality'. Modelled on intertexuality, it attempts an articulation of the relationships between theatrical texts. Crucially it goes beyond the written to look at a shared language of entertainment which includes the 'systems of the stage', genre, convention and memory. All entertainments 'within a single theatrical tradition' are interdependent, although the single performance is a moment of crystallisation (Bratton 2003: 37–8). But as Bratton notes, the problem, as ever, is accessing the non-written. By way of attempt, and illustration, she analyses playbills.

Intertheatricality reverses the process of lifting apparent facts out of their surrounding materials. It extends the notion of what a fact might be, and drops it into a continuously moving web of relationships. In a sense theatre history here is being revised by connecting drama and theatre more firmly into the layered and interlocked processes of society at large. That connection, abjured by so much theatre history, has its own range of possibilities.

DRAMA AND SOCIETY

In his radical democratic journal *The Black Dwarf,* T.J. Wooler adopted a particular technique for mocking state ceremony: in the February issue, 1817, he reports on a 'military melo drame, called the Procession' (p. 31), which is part of the 'state theatricals'. By encouraging his readers to see state ceremonies as theatre Wooler is partly stripping them of dignity. But perhaps more importantly he is suggesting that ceremonial activity is the means by which state power constructs, and maintains, its own authority. The ceremony is part of the state's daily life while being at the same time a performance. Once we view ceremonies as theatricals we see that what has been taken for granted as real life is often at the same time a negotiation between people conducted by means of performance.

Performing social life

Although Wooler's purpose in *The Black Dwarf* was satirical he had a deep interest in the theatre itself. His journal *The Stage* had tried to develop a new mode of theatre criticism, and had included essays on the theatre as an institution. But it is the identifying of the theatricality of non-theatre events which concerns us here. Contemporaries of Wooler were in their separate ways attempting to defamiliarise the dignity of the state and to develop ideological critique, as, say, in Shelley's poem *The Mask of Anarchy*. But Wooler's focus on what we might call the performative transactions of the ceremonial event led him into territory which would later be occupied by anthropologists and ethnologists.

That territory was mapped in the early twentieth century by such thinkers as Marcel Mauss and Norbert Elias. In Mauss's essay on techniques of the body (see Keyword: Embodiment) he observes that seemingly natural activities such as swimming and digging are carried out with physical techniques that are specific to particular periods and peoples. So too, Elias's account of the civilising process shows how, in the development of techniques for eating and human waste disposal, societies enact their respect for the distinction between decorum and dirt. In adopting table manners which are deemed 'correct' a person demonstrates, in almost every sense, their class. Not only are bodily techniques learnt rather than natural, therefore, but some of them also amount to performances of social competence and authority.

From here it is a relatively short intellectual step to the suggestion that all social interactions are shaped by an intention, conscious or otherwise, to construct and maintain the impression of one's self given to others. This was the theme of Erving Goffman's (1922–82) book, *The Presentation of Self in Everyday Life*, which first appeared in 1956. In his preface Goffman acknowledges the influence of an unpublished paper by Tom Burns of Edinburgh University which argued that in interactions individuals desire to guide and control the responses of others. He also acknowledged the work of the literary scholar Kenneth Burke who had attempted to describe the general rules which governed people's attempts to attribute motives to human activities. In *A Grammar of Motives* (1945) Burke employed a model which he referred to as a 'dramatistic pentad', because it consisted of five terms all loosely derived from dramatic writing: act, scene, agent, agency and purpose. These elements, in varying relationships with one another, are to be found in the attribution and explanation of human motives.

Burke described his pentad as 'dramatistic' not as 'dramatic'. Although he was using a language derived from drama, he was not concerned with drama as an artform. Similarly Goffman's language of cues and parts, routines and dramaturgical strategies was also clearly derived from drama, but was being applied to human interaction rather than an artform. By contrast an attempt to describe a sociological approach to theatre, rather than vice versa, was undertaken by Georges Gurvitch.

In 1956 Gurvitch set out a programme for what such an approach might involve. Up till then, he said, only the theatre's public had been analysed. Now other branches of study might comprise analysis of theatrical performance as 'worked out within a specific social framework', where the two frameworks of social and theatrical might clash; or the study of 'actors as a social group'; or the study of the 'functional relationship between the *content* . . . of plays and the actual social system'. Most important might be study of the '*social functions of theatre* in different kinds of society' (in Burns and Burns 1973: 77–8, original emphasis).

While theatre as such is framed within functionality, the conception of the social is significantly more dynamic. He notes the pervasiveness of theatricality in social life, the playing out of roles, the affinity of society and theatre: 'the social ceremonies, and the individual and collective roles which we play in them (sometimes without knowing it), present an astonishing analogy with what we call the theatre' (p. 72). In these observations he seems very typical of his time. Coinciding with the publication of Goffman and with the emergence of Singer's concept of 'cultural performance' (1955), Gurvitch is expressing a very 1950s interest in performance within the political everyday.

This 1950s interest in sociology and theatre helped to set a trend for, and chimed with, a number of other books which saw everyday life as a domain in which people negotiated, through daily human exchanges, for power and prestige: learning how to win friends and influence people, achieving oneupmanship, working out the games people play, to use some of the relevant phrases. In retrospect, this account of a competitive, performed everyday life coincides in the West, and the United States especially, with a sense, particularly on the left, of the evaporation of great liberal causes in the grip of a culture of conformity and commodity acquisition. In 1959 the sociologist C. Wright Mills announced the end of 'what is called The Modern Age', to be succeeded by 'a post-modern period' (*The Sociological Imagination* 1999: 165, 166).

Into this summary, however, we need also to take account of another, currently influential, approach to everyday performance, that of anthropology. Let us try to clarify the differences between the two approaches. Under the influence of Victor Turner (whom we discuss in more detail in chapter 8) anthropology analysed social events which, while not being theatrical, were still explicitly performed, such as initiation rites, wedding celebrations, funeral ceremonies. Turner coined the term 'social drama' for a particular phase of the process dealing with a conflict situation. In studying social dramas the anthropologist can reveal the values of a community. But the concept of social drama also offers a way of thinking about the work done in theatres. By contrast a sociologist such as Goffman is much less interested in what is explicitly performed and rather more interested in the concealed or unconscious performances of everyday life. Instead of producing a new model for thinking about drama, his work simply draws on the language of drama and theatre in order to analyse everyday life.

Thereafter, in the early 1970s, when Richard Schechner embraced ethnology and anthropology (see p. 119) it actually amounted to a functionalist sociological approach. And, as with Goffman and Turner, there was once again a disengagement from analysis of the formal art of the artwork. This observation brings us to a crucial point.

Society and form

There seemed to be a large gap between approaches which addressed society and those which formally analysed artworks. This gap was explained by the cultural critic Raymond Williams in 1971: formal analysis of dramatic text was done mainly in university English departments, but these were hostile to sociological approaches and especially Marxism. In exploring that hostility he noted that Marxism was weak in its ability to work in detail with the products of human imagination and consciousness. Marxism, as practised at the time, seemed to deal in mechanical generalities. In contrast the critical mode that dominated English departments, practical or 'New' criticism, dealt with very specific nuances of text. And it had no interest in addressing itself to wider social concerns. This hostility set the frame for Williams' own work. Since the mid-1950s, that period of Goffman and Gurvitch, he had been trying to reconcile sociology and practical criticism. He did it, as we suggest in chapter 2, by locating dramatic forms within a larger 'structure of feeling'. He wanted both a less mechanical Marxism and a critical analysis that was socially aware. As he described it later, in 1971, the central project was an attempt to find ways of studying structure, in particular works and periods, which could stay in touch with and illuminate particular artworks and forms, but also forms and relations of more general social life (1981: xiii–xiv).

The significance of this summary in 1971 was that Williams had now discovered, and could tell his audience about, a Marxist writer who had very similar concerns. This was Lucien Goldmann (1913–70). In the lecture printed as the introduction to Goldmann's *Racine* (1981) Williams sets the scene for his encounter with Goldmann. Here he found a concept very like his own structure of feeling: 'genetic structuralism'. Within this model the relation between 'social and literary facts' is a matter of 'mental structures', those ways of thinking which organise, simultaneously, the consciousness of a social group and the imaginative creation of a writer. These mental structures change in history; they come into being, they decline. Their mutations and interconnections across time require an account which is genetic.

Goldmann had first developed his ideas in *The Hidden God* (1955, translated into English in 1964). It declares its method as an approach to works through the 'world vision' they express. 'World vision' is defined as the conceptual extrapolation in the most coherent possible manner of the real, emotional, intellectual and even motory tendencies of the members of a group. It is a coherent pattern of problems and replies which is expressed, on the literary plane, by the creation through words of a concrete universe of beings and things.

(1964: 314–15)

There is a qualification here, though. Goldmann suggests that world vision only applies to 'great' or 'valid' works of art:

all valid literary works have an inner coherence and express a world vision; most other writings, whether published or not, are incapable – precisely because of their lack of such coherence – of expressing either a true universe or of finding a rigorous and unified literary genre.

(p. 315)

The overall task of a 'sociological aesthetic' is 'to bring out the relationship between one of the world visions and the universe of characters and things created in a particular work' (p. 316). Later, in 1967, Goldmann refined his concept of world vision as cultural activity which achieves 'a roughly coherent and significant structure, i.e. in so far as it approximates towards a conclusion *towards which all the members of a certain social group are tending*' (Burns and Burns 1973: 113, original emphasis). The suggestion that materially concrete human activity organises itself into a 'roughly coherent' structure is one which closely coincides with Williams' formulation of 'structure of feeling', which he was developing at the same time. Both models attempt to provide an overview of artistic activity in a society without losing a sense of human particularity: the concreteness of the felt and the imagined.

Williams observes that there are a number of contact points between literary and social studies: analysis of the reading (or watching) public, the history of writers as a social group, the social history of literary (or dramatic) forms. But what most excited him about Goldmann, he says, was the emphasis on *forms*. He had become convinced that

changes of viewpoint, changes of known and knowable relationships, changes of possible and actual resolutions, could be directly demonstrated, as forms of literary organization, and then, just because they involved more than individual solutions, could be reasonably related to a real social history.

(Williams 1981: xix)

He had attempted just such an analysis in *Modern Tragedy* (1966). As a model for the connections between social life and dramatic or literary forms this is very different from a narrowly conceived sociology of drama.

The alternative to that sociology, so-called practical criticism, had never been an option for Williams. When he lectured about Goldmann in 1971 he was pointing the way out of an impasse that had debilitated approaches to drama and performance. But he was not alone in his position. The early 1970s saw a shift in the relationship between social science approaches and the study of drama. Williams' lecture was published in 1972. The same year Elizabeth Burns' *Theatricality* was published. Here Burns begins from the familiar position of the 1950s, which assumes a continuity between ordinary social behaviour and performed or 'theatrical' occasions such as weddings and civil ceremonies. She then turns the argument in order to demonstrate that the activity of theatre-going is very different from the process of everyday life. In the theatre there are two simultaneous interactions, that of performer and audience and that of fictional characters with each other. These interactions are governed by different sets of conventions: the audience's agreement to allow themselves to be persuaded by the performers is governed by 'rhetorical' convention; the performed work, the fiction that aspires to be effective by seeming truthful, is governed by 'authenticating' convention. For the persuasiveness to be effective, the feeling of authenticity has to be constantly renewed. The presence of these two conventions marks the difference from everyday behaviour. Whenever behaviour appears to be composed 'according to this grammar of rhetorical and authenticating conventions' there is a sense of 'theatricality' (Burns 1972: 31–3).

Burns concedes that ordinary life draws on the same references and 'typifications' as playwrights, actors and audiences do. This, she says, is what has led to a 'dramaturgic' vocabulary being employed by social scientists. But theatre is clearly distinguished from everyday life by its 'compositional quality'. This appears in three areas: the 'doubled' interaction of the theatrical event; the acceptance in the theatre of the sort of composed behaviour which would be rejected as false outside it; the ability of theatre to state articulately 'paradigmatic values' which are normally difficult to distinguish coherently in ordinary life. Thus by drawing on perhaps more literary and linguistic concerns with rhetoric and convention, the 'sociological' approach here makes the break from previous assumptions about everyday performance. It reinstates the difference between theatre and ordinary life.

An extract from Burns' book, the crucial chapter which we have summarised here, appeared the following year, 1973, in an anthology called *The Sociology of Literature and Drama* which she edited with Tom Burns, Goffman's former colleague at Edinburgh. The introduction to the anthology incorporates a short extract from the opening to Burns' *Theatricality* which comments sceptically on the social science analogy between staged and social behaviour. It highlights in particular Goffman 'whose elaboration of this similitude in his best known work takes him through chapter after chapter dealing with "performances", "team-play", "front-stage"', etc. It then quotes Goffman's addition to the second edition of that work where he admits that 'this attempt to press a mere analogy so far was in part a rhetoric and a manoeuvre' (in Burns and Burns 1973: 23).

Taken together, Williams' 1971 lecture on Goldmann, Burns' *Theatricality* (1972) and Burns and Burns' anthology (1973) all seem to coincide with, possibly even inaugurate, a rethinking of the relationship between social science and literary and dramatic studies, which acknowledges specific difference as well as connection. At the same moment the Centre for Cultural Studies, at Birmingham University, was in its most influential phase under the leadership of Stuart Hall (from 1967 onwards) and the film journal *Screen*, launched in 1969 (and re-launched in 1971), began to publish film theory influenced by French poststructuralist Marxism and psychoanalysis.

And so to the USA

This turn towards the 'cultural' which arose from, and created, a new relationship between social science and artwork seems not to have travelled, however, across the Atlantic. For it was some years later, in 1983, that the Yale-based journal *Theater* announced the entry to the United

States of a sociological approach to theatre. This inaugural moment was followed in 1984 by John MacAloon's *Rite, Drama, Festival, Spectacle* which presented itself as 'Rehearsals Toward a Theory of Cultural Performance'. In the introduction MacAloon attempts to track the concept of cultural performance. He begins with Turner's 'social drama', moves to Singer's 'cultural performance', then to Burke's grammar of motives, then to Goffman. As may be clear, there is considerable sliding about of the categories both of everyday and of performance here. More strangely, nowhere in his overview does MacAloon mention Williams or Goldmann or Burns. His grand looking-foward to the development of the subject in the next decade is thus somewhat vitiated by his apparent ignorance of what had already been not only rehearsed but performed.

A similar but more significant omission characterises that 1983 issue of *Theater*. The issue editor, Michael Hays, introduces four essays with the observation that during the nineteenth century criticism came to focus on the dramatic text as the object of literary study. To reverse this trend he calls for an 'integrated theory and method for understanding the theater as a social institution'. The absence of such a theory and method from the Anglo-American tradition is attributed to the fact that the tradition is 'unable to free itself from the idealism that has infected all its recent avatars from Eliot to Leavis, to the new criticism, and, finally, much of the Americanized version of post-structuralist theory' (Hays 1983: 5–6). By 1983 the reaction against Leavis in British literary studies was, after some years of stridency, virtually complete. It had been fuelled by the development of a more cultural focus during the 1970s. Indeed the Anglo bit of the 'Anglo-American tradition' had seen not only the translation into English of Lukács and Goldmann but also the publication of those works by Burns and, pre-eminently, Williams. On the American side, even so, Hays had Singer's model of cultural performance to refer to, and Goldmann had been published in *The Drama Review* around 1970.

The silence around an already developed British theory of theatre as institution was filled by *Theater* with the publication in English of work by Patrice Pavis and Marco de Marinis. The latter's essay is entitled 'Theatrical Comprehension: A Socio-Semiotic Approach'. Its argument is that the audience is not only a receiver but also an active 'maker' of the performance's meaning. Semiotics, says de Marinis, has hitherto been limited by concentration on performance as 'finished product'. His essay proposes to deal with the following 'micro-levels' of reception: perception, interpretation, emotional and cognitive reaction, evaluation, memorization. But, despite its insistence that semiotic interpretation involves the work of recognising larger conventions and codes governing production of theatrical experience, the essay does not get much closer to the other aspects of the social, which, as Williams describes them in *Culture* (1981), might include institutions and social formations such as guilds, class fractions and academies, and modes of production, reproduction and dissemination.

A similar slippage away from the concreteness of the social occurs in the essay by Pavis on 'Socio-Criticism'. The term is not his own, but comes, as he acknowledges, from Claude Duchet. It aims to 'confront the approaches of sociology and formalism dialectically', a confrontation Williams had explored over ten years before. By 1983, however, Pavis has a new generation of terminology at his disposal: 'Fundamentally, socio-criticism supposes that the dramatic text carries within itself ideological contradictions more or less visible in the conflict of ideologemes or the configuration of the dramatic system' (Pavis 1983: 10).

The word 'ideologemes' is taken from Fredric Jameson's *The Political Unconscious* (1981). Here Jameson develops his own method of reconciling a larger social exploration with detailed formal analysis. Each literary text is seen as a particular utterance within and contributing to the larger statement through which a social class represents itself. Shaping the literary text and supplying its terms of reference is ideology. In this respect Jameson's work, like the overall model of socio-criticism, attributed to Duchet and other French critics of the early seventies, links back to the work of Pierre Macherey whose *Theory of Literary Production* appeared in 1966. In Macherey's model, however, the ideological contradictions of an artwork are intrinsic to its mode of production. Pavis's version, by contrast, tends to focus rather more single-mindedly simply on text and language.

In doing so it causes to vanish the primary category of *production*, which, for Macherey, is indispensable. For his is an explicitly Marxist critique, albeit derived from the (post)structuralist Marxism of Louis Althusser (which in turn so infuriated Raymond Williams). What is going on, in short, is that at its self-declared inception into the American tradition, despite Hays' acknowledgement of the previous work of Lukács and Goldmann, the sociology of theatre has effectively weakened the category of that which is concretely social and drawn a veil over the major influence of Marxism.

Drama, life and history

For Marxism has been in there all along. While Williams may have rejected its poststructuralist Parisian version, he linked himself to Goldmann, and to the figure back behind Goldmann, Georg Lukács.

While in the mid- to late 1930s Mauss and Elias were paving the way for the study of 'everyday' performance, Lukács at the same time was trying to engage with the importance of literary form within the context of social revolution. To this end most of his literary critical work was done on 'realist' texts, relating drama and novels to society. But that work was driven by a very simple and profound question. He wanted to explain why drama is important in human culture. The answer he gives, in his most extended consideration of drama, in *The Historical Novel* (originally written 1937, revised 1960), is that drama 'aims at a total embodiment of the life-process' (Lukács 1969: 106). Epic too can be said to have a similarly wide scope, but whereas epic can contain a wealth of detailed circumstances, drama works by selection. The sense of 'totality' is 'concentrated round a fixed centre, round the domestic collision' (p. 105). The collision consists of human aspirations coming into mutual conflict. By way of illustrating how an impression of totality is generated out of a selective attention to collision Lukács refers us to Shakespeare's *King Lear*: 'Shakespeare portrays in the relations of Lear and his daughters, Gloster and his sons the great typical, human moral movements and trends, which spring in an extremely heightened form from the problematicalness and break-up of the feudal family' (pp. 106–7).

Lukács' emphasis on the collision is derived, as he notes, from Hegel's theory of drama, and in particular tragedy. In Hegel and in Lukács this collision is dialectical, born out of internal contradiction and necessary to development. But, for Lukács, Hegel's approach was slightly too idealised, too separated from concrete historical process. So the move Lukács makes is to note that this collision has a particular characteristic which is stressed in all 'genuine and deep' theories of tragedy, namely 'the necessity, on the one hand, for each of the conflicting forces to take action and, on the other, for the collision to be forcibly settled.' By translating these formal aspects into 'the language of life' it then becomes possible to 'see in them the most highly generalized features of revolutionary transformations in life itself, reduced to the abstract form of movement.' It is 'no accident' therefore 'that the great periods of tragedy coincide with the great, world-historical changes in human society' (p. 111). Such changes may be observed in ancient Greek and Renaissance societies, as Engels and Marx had noted.

But, says Lukács, it would be mechanistic simply to link dramatic form and historical revolution in this narrow way. For life itself has its own dramatic shapes: 'The contradictoriness of social development, the intensification of these contradictions to the point of tragic collision is a *general* fact of life' (p. 113). And it is life that produces a (fictional) dramatic embodiment of these shapes. The mode of that embodiment is crucial to drama's capacity both to reflect the totality of life and to engage its spectators. Key here is the technique of dramatic characterisation. As Lukács explains, 'the social collision, as the centre of drama . . . requires the portrayal of individuals, who in their personal passions directly represent those forces whose clash forms the material content of the "collision"' (p. 119). In, for instance, *Romeo and Juliet* Shakespeare's 'poetic depth and tragic wisdom are revealed here in the inseparable, organic unity between the uttermost emphasis of individual qualities, of the subjectivity of the passion, and the universality of the collision' (p. 130). He goes on from here to generalise the point about great characters in drama: 'If their tragic passion coincides at its heart with the decisive, social moment of the collision, then, but only then, can their personalities acquire a fully unfolded and rich, dramatic relief' (p. 132).

Note the insistence here on what needs to happen if a character is to be full and richly dramatic. Lukács' explanation of the importance of drama has led him towards a formula for evaluating drama:

> The greatness of *dramatic characterization*, the ability to make characters live *dramatically* does not only depend, therefore, on the playwright's ability to create character, in itself, but rather, indeed above all, upon how far it is given him, subjectively and objectively, to discover the characters and collisions in reality that will correspond to these inner requirements of dramatic form.
>
> (p. 132, original emphasis)

Where the correspondence does not exist, the play is weak – he has just cited Ford's *'Tis Pity She's a Whore*, where the struggle of social systems has no bearing on the drama, but he is also thinking of many modern(ist) plays which he would dismiss as 'formalist' – not derived from life – including the work of Brecht.

In really great drama Lukács says there is an expression of the drama of history itself. Even the most intimate subtleties of character are 'coloured by the age' (p. 137). The connections between drama and life lead inevitably to consideration of the connections between drama and history. This relationship has to do not with a painstaking accuracy in the depiction of details but in an understanding, and presentation, of the key shapes. Shakespeare's *Henry VI* is 'historically faithful and authentic because the human features absorb the most essential elements of this great historical crisis' (p. 182).

The importance of the dramatist's ability to find the key historical collisions, and to embody them in appropriate 'world historical indi viduals', is that this way of writing has an effect: 'while the essence of a collision must remain historically authentic, historical drama must bring out those features in men and their destinies which will make a spectator, separated from these events by centuries, feel himself a direct participant of them' (p. 179). For Lukács the connections of drama and society are also connections with history. And they have their final – political – reference point in their capacity to transform a spectator into a participant in the collisions of history.

4

THE ESSENCE OF DRAMA

In a much used textbook published in 1987, Martin Esslin said that the 'essential ingredients' of drama are 'heightened intensity of incident and emotion' (1987: 23). What all types of drama have in common, he suggests, is that they are 'mimetic action' (24).

THE NATURE AND ORIGINS OF DRAMA

In saying this he was re-stating an idea that he had developed in an earlier book, *An Anatomy of Drama* (1976). There he looks at drama alongside play, ritual and spectacle, and identifies drama's key quality: 'What makes drama drama is precisely the element which lies outside and beyond the words and which has to be seen as action – or *acted* – to give the author's concept its full value' (1976: 14).

Esslin's definition is fairly neatly in line with the opinion of one of the earliest commentators on Western drama, the ancient Greek philosopher Aristotle (384–322 BCE). In his *Poetics* Aristotle described tragedy as 'representation of an act which is serious, complete, and of a certain magnitude . . . in the mode of dramatic enactment, not narrative' (Halliwell 1987: 37). Note, though, that we say 'described'. Aristotle attempted descriptions and categorisations of many of the phenomena he saw around him, including the weather. When he turned his attention to 'poetics' he thought it necessary to try and account for the power of an artform that had held a significant place in the culture of Athens nearly a century earlier, drama. Although he had not seen this drama for himself, Aristotle tried to describe how it worked.

The problem, for us, is that in the centuries after Aristotle commentators on his work lost sight of how provisional it was. They turned his descriptions into prescriptions, implying that a play could only be a proper play if it had the features Aristotle suggested. A case in point is the sixteenth-century Italian literary theorist Lodovico Castelvetro. He produced the first vernacular translation of *Poetics* (1570), with a commentary that appeared to identify as rules for proper drama the unities of time, space and action.

We have seen (in chapter 2) how critical commentary wrestled with these prescriptions attributed to Aristotle. In this opening section, however, we try to range more widely across the various attempts to define drama. In doing so, we encounter two different strands of argument: (1) identification of the key features, what Esslin called the 'essential ingredients', of drama; this is usually done by tracking back to drama's supposed point of origin in human society; (2) suggestion that drama connects with, and expresses, certain basic, essential, features of the human mind and emotions (assuming that you can generalise about human beings in this way).

Esslin's definition is in line with traditional thinking. But his insistence on action also comes out of a more local contemporary battle. Literary studies in general, including drama, had been dominated by a critical approach that focused on the artwork as a free-standing verbal construct that will yield up its meaning through detailed and subtle reading. For example, in a textbook from an earlier generation, Brooks and Heilman's *Understanding Drama* (first published in 1945), the student is told that

> costumes, setting and even acting itself are, finally, secondary. It is the word which is primary here; and this fact may explain why a good play retains so much of its dramatic power even when merely read in the study or the classroom.

> (p. 12)

Understanding Drama came out of the critical approach called New Criticism (see p. 28). This was dominant in the mid-1940s, and remained influential for two or three decades afterwards. Nevertheless there was an early riposte to Brooks and Heilman, in 1949, in the shape of Francis Fergusson's *The Idea of a Theater*. Separating drama from lyric poetry, Fergusson reinstates Aristotle's insistence that the dramatic poet imitates 'action'. It is here, he says, that he diverges from the approach of the literary critics. He is 'in search of that dramatic art which, in all real plays, underlies the more highly evolved arts of language'. And he says he is not alone:

> This idea of drama, as an art which eventuates in words, but which in its own essence is at once more primitive, more subtle, and more direct than either word or concept – the irreducible idea of the dramatic – appears in a number of contemporary writers who are students of culture rather than literary critics.
>
> (Fergusson 1953: 21–2)

DRAMA'S ORIGIN AND HUMAN NATURE

'The irreducible idea of the dramatic': it is the persistence of this concept, the concept that drama has a particular specific essence, which we need to track further. Fergusson traces his own position back to the Cambridge School of Classical Anthropologists, who published significantly from 1912, and beyond them to the German philosopher Friedrich Nietzsche (1844–1900). The Cambridge School was a group of scholars who, developing Aristotle's own remarks on the dithyramb, traced the roots of Greek tragedy to Greek myth and ritual. As Fergusson put it, they thus 'suggest that drama is prior to the arts, the sciences of man, and the philosophies, of modern civilization' (1953: 22). We shall return to these scholars in a later section on ritual (and there too we will look at the idea that drama also originates in play). Here we need simply to note their search for a 'primal ritual' underlying Greek tragedy. This confirmed for Fergusson that drama connects back to something fundamental in human behaviour, with a point of origin in primitive ritual.

Fergusson was not alone in assuming the link between tragedy and ritual. A couple of decades or so later Martin Esslin said 'in ritual we have the common root of music, dance, poetry and drama; in the subsequent process of further differentiation, drama developed into spoken drama, ballet, opera, musical comedy' (1976: 28). Esslin's restatement of the emphasis on ritual was typical of his period (though we should note the dissenting opinion from all this that had come from Eric Bentley in 1954). Contemporary theatre makers and critics had been searching for a practice that might engage, and re-stage, the primordial. Peter Brook's *Orghast* experiment in Iran in 1971 had a sense of deliberate return to ancient dramatic-ceremonial languages in order to recover the fullness which had shrivelled in modern speech. In 1973 the critic Jan Kott analysed *The Bacchae* to show how 'The myth and the rite . . . reach deep into the structure of performance' (1998: 272). Contemporaneously the Polish director Jerzy Grotowski (1933–99) had developed his idea of the 'holy actor' in performances which had ritual function. His theatre of sources project, from 1976, had at its heart the attempt to rediscover human essence beneath the influence of culture. But this now is more than a connection with ancient ritual. The assumption is that drama can put us in contact with basic humanity itself. As Esslin put it, drama is 'properly linked to the basic make-up of our species' (1976: 20).

We are encountering here the two contrasted positions that we flagged earlier on. One is that drama is powerful because it has its origins in an ancient primal ritual, a cultural activity. The other is that drama is powerful because as a form it is linked to the make-up of the species, an expression of 'human nature'. On one hand, deriving from something humans do; on the other, deriving from what humans supposedly are.

The first position has a habit of sliding into the second one. There is an instance of this in Fergusson. He links to the Cambridge School, whose search for primal ritual origins aims to be a historical study of ancient culture. But he also connects to the literary theorist Kenneth Burke. Burke's work, from 1945, was principally engaged with analysing the attribution of motives to human behaviour and the human use of symbol systems. To this end he proposed a model using a 'dramatistic' terminology which could arrive at some general insights. Burke is not interested in the origin of drama but instead in drama's ability to provide a model, a 'grammar', for describing human interactions (see p. 45).

There is something else of importance happening here. The Cambridge School concentrated on ancient Greek tragedy, an artform. Burke is concerned with how people use rhetoric to 'perform' socially. There is a distinction between 'drama' as art – aesthetic drama – and the performance of social interactions in everyday life. But that distinction tends to get blurred. When it happens, the slippage between aesthetic drama and social performance creates a sense that drama is important and powerful because it can express the 'make-up of our species'.

DRAMA'S ORIGIN AND HUMAN ORGANISATION

Esslin explained drama's power by linking it back to an ancient artform, ritual. Other descriptions of the origins of drama, however, connect it to modes of social organisation, to various practices by which ancient people tried to ensure their continued survival. So we now have to recognise that the argument about origins can point two ways: to a specific archaic form, ritual, or to a more general social process.

One of the clearest and most comprehensive accounts of drama's emergence from basic human processes was published by George Thomson in 1941 as *Aeschylus and Athens*. He argues that ancient hunters studied the behaviour of the animals they wanted to catch. From here developed 'mimetic rites' in which the animal is imitated, and where the rite functions to anticipate the success of the search for food. Its sympathetic magic creates the illusion that reality can be controlled. Back behind ancient ritual is the work of securing food. The 'mimetic dance . . . originated as part of the actual technique of production', and from here 'passed into a dramatisation of the activities of the clan ancestors' (1973: 96). Poetry and dancing, 'speech and gesture raised to a magical level of intensity', derive from and are fused together in the mimetic rite. They then become separated with 'the rise of a ruling class whose culture was divorced from the labour of production' (p. 59).

Thomson's approach is Marxist, displayed in his tracking of an artform back to a mode of production which sustains basic human life. Ritual behaviour falls into place as part of a process that enhances and reflects upon this production: imitating the animals you hunt. Later forms of aesthetic drama, including tragedy, enhance and reflect later modes and relations of production.

The analysis based on mode of production has some similarities to other analyses which connect tragic form to the ancient process and organisation of society. In *Violence and the Sacred* (1996) René Girard describes processes whereby the sinner/outsider/ traitor is expelled from human society. The 'original act of communal violence' produces religious imitations which commemorate it, and thus perpetuate unanimity. Games of chance originate in rites of victim selection. Theatre too plays a part in the operation of the 'sacrificial principle' through the close relationship between tragedy and the divine (Girard 1996: 26, 28). Following the late nineteenth-century anthropologist James Frazer, tragic form is associated with the processes by which society purges itself of alien matter. The classical scholar Jean-Pierre Vernant describes how in an afflicted society the king or his delegate, a carnival king, 'is expelled or put to death, carrying away with him all the disorder that he embodied and of which he thereby purges the community' (Vernant and Vidal-Naquet 1990: 132–3).

The approaches of Thomson, Girard and Vernant all contrast with accounts which present ritual as itself the point of origin of tragedy and drama. In Thomson's Marxist argument the productive practices are rooted in the conditions of a very specific society, and dramatic form, far from having an essence, changes as society changes. Vernant too outlines what he sees as a feature specifically of ancient Greek thought and culture. Girard's argument, though it begins in a specifically organised society, tends towards an assumption that these activities are generally recurrent in human societies. So once again we see our main basic contrast, and how its elements slide together: drama's power and characteristics are attributed to specific forms of human organisation; but the very ancientness of these forms seems to show human nature in the raw. The attempt to explain a specific shape which originates in a particular society ends up being a claim for an artform that expresses the 'make-up of our species'.

NIETZSCHE

What we have seen so far in the definitions of drama's essence and power is an alternation between emphasis on its historical, specific, origin and emphasis on its link with a generalised notion of humanity. Drama is powerful because, on one hand, it carries traces of very ancient human activity; or, on the other hand, because it expresses basic human impulses. We now follow this alternation through the work of two influential figures and then into approaches to interpreting and categorising drama. We begin with Nietzsche and Artaud.

Friedrich Nietzsche's *Birth of Tragedy* was an early work, first appearing in 1872. Its argument is that Greek tragedy emerges from the interaction between two fundamental human drives, which he names the Dionysian and the Apollonian. He likens the distinction between them to that between intoxication and the dream. In the dream the emphasis is on appearance, and he links this to the human artist as someone who is concerned with spectacle, interprets images, builds understanding. Intoxication on the other hand is predicated not so much on standing outside as loss of self into, a collapse of individuality, a merging with nature. Dream and intoxication are both, says Nietzsche, 'physiological phenomena'. Later in the argument these drives are mapped onto racial and sexual difference, but the central and persistent point is that they are anchored in bodily materiality.

Having set up the opposition between drives, Nietzsche proceeds to explain not just the origin of Greek tragedy but also the origin of drama itself. Distinguishing between the poet and the dramatist he says that while a poet sees the play a dramatist 'feels the drive to transform oneself and to speak out of other bodies and souls' (Nietzsche 2000: 49). Dionysiac intoxication produces transformation of self. This physiological process

> stands at the beginning of the development of the drama. Here there is something different from the rhapsode who does not fuse with his images, but like the painter sees them outside himself with an observing eye; here there is already a surrender of the individual through an entering into an unfamiliar nature.
>
> (p. 50)

But although this 'enchantment' is 'the precondition of all dramatic art', another element is necessary to make it drama. For the Dionysian 'enthusiast' sees himself as a satyr, and as satyr sees the god. We are now back in the territory of the Apollonian, of images outside oneself, of representation. Greek tragedy consists of the Dionysian chorus discharging itself in 'an Apollonian world of images' (p. 50). The two drives are opposite but inextricably connected, dialectical: 'drama is the concrete Apollonian representation of Dionysian insights and effects' (p. 51).

By contrast with Greek tragedy, in the drama of his own time the dialectical relationship seems to be lost. Nietzsche describes a 'reverence for the natural and the real', which produced a superficial and banal realism of style. He would presumably have felt his point was confirmed by the plays of Tom Robertson in England in the 1860s. They were celebrated for their 'cup and saucer realism', which avoided the excesses of melodrama: realism as containment. What is lost in this containment is the social effect of the Dionysian element. This began to happen as soon as drama was conceived in its 'narrower sense', stage plays. It came from a strengthening of the Apollonian element, that drive to make images, the need to show the god as real, to make its power visible to all. And the cost of it is the disappearance of the chorus, the pre-eminently Dionysian element which set up the conditions for loss of self into the crowd. Dionysian tragedy, argued Nietzsche, reintegrated human beings with nature, a process which had two important aspects. First, there is an 'overpowering feeling of unity which leads back to the heart of nature' (p. 45). Second, the feeling of unity suppresses any sense of individuality. For Nietzsche 'individuation' is 'the original cause of evil' (p. 60).

In Nietzsche's attack on contemporary stage plays just as in his account of the origin of drama, we can see a familiar idea. He assumes that drama has a connection to particular aspects of the 'make-up' of the human species, which he conceives as two opposed but connected drives. This gives drama its essential quality. Where an element is missing, as in realist stage plays, it is no longer properly drama in its fullest sense. So there is a clear idea of what proper drama is. On the other hand, and this is what gives Nietzsche's work greater profundity than much of what followed it, the essence of drama is not one singular thing, such as a primal ritual or a human behaviour pattern. It is a dialectical relationship between two opposed connected drives. From this relationship flows constant restlessness, where one thing has always to be considered relative to another.

ARTAUD

Half a century later Nietzsche's rejection of contemporary stage plays was echoed by the French actor and visionary theorist Antonin Artaud

(1896–1948). While Nietzsche was writing within the context of an emergent Naturalism, Artaud's work coincided with the point where it was dominant, and starting to become hollow. One of the major faults of contemporary realist theatre was that it depended on words or, to be more precise, 'dialogue form'. Dialogue 'does not specifically belong to the stage but to books' (1970: 27). In opposition to dialogue Artaud places 'poetry', which has an anarchic spirit, questioning the apparent purposes and logic in objects and natural forms (p. 31). This poetry is not so much verbal as spatial.

Artaud found this poetry in Balinese theatre (even though he actually misunderstood it), which became for him the stick with which he could beat literary, word-bound Western theatre. Just as for Nietzsche Dionysian music took spectators deeper than a mere imitation of nature, so for Artaud Balinese theatre offered something deeper than, and prior to, words. In this theatre the 'stage production language', as he called it, was made up not of words but of 'gestures, signs, postures and sounds'. Against the 'psychological' inclinations of Western theatre, he sets the 'metaphysical' inclinations of Oriental theatre. Its stage language 'develops all its physical and poetic effects on all conscious levels and in all senses' and leads to 'thought adopting deep attitudes which might be called *active metaphysics*' (p. 33). This depth goes beyond everyday discourse: Balinese theatre 'has invented a language of gestures to be spatially developed, but having no meaning outside it' (p. 43). Nietzsche similarly claimed that the Dionysian chorus expresses nature in 'a new world of symbols . . . a symbolism of the body for once, not just the symbolism of the mouth, but the full gestures of dance, the rhythmic movement of all the limbs' (Nietzsche 2000: 26).

'The dancer's feet', says Artaud, 'dissolve thoughts and feelings, returning them to their pure state' (1970: 48). Thus spectators can be put in touch with something hitherto lost. The actors, costumes and gestures become 'strange signs matching some dark prodigious reality we have repressed once and for all here in the West' (p. 43). Oriental theatre's general effect is then likened to something which is already familiar from Nietzsche: 'All of this is steeped in deep intoxication, restoring the very elements of rapture' (p. 47). Rediscovering the repressed, restoring rapture: theatre functioning at its best can connect performers and audience alike with something that lies deeper than history or culture, a 'theatre that vibrates with instinctive things' (p. 43). The language of this theatre doesn't merely express such 'instinctive things', it has its source in them: 'All creativity stems from the stage in this drama, finding its expression and even its sources in a secret psychic impulse, speech prior to words' (p. 42; see Keyword: Presence and representation). It is not a matter simply of rediscovering that which has been repressed in the West: the performance of oriental theatre is continuous with buried 'psychic impulse'. In the same way the chorus for Nietzsche articulated the Dionysian 'physiological drive'.

Here, however, we need to acknowledge a crucial difference. For Nietzsche the Dionysian drive was inextricably connected with the drive to which it was opposed, the Apollonian. Each drive is as physiologically real as the other. By contrast, Artaud's opposition between Western and Oriental theatres is a straightforward confrontation, not dialectical and dynamic. This straightforwardness allows him to decide that one of them is not a form of theatre at all. With the expression of its thoughts locked entirely into spoken words, Western theatre is not theatrical. It has no stage production language of its own (pp. 27, 50).

Artaud's polemical insistence here speaks the urgency of his opposition to a dominant word-bound realism and of his desire to escape repression. But it leads him to a position that is both more simplistic than Nietzsche's and, at the same time, seductively eloquent in its definition of what the essence of real drama/theatre is. It not only expresses but connects back into essences of life, the psychical and instinctive, elements of the 'makeup of our species'. As a formulation for defining the essence of drama it is a lot more generalised than reference to primal ritual or processes of hunting and sacrifice. Its greater generality, combined with its simplicity, gave it substantial power.

DRAMA'S PSYCHOANALYTIC TRUTH

Artaud is allocated a place alongside Aristotle in the critic André Green's development of an approach to interpreting tragedy in *The Tragic Effect* (1979). But he is also a stepping-stone to enable Green to get somewhere else: after Artaud comes Freud. Green's purposes are clear in the title to this part of his book: 'Prologue: The psycho-analytic reading of tragedy'.

In this section of our chapter we engage with the approach to drama that has been developed by psychoanalysis. Our logic for doing this is partly derived from the fact that it builds on the implications of Artaud's work. But we also want to look at the activity of explicating dramatic text. Hitherto we have looked at how the essence of drama has been defined in generalised accounts of its nature and origins. We suggest in this section that one of the abiding assumptions about drama – namely its relationship with the basic reality of 'human nature' – is perpetuated and reinforced in some of the ways that dramatic texts are explicated. Psychoanalytic 'readings' are a good case in point.

In his 'Prologue' André Green puts Aristotle and Artaud into a psychoanalytic context. For instance the arousal of pity and fear is best achieved in 'relations of kinship' and thus 'The family . . . is the tragic space *par excellence*' (1979: 7). Artaud's 'theatre of cruelty' is depicted as an attempt to lift repression. This then links to Freud and the death drive (p. 13). Having planted Aristotle and Artaud into the landscape of psychoanalysis, Green then gets on with the business of explicating written texts. This activity of psychoanalysis with regard to drama is there right from its start, with the work both of Freud himself, in his 1905/6 essay 'Psychopathic characters on the stage', and his follower Ernest Jones, in his 1949 book *Hamlet and Oedipus*.

In describing the method of psychoanalytic explication Green says that, while being careful to recognise that artworks are not real human behaviour, the psychoanalyst is nevertheless 'right in thinking that works of art may help him grasp the articulation of actual but hidden relations, in the cases that he studies' (1979: 22). Thus, a psychoanalytic reading of tragedy 'will have as its aim the mapping of the traces of the Oedipal structure concealed in its formal organization'. In making this map, we can observe that, despite what Green has said, the shape of the general Oedipal structure comes to replace the work's specific form; the hidden human relations, or rather their archetypal structure, really are more important than the art of the artwork. As he has already put it, 'Tragedy . . . is the representation of the phantasy myth of the Oedipus complex, which Freud identified as the constitutive complex of the subject' (p. 27). Here, rather clearly, is the idea that tragedy and drama express the supposed essence of humanity, the make-up of the species.

For another example of this sort of explication, let us look at how the famous French psychoanalyst Jacques Lacan (1901–81) analyses *Hamlet*. Like Green, he tries to tease out what may lie beneath the formal organisation of a dramatic text. Thus, in his account of the 'nunnery' scene (3.1), where Hamlet verbally abuses Ophelia, he detects a 'trace' of 'the perverse imbalance of the fantasmatic relationship, when the fantasy is tipped toward the object'. The meaning of 'object' here is as in the phrase 'the object of my hatred': the object can be that 'through which the instinct seeks to attain its aim' – to get satisfaction, or it can be the total object of attraction, usually a person (Laplanche and Pontalis 1983: 273–6). Hamlet, says Lacan, 'no longer treats Ophelia like a woman at all. She becomes in his eyes the childbearer to every sin'. In short, 'what is taking place here is the destruction and loss of the object' (Lacan 1977: 23).

Lacan treats the theatrical scene as an elaborated version of a psychic one. Its essence for him is its universal psychic content, for which the stage action is merely a metaphor. The formal organisation of the scene is simply to be bracketed off. And with that, any sense of stage convention is also discarded. The persons in the scene, for instance, are taken to correspond to 'real' people: Lacan seems to be looking in on this scene with very naturalistic eyes. But if for a moment we move away from Lacan and attend to the formal organisation itself, we can note how the Hamlet/Ophelia dialogue is framed by two onstage watchers; and how the changes in verbal and physical register within the scene as a whole produce a sense of quotedness, of which the most obvious example is Ophelia's highly ornate speech after Hamlet's exit. At such a moment the formal organisation calls attention to itself, and when that happens it is clear that the stage is producing these figures as quotations and representations rather than as 'real' people. Ophelia in particular is explicitly constructed in various ways during the scene, so that the failure to treat her 'like a woman' may be said to be less a symptom of Hamlet's neurosis than of the text's interest in the mechanics of representation, which might ask, among other things, what 'woman' is.

This essentialising and universalising activity distracts from other significant concerns. For example, Lacan claims that the motivation for Hamlet's hiding of Polonius's body is 'just another mockery of that which is of central importance: insufficient mourning' (p. 39). Within its moment of original production the attitude to Polonius's body would have been in tense relation with deeply held assumptions about funerary protocols, especially for aristocrats. In its construction of Hamlet's activity at this point the play stages a relationship between individual wit and social protocol. Hamlet's very contemporary wit enables him to be the focus of attention in a space hitherto controlled by the decorums for the dead that were fetishised, and fetishistically transgressed, by tragedies of vengeance. The play itself also repeatedly ostends its own wit and modernity. In the complex relationships between gendered persons, stage and auditorium, residual and emergent cultural conventions, psyche and history, there would then seem to be more for psychoanalysis to do here than focus on 'insufficient mourning'.

This sort of psychoanalytic reading seductively draws its readers into its central focus by suppressing any difference between them and the strange world of the artwork. It thereby actively perpetuates an essentialist definition of drama. Lacan's 'seminar' does just this when he formulates, in parentheses, a definition of 'the' tragic hero – 'both Oedipus and each one of us potentially at some point of our being, when we repeat the Oedipal drama' (p. 42). Not only fictional characters are generalised in this way, but so too is the author. Ignoring the real history of dramaturgy, Green represents the author as having phallic authority over the artwork he has fathered. So every hero and thus every spectator 'is in the position of the son in the Oedipal situation' (Green 1979: 27). All tragic narratives and all theatrical experience are subsumed into one particular mode of action and viewing relation: 'The hero is the locus of an encounter between the power of the bard, who brings the phantasy to life, and the desire of the spectator, who sees his phantasy embodied and represented.' This observation takes us a long way from historical realities, for not all plays were written by individual male bards, nor were all audiences solely male. It is an abstract model of the supposed essence of drama which is perhaps even more imaginary than the primal ritual.

Through psychoanalytic explication of text, back through Nietzsche and Artaud trying to articulate the power of drama, to the attempts to think about drama's origins: over the chapter we have seen, mutating in different ways, a basic pair of ideas. Drama is assumed to be derived from primal human behaviour, 'ritual', or to express basic human 'nature'. These ideas contrast with and slip into one another. They are often called upon to define drama's difference from non-drama, or to specify the difference between serious drama and trivial. When one makes these assumptions and distinctions one often buys into the mindset that looks for essences.

5

WOMEN, THEATRE AND THE ETHICS OF THE ACADEMY

FEMINISM AND THE DISCIPLINE OF THEATRE STUDIES

In 1981, Nancy S. Reinhardt reviewed the impact of feminism on American theatre studies since the rise of the women's movement, and found that it was lagging behind other disciplines. While feminism had inspired new developments for nearly ten years in film studies, for instance, both a feminist theatre criticism and theatre history remained quite new. Theatre scholars were now importing models from other disciplines, such as semiology from film studies, a decade after its impact there. This was despite the development of a lively feminist theatre in the 1970s as part of the politics, as had been the case with Black Liberation in the 1960s (Reinhardt 1981: 25–6).

Reinhardt suggests three reasons for this. First, film and media studies were not hampered by the 'critical baggage' of older disciplines, and were thus open to 'new perspectives and challenges'. Second, the exploitation of women in mainstream media is so patent as to demand critical attention. Third, 'theatre is essentially – almost by definition – a public, social and hence male-dominated art' (Reinhardt 1981: 26–7). This third reason for critical tardiness is also the opening for critique: 'The dominant *public* action both on stage and in the audience stresses a male world in which women are either kept to the sides, in recesses, or are placed on display for the male viewer' (Reinhardt 1981: 29).

Jill Dolan could attest a decade later to the rapid transformation of the 'critical and creative terrain' of feminist theatre and its associated studies in the two decades from the mid-1970s, figuring the journal *The Drama Review* as part of the academic and experimental performance matrix of New York, where a consciousness of the need for interdisciplinary work was emerging in both spheres. In line with emphases in the feminist mainstream, the early concern was with the recovery of histories of women's performance (see Reinhardt 1981: 49, n. 3). But, as poststructuralism gained a general ascendancy in the academy, and psychoanalysis especially became recognised as a powerful tool, the perspective changed from biography to the interrogation of representations of gender, sexuality and race. This new emphasis brought in train 'questions of form, context, history, and representation' (Dolan 1996: 2).

While feminists were thus instrumental in effecting a shift towards theoretical models in theatre and performance studies in general during the 1980s, they met hostility and resistance. In 1990, Sue Ellen Case published *Performing Feminisms,* a collection of essays mostly drawn from *Theatre Journal,* the house journal of the Association for Theatre in Higher Education (ATHE). Case claims that the journal had been criticised for its emphasis on 'theory and specifically political theory' during her co-editorship. A 'schism between theory and history' in the journal, ATHE and theatre departments continued still. Some claimed that a move to interdisciplinarity threatened the integrity of theatre studies as a discipline (Case 1990: 1).

Besides ideological resistance to feminism as such and fears about disciplinary integrity – fears in themselves with a long history open to feminist critique as we shall see – Case suggests more local historical reasons why feminist theory came late to Theatre Studies. Theatre criticism had been most developed in departments of English, where the emphasis was on playtexts, especially from the Renaissance. Theatre departments were relatively new, and in the United States still maintained the training of practitioners as their primary function, accompanied typically only by theatre history as the main area of academic study. Thus both feminist and other critical approaches to contemporary texts and practices inhabited still in 1990 'a severely marginal position' (Case 1990: 2).

FEMINISM, TRAGEDY AND THE PATRIARCHAL ACADEMY

Reinhardt argues that the masculine gendering of the public sphere in theatre is most true of tragedy, and asks why such a partial model as Aristotle's should have dominated the academy for so long. Her answer is twofold: that Aristotle is 'the paradigmatic spokesman for the ancient male-centered society (of) the city-state'; and that traditional university scholarship has its roots in the same soil. The original Greek concept of the university is of a lively struggle through debate between master and pupil. And this, argues Reinhardt, is cognate not only with the training of Greek male citizens in physical combat, but also with Aristotelian tragedy, which, like much traditional Western drama since, is linear, based on the *agon*, leads to climax and resolution and discards 'anything inconsistent or superfluous' – arguably the feminine. She cites Adrienne Rich's quotation of Walter J. Ong's view that adversarial practice dominated the academy until Romanticism (Reinhardt 1981: 29–30, 35–7; see also Rich 1980).

Aristotle notoriously finds women less appropriate than men (and slaves not at all) as tragic heroes. In *Feminism and Theatre* (1988), Case observes that while the dithyramb involved both male and female choruses, the competitive festivals that founded the drama emerged from only the male. And if women were present in the audience at all, they are thought to have had marginal status. As she reports, feminist historians have argued that this foundational exclusion of women from the drama constitutes it as 'a political and aesthetic arena for ritualised and codified gender behaviour' in support of 'civic privileges and restrictions' in fifth century Athens (Case 1988: 11). Theatre is thus one of several institutions and cultural practices – including the law, religion, architecture, sexuality, the family and learning – that embody a shift towards the patriarchal state.

Case reviews the socio-economic and ideological parameters of this shift. Men headed families and owned wealth; citizenship was dependent on male lineage, and women became objects of exchange through marriage, confined to the domestic sphere. Women in these conditions are rendered culturally invisible, their invisibility providing 'the empty space which organises the focus on the male subject'. Learning and the appreciation of art, both understood as 'the pleasure of mimesis', are presumed to be the province of the male. It follows that the drama can have 'no function' for women, since they do not have 'the authority of choice' (Case 1988: 8–9, 17–18).

'Woman' was fashioned as a polar opposite to 'Man' to contain and define women from a male perspective of privilege. Mythical narratives of the suppression of the cthonic (earthly, 'womanly') were constructed to justify the cultural shift. Reinhardt and Case follow Millett (1972) and others in regarding Aeschylus' *Oresteia* as a foundation myth for the *polis*, with Athena presiding over newly instituted rational justice, the irrational vengefulness of the feminine Furies having been suppressed (Case 1988: 7–12 *passim*).

A number of issues arise from this anti-patriarchal critique. It raises fundamental questions about Western theatre as a general form. With regard to the plays, it can be argued that any culture that values them 'actively participates in the same patriarchal subtext' (Case 1988: 12). Reinhardt suggests that if we do use the Aristotelian model to explicate *Oedipus Rex*, we need to understand that both the play *and* Aristotle's prescriptions enact the struggle of male rationality to control supposed female irrationality (Reinhardt 1981: 31).

Seven years after Reinhardt's review, Case could invite feminist scholars to link 'practice, text and cultural background' in a 'new way' that had evolved since (Case 1988: 15). The growth of materialist feminism in particular had opened up both theatre and theatre studies to critique as patriarchal institutions engaged in the reproduction of gendered power relations. In the next section, we turn to divisions within feminism itself, and their partial resolution in the formula of 'positionality'. The concern here is with critical praxis, the ways in which theory is performed by individuals and collectives, and its relationship with the performance of identity.

FEMINIST ETHICS AND POSITIONALITY

Jill Dolan observes that, by the time of its 1994 conference in Chicago, the once 'upstart' and 'outlaw' Women and Theatre Program had become

both 'oppositional and institutional'. She addresses this new and contradictory centrality from two angles. First, since texts and traces of feminist
performance have now thereby become commodities, feminist critics
need to intervene in their reception. Second, gaining the centre must
foreground the 'exclusionary problems of all sites, identities, communities
and methods'. The questions 'what feminists are doing, what they're forgetting, and who they serve' must remain continually open (Dolan 1996:
2–3, 16). An emblematic prompt for such foregrounding was the criticism
of typologies developed from the mid-1980s, such as Gayle Austin's
summary identification in 1990 of 'radical', 'liberal' and 'materialist'
feminisms. Austin's basic distinction was between a separatist politics that
champions qualities it presumes are essentially womanly ('radical'); the
pursuit of equality with men on the basis of a shared humanity ('liberal');
and a focus on gender as being culturally produced, implying a necessary
engagement with the class politics of the political left ('materialist') (Austin
1990: 6; see also Aston 1995: 8–9; Carlson 1996: 145; Reinelt and Roach
1992: 229, n. 2). Thus, the arguments we have rehearsed above about
ancient Greece hover between materialist and radical or essentialist
feminist discourses.

Categorisations such as Austin's were criticised as being not only
partial but also exclusionary, being based on forms of political organisation dominated by white middle-class women. The criticism gained
prominence in a number of publications around 1980 by women of colour
(for references, see de Lauretis 1987: 10; Case 1990: 56–7; and Dolan
1993: 417).

In a retrospective of the 1980s, Case maps a number of areas and
issues that inform the academic response. Central to her argument is the
dialectical relationship between the two major theoretical strands in
feminist theatre studies during the 1980s – poststructuralist materialism
and feminist psychoanalysis. One psychoanalytic perspective that was
developed within gender politics was a critique of phallic regimes of truth-
construction that ignored women's experience. This was in tune with the
way in which materialist feminists were now using poststructuralism
to destabilise conventional materialist categories like 'class'. But psychoanalysis also offered essentialist models amenable to radical feminism,
which in turn tended to install a unitary and hence 'exclusionary' concept
of Woman. Clearly, there is a contradiction between essentialist feminist

psychoanalysis and poststructuralist materialist feminism. But for Case, they emerge as a dialectical pair. While materialist poststructuralists properly destabilise 'exclusionary' essentialist feminist categories like 'women' and 'lesbian', this is at the cost of 'an actively resistant praxis', sorely needed in the face of attacks from the political right (Case 1990: 7–8).

Case considers the dialectic between the two paradigms through the metaphor of movement. The dialectic had paradoxically constituted both a 'stall' and 'motive force'. Its maintenance as motive force was greatly helped by the development of the idea of feminist critical 'positionality', prompted by the challenge to white feminist hegemony noted above. The performance of critical positionality insists simultaneously upon 'the positioning of agency' as well as its 'materialist deconstruction' and thereby, writes Case, facilitates 'accuracy and therefore efficacy' (Case 1990: 6–7). Dolan notes its specific usage from 1988 (Dolan 1993: 417, n. 1).

The both–and of positionality modulates into the tactic of 'strategic' or – as Gayatri Spivak terms it, 'operational' – essentialism (Spivak cited via Judith Butler 1990: 325 in Harris 1999: 18) whereby a basic commitment to deconstructive critique is paired with the performative adoption of secure subject positions for particular political purposes. Carlson suggests that other groups of oppressed people, such as gays, Blacks and Latinos, will logically also be drawn to the position of strategic essentialism (Carlson 1996: 182–3). We would argue that Carlson's observation is specific to an individualist, ultimately liberal, perspective in which the politics of identity and group representation dominate. Janelle Reinelt suggests that Austin's typology of liberal, radical and materialist feminisms remains useful to 'those beginning' undergraduate study of feminist theatre and criticism, provided warning is also given of its inadequacy (Reinelt 1992: 227). While such an approach will give the student a useful framework for reading earlier feminist criticism, it nevertheless threatens to lay specific foundations for understanding that are aligned with the culture of only some, relatively privileged, students. As Dolan insists, in joining a university, one enters into a realm of discourse. To what extent does rehearsal of its genealogy set a limiting frame? To what extent can it be used to encourage different narratives? What of our own declared exclusions in making this book?

FEMINIST COMMUNITIES, TEXTUALITY AND TRANSCENDENCE

We now turn to two further questions of praxis considered in terms of performativity. First are claims about the nature and effects of feminist practice in the academy. Second is the question of the relationship between the academy and the wider feminist movement: we review another dialectical model, structurally related to the issue of 'positionality'.

As do most feminist academics, Case situates herself in a community of scholars in creative dialogue both with the wider social movement and amongst themselves. She recalls that feminist scholarship in the journal she edited enjoyed a richness of 'intercitation' and 'self-criticism'. In a revivification of 'vestigial processes from Marxism', a nourishing and mobile sense of agency continually tested itself 'within the context of dominant and collective ideology'. This sort of feminist critical discourse not only mediates creatively between 'inclusion and social specificity' but is also able 'to move in and out of oppressive operations'. The feminist critic is able to engage productively with critiques that are ultimately based in patriarchal assumptions, while maintaining a 'liberative distance'. She thereby avoids 'collusion'. Case disdainfully contrasts 'the economy and grace' of feminist critical theory with 'the puffing "projects" of unaligned postmodern theorists' including the New Historicists (Case 1990: 4–6).

Feminist theory brought to the academy both interdisciplinarity and an active link between academic feminism and the wider social movement. Case argues that feminist theoretical practice had 'shaken departmental and genre assumptions'; raised fundamental questions about 'what constitutes scholarship and . . . what constitutes epistemology' (constructions of 'truth'); and blurred the line between 'disciplinary and performance practices' (Case 1990: 3). But if women in the social movement had challenged academic categories within this symbiotic contract, there was also the question of the relationship between academic praxis as such and the wider political struggle. She addresses this problem through the lens first of textualisation, and then of elite forms.

Case argues that feminist theatre criticism in the 1980s that deployed psychoanalysis tended to limit history to the transcendental sphere of 'textual operations'. The fetishised text obscured the real workings of history. This constituted a 'modernist refusal of reference' – the repeated deferral of actively resistant praxis (Case 1990: 8–9). According to Case's earlier argument such textualising tendencies were of course already active in the literary critical establishment that adopted psychoanalytic theory.

Case considers whether, indeed, academic feminist criticism as a whole and its attendant performance culture might be accused of a modernist withdrawal from the popular. Against this, she argues that avant-garde feminist criticism and performance have a particular role to play; they have a 'community-specific address'. If avant-garde forms 'do not reach out to a majority of women as effectively as popular culture' they 'do adequately perform feminism for some members of the movement'. The 'psychosemiotic approach' in particular has enabled 'interaction directly with the frightening world of the fathers in which the feminist must negotiate with violent misogynistic inscriptions, or the devastating effects of total absence'. The feminist critic has a specific 'locus of labor' that requires particular tools. She cites Brecht's *lehrstücke* as a parallel (Case 1990: 10–11).

With respect to the social side of the symbiotic bond, Case asks astutely, 'Why does the feminist community need the deconstruction?' Does it really matter in practical terms if lesbian essentialism adheres to notions of the Real, and hence the 'binding ontological bond' of mimesis? The dialectic between poststructuralist materialism and psychoanalytic essentialism operates, then, in the embrace of another: between avant-garde strategies of resistance that bring elitism in train, and a broader practice that attends to the specificities of race and class but is also inclined to use transcendent categories (Case 1990: 10). Neither is perfect, but each is more adequate to its purpose than the other. Each has its own sphere of performativity.

Precisely who is it that decides on this division of labour? Is critical deconstruction something with which only academics need be bothered, to sustain their critique in the academy, but take no further? What implications are there here for the active dialogue between the feminist academy and the rest of the social movement?

Case reports that the 'romance with postmodernism' as a means 'to intervene in discourse' has 'abated'. This presumably refers to the 'media generation'. But the question nevertheless remains of how to develop 'a form, tied to a critical methodology that enables the perception of the masks of dominant ideology and tactics' capable of being read by a popular audience. Case has raised Brecht's *lehrstücke* as a model. But these, after all, were designed as public events, engaging schools and radio – even though he also suggested that they were rehearsals for a future socialist pedagogy, rather than fully effective now. Could Leninism have a vestigial echo in Case's position here (Case 1990: 9)?

In the final two sections, we turn to another dimension of performativity, specifically the theorisation of gender as a scripted performance and its implications for feminist arts practices outside conventional theatre. We find again dialectical models, but also appeals to margins and gaps.

TECHNOLOGIES OF GENDER AND THE FEMINIST SUBJECT

Shortly before Case's retrospective, film theorist Teresa de Lauretis published *Technologies of Gender* (1987). In *The History of Sexuality* (volume 1: 1981), Foucault had demonstrated that human sexuality was not natural but cultural, a 'technology of sex' both fashioned and sustained by medical, legal, educational and other institutional discourses. De Lauretis suggests by extension that gender is the product of 'technologies of gender'. Let us foreground the performative character of this model. Gender for de Lauretis is, as Foucault says of sexuality, 'a set of effects produced in bodies, behaviours, and social relations' (de Lauretis 1987: 1–3).

De Lauretis argues that feminist critique of patriarchal systems and the building of a women's culture during the 1960s and 1970s assumed the alignment of *gender*, understood as a set of qualities, with *sexual difference*, the basic biological distinctions between men and women. She finds the same alignment within later feminist appropriations of Derrida's notion of *différance*. She writes to disrupt it.

Gender, de Lauretis argues, is simply a system of *generic* classification: it places individuals within groups defined by a set of common characteristics. But gender is a strictly binary system. The male or female child is without gender until identified as a boy or girl, after which it is entrained to conform to and identify with a preordained model of masculine or feminine. No other class is available. But while such binary classification is shared across cultures, the definitions of masculine and feminine vary widely between them. And within any one culture, the subject is also 'en-gendered in the experience of race and class, as well as sexual, relations'. The defining characteristics of masculine and feminine are culturally specific sets of representations that have real social and subjective consequences. Representation constructs, rather than reflects, gender (de Lauretis 1987: 2–6).

Following Althusser's model of ideology, de Lauretis suggests that gender 'hails' or interpellates the subject. Becoming gendered means participating in that realm of representation. And she insists that the construction goes on even in avant-garde artistic practice, critical theorising and political practice, including feminism. There is 'no social reality . . . outside the sex-gender system', and theorising is part of that social reality. While Althusser felt able to posit 'science' as being outside 'ideology', feminism challenged the very construct of scientific objectivity as masculinist. De Lauretis proposes a solution to this conundrum in a way that anticipates Judith Butler's work on performativity (see Keyword: Performativity). She proposes a 'subject of feminism', distinct from both abstract Woman and real women 'actually engendered in social relations'. This subject 'in process' is simultaneously 'inside *and* outside the ideology of gender, and conscious of being so, conscious of that twofold pull'. While the subject of feminism is a 'theoretical construct', de Lauretis considers how that self-determination might be performed, in 'subjective, micropolitical and everyday practices'. It means deliberately living a contradiction (de Lauretis 1987: 3–10 *passim*, original emphasis).

The position de Lauretis develops has much to say of pertinence to feminist theatre and performance practice and theory, and her work has been influential. She provides a performative model of subjectivity geared to the subversion of the sex-gender system. And she helps foreground the theatrical apparatus as one 'technology of gender' amongst many. As de Lauretis points out, the identification of a 'cinematic apparatus' that does ideological work had developed coincidentally with but independently from Foucault's work on sexuality. Laura Mulvey's influential essay on the male gaze comes from this period (Mulvey 1975). Radical film makers had since subversively experimented with the cinematic 'space-off'. The film frame selects what we see. Cinematic illusion depends on our capacity to imagine what lies outside it within the fiction. But in reality, there are for instance the camera, technicians and the reality of the film studio or location, and, somewhere, an editor. We are supposed to be unaware of them. The radical strategy was to put the 'space-off' at the centre. This had implications for feminist performance (de Lauretis 1987: 13–26).

MARKED AND UN(RE)MARKED

Moving 'in and out of gender as ideological representation' is a strategy recognisable in queer performance, such as that by Split Britches (see Case 1996). Their queer pastiche moves swiftly and undecidably between gender roles that may or may not at any one moment be psychically invested for performer and audience alike. Just as 'the terms of a different construction of gender' exist 'in the margins of hegemonic discourse' (de Lauretis 1987: 18), so Split Britches generate such margins in the full 'frame' of the stage. This search for a space between the always male-centred secure representation of gender and 'what that representation leaves out or, more pointedly, makes . . . unrepresentable' (de Lauretis 1987: 26) links to the perspective developed by Peggy Phelan in *Unmarked* (1993).

Phelan develops a thesis around the proposition that to participate in a realm of representation is to become marked. Following Derrida and Lacan, she argues that, in Western cultures, males are marked with value and females are not. But then, within this 'psycho-philosophical frame', cultural representation including art re-marks the woman as a signifier or metaphor; and the man becomes the un(re)marked norm, the point of view. Women in art always stand for something from the point of view of the male, which is presumed to be normative (Phelan 1993: 5).

Phelan wants to reinvest value in a subjectivity or identity that is not, or cannot be, represented in these terms. This runs counter to the presumption held by left and right alike that to gain visibility is to attain political power. Her specific focus on Performance is framed by the way in which, in more conventional art forms, 'the pleasure of resemblance and repetition' both reassuringly centres the spectator and fetishises what is being looked at. In theatre, an apparatus of conventional representation, the 'Other' on stage is incorporated by the spectator as 'the Same'. What Phelan develops, by looking at the work of Angelika Festa, Cindy Sherman and others, is a sense of Performance as 'a model for another representational economy, one in which the reproduction of the Other *as* the Same is not assured.' What Festa performs, for instance, in her complex solo pieces, is 'a deliberate and conscious refusal to take the payoff of visibility' that also bears witness to 'the loss and grief women in patriarchal cultures suffer in 'the chasm between presence and re-presentation' (Phelan 1993: 1–3, 19, 163, original emphasis).

We can link Phelan's search for 'another representational economy', rather than an escape from representation altogether, to Derrida's symptomatic reading of Artaud as being deeply locked into Western metaphysics (see Keyword: Presence and representation). And both her search and de Lauretis's for 'the terms of a different construction of gender' are geared to a politics that recognises difference rather than imposes differentiation. While Phelan seems to depend more on abstract linguistic models, both she and de Lauretis start from the assumption that any Western philosophical and other theory appropriated by feminism is to be understood to operate within the same 'hommo-sexual' frame, as Irigaray has it, as the rest of Western patriarchal culture. De Lauretis for instance cites Rosi Braidotti who in 1985 complained that the frequent championing of the 'feminine' as the future of humanity by Deleuze, Derrida, Foucault and Lyotard merely once again translated women into metaphors. These male theorists consistently displace 'the historicity of gender onto (the) diffuse, decentered, or deconstructed (but certainly not female) subject'. Real women did not figure (de Lauretis 1987: 23–4). Some, meanwhile, find Braidotti inclined to essentialism.

6

PERFORMANCE, ART AND THE AVANT GARDE

We start this chapter by reviewing some established accounts of the emergence of contemporary Performance. Then, by widening the frame to include a less known narrative, we attempt to defamiliarise those established stories and maps. From here we arrive at the event – May 1968 – that generated the problematic underpinning so much of the poststructuralist theory that was to impact on performance and its associated studies in the 1980s. Occasionally in what follows, we refer to practitioners. There is not room here to describe their work. But reference can of course be found in the books and articles cited.

NARRATIVE DEFINITIONS OF PERFORMANCE

Introducing a retrospective collection of her own critical writings, Sally Banes reviews definitions and classifications of Performance made by practitioners and critics during the 1970s. She demonstrates that each was ultimately partial. The 'mediumless genre' of Performance is too heterogeneous to be captured by 'essential definitions'. A better ploy is to develop historical narratives about it and its genealogy, or 'genetic codes' (Banes 1998: 1–7). Nöel Carroll had argued similarly in 1986, adding that indeed every art comprises 'a plurality of developing interests whose intelligibility is best conveyed by a narrative' (Carroll 1986: 79). These postmodern positions have an anti-essentialist cast.

Carroll maps Performance as emerging from two dominant sources, each rooted in the 1960s. He designates work by painters and sculptors who reacted against formalist gallery aesthetics '*art performance*'; and work by theatre artists reacting against established modes of theatre making '*performance art*'. He presents Performance as a dialogue between these two strands, 'a connected and living tradition' based on 'shared concerns and preoccupations' (Carroll 1986: 65).

'Performance art' emerged out of 1960s avant-garde theatre practices that opposed dominant text-based theatre. The aim was to be reflexive, presentational rather than representational, and to situate the audience as participants rather than as spectators. The focus was on the 'performative' of theatre, in the sense of its being here and now. The ultimate key influence here is Artaud and *The Theatre and its Double* (Carroll 1986: 71–2) (see Keyword: Presence and representation).

In chapter 9, we explore the proposition that 'art performance' emerged as a radical break with modernist formalism in fine art, associated in particular with the influential critic Clement Greenberg. Carroll suggests that art performance can also be seen as being in *continuity* with certain 1960s fine art discourses and practices. Key here is abstract expressionist painting. For Greenberg, it was the latest articulation of the essence of painting. But, says Carroll, Harold Rosenberg's designation of Jackson Pollock's (1912–56) abstract expressionist practice as 'action painting' foregrounded the performance and process of painting rather than the finished object (Carroll 1986: 66–7).

Carroll maps 'confluences' between art performance and performance art – typified respectively by, say, Happenings and Living Theatre. Both want to dissolve the distance between spectator and performance, and they share the common 1960s 'utopian urge to break down barriers'. Further, the Artaudian emphasis on spectacle brings performance art into the realms of visual arts practice. But, he argues, they differ on one fundamental count. Art performance is founded on an anti-essentialist resistance to formalism; and performance art is founded on an essentialist resistance to the representationalism of dominant theatre practice. Despite this contradiction, they met on the ground of performance as a 'real event' and

were 'perceived to be connected'. A 'new terrain of practice was carved out
. . . at points of tangency' (Carroll 1986: 72–3).

After this foundational confluence, Carroll narrates the semi-
autonomous development of both strands, with a dialogue between them
occasionally issuing in major points of coincidence. In his later contribution to the entry on 'performance art/art performance' in the *Oxford
Encyclopedia*, this has consolidated into 'a braiding narrative' – a rather
banal nod towards Schechner (see p. 119). The nodes of the braid
comprise shared preoccupations with the real in the 1960s, representations
(especially popular) in the 1980s; and, at the end of the twentieth century,
'with political realities as well as political identities, often constructed
and experienced through a mass media and increasingly virtual culture'
(Kennedy 2003: 1019–23).

In 1986, Carroll addressed the 'symbolic resonances' of Performance
as a 'self-appointed title'. It suggests both the immediacy of the performance event as authentic and theatrical representation as inauthentic.
Carroll suggests that while a shift from discourses of authenticity to those
of simulation and disjunction might be mapped from the 1960s to the
1980s, a more persistent dialectic between these poles informs 'the popular
metaphysics of our culture' (Carroll 1986: 63–71). Performance captures
this 'structure of feeling' (see p. 32). The *Encyclopedia* entry of 2003
ends with a more heroic synthesis. It implies a narrative whereby an
embodied and critical understanding of the Western dialectic between the
Real and representation has progressively emerged and now underpins
radical Performance practice (see chapters 5 and 9). The figure here is
of a braiding of political currents, whereby 'Feminism was by the 1990s
only one branch of multiculturalism, which also included the politics of
ethnic identities, sexuality, and ability'. On this terrain, 'the concerns
of art performance and performance art overlapped and intertwined'
(Kennedy 2003: 1023).

Let us turn to another narrative. It foregrounds the influence of the
avant garde of the early twentieth century. Roselee Goldberg wrote
Performance: Live Art 1909 to the Present (1979) when performance
had just begun to gain acceptance as 'a medium . . . in its own right'.
She argues that the recent practices she maps had laid bare a 'hidden
history' that she also traces, interwoven with the standard art histories.
While the latter have been dedicated to the enduring object (the painting,

building or poem, say), 'artists have always turned to live performance as one means among many of articulating their ideas'. Formally, Performance as considered by Goldberg 'denies precise or easy definition beyond the simple declaration that it is live by live artists'. It draws on a wide range of influences, including 'literature, theatre, drama, music, architecture, poetry, film and fantasy'. Culturally, Goldberg considers Performance as constituting an 'avant avant garde' in the twentieth century, it being the chosen recourse of artists 'who led the field in breaking with each successive tradition'. She figures Performance as the quintessence of the avant garde, its self-doubling and its sharpest point. Meanwhile, Goldberg provides no evidence for her contention that 'live gestures have *constantly* been used as a weapon against the conventions of established art'. It seems designed to stake a special claim for Performance as agent. Goldberg conceptualises Performance both as the quintessence of the historically specific avant garde and as a transhistorical mode of artistic innovation (Goldberg 1979: 6–7, emphasis added).

Tracing a route from the Futurists to the work of Wilson and Foreman, Goldberg aligns Performance with the manifesto in the opening stages of her narrative. Futurists, Constructivists, Dadaists and Surrealists typically only turned to the making of objects *after* a declamatory phase of live performance. The anarchic and utopian 'performance manifesto' challenges not only dominant artistic conventions but also the division between the major genres themselves (Goldberg 1979: 6). Her narrative embraces a wide range of aesthetic performance practices thereafter. Covering a vast and complex field in a short space, the chapters on contemporary Performance have the feel of a card index organised into chronological chunks with only the occasional formal map or cultural signpost. The book has been challenged both for its inclusiveness and for its exclusions. Kershaw (1999) argues that by lashing together, for instance, the historical avant garde and the 'media generation' of the 1980s, she dilutes the category of Performance to the point of evacuation.

Marvin Carlson (1996) meanwhile challenges Goldberg for historically aligning Performance with the twentieth-century avant garde in the first place. It limits our understanding both of how contemporary Performance works and of its relationship to historical performance. Goldberg makes an inadequate attempt to draw, for example, medieval and renaissance non-theatrical performances into her own schema. Carlson suggests how such manifestations might adequately be included in a more complex narrative. His focus is on the 'manifestation of the artist's "presence" through a striking display of technical accomplishment and virtuosity', and he deploys Jean Alter's distinction between theatre's 'referential' and 'performant' functions, the latter embracing not just the performer's presence, but 'the direct physical experience of the event' (Carlson 1996: 80–2, citing Alter 1990). There is a history to be told, then, of performances that comprise, in Alter's terms, predominantly 'performant' elements.

Carlson argues that the most adequate way to consider contemporary Performance is to see it as being, if not always in continuity, at least cognate with performances in 'the marketplace, the fairground, the circus' or 'private court entertainments, aristocratic salons and soirées'. And, as he notes, very many dramas that have since been corralled into the literary sphere were produced for a theatre ablaze with non-referential activity, popular renaissance theatre perhaps providing the most poignant example. He joins Kostelanetz (1968) in arguing that 'the almost universal attempt by theatre scholars to develop a European-style history of literary theatre for the United States has been misguided'. The key term is performance rather than literature. From this perspective, the significance of cabaret is much less that it was appropriated by the European avant garde, than the persistence of the popular form itself. Most importantly, it more closely 'prefigures the dynamic' of contemporary Performance (Carlson 1996: 83–7). But in the event, Carlson does relatively little to substantiate this sense of the popular tradition as a determination on American Performance.

Carlson, as others, identifies nodal points of innovation in American experimental performance. First is the event at Black Mountain College mounted by Cage, Cunningham, Rauschenberg and others in 1952. Carlson cites Natalie Crohn Schmitt's argument, in 1990, that Cage effected a category shift in the arts that parallels the collapse of positivist science. It displaces traditional Aristotelian aesthetics with an 'emphasis on the phenomenal experience of performer, performance event and audience'. Carlson figures the Black Mountain College event as a transformative recapitulation of many aesthetic characteristics of the earlier avant gardes. But for him it also exemplifies the individual dancer as the United States' particular contribution to experimental performance since those earlier decades. He draws on a well-established three-step narrative in dance history: pioneer solo work in Europe before 1914 by Duncan and others; a concern with abstraction and allegory in the Graham generation that defined modern dance; and the rejection by a third generation of an emphasis on content in favour of 'individual clarity and independence'. And, of this generation, Merce Cunningham emerges as the pivotal link, especially in his collaboration with Cage. Parallel to Cage's work in music was Halprin's dance practice on the West Coast, developing earlier work on everyday activities and scripting task-oriented movement, helping 'prepare the way for happenings and other performance activities of the 1960s', partly through the development of such work at Judson Church in New York (Carlson 1996: 93–5).

Carlson's second nodal point is Kaprow's *18 Happenings in 6 Parts* of 1959. Kaprow used 'happening' in contradistinction to 'theatre' or 'performance' to evoke the idea that the event, in Kaprow's words, 'just happens to happen'. Yet, Carlson observes, the event was typically 'scripted, rehearsed, and carefully controlled' (see Keywords: Aleatory). Kaprow scripts a slippage between art and the rest of life. The possibility of theatrical 'occasion' and its passive audience is obviated in particular by discontinuities of time and place. Kaprow hated the aura of theatricality that adhered to his happenings when audiences began to gather. Such an aura was the opposite of 'art' and 'purposive activity' (Carlson 1996: 96–7, citing Kaprow).

Carlson suggests that similar events, but conducted by single artists, more closely prefigure 1970s Performance. He judges that field as it developed into the 1980s to be so complex that little more than a map of its 'general parameters' can be accomplished. But he distinguishes between two general types of quasi-theatrical performance that for the most part developed along separate tracks through the 1970s. One is the typically one-person show using life materials, often done in a gallery space. The other – not designated 'performance' at the time – is what Kostelanetz (1968) and Marranca ([1977] 1996) treat under the rubrics of 'the theatre of mixed means' and the 'Theatre of Images' respectively. These multi-media theatrical shows typically foregrounded 'both process and reception'. Carlson meanwhile suggests that early Performance itself signalled a potential cross-over between the two modes of work, with Laurie Anderson and Robert Wilson as prime examples. And it is

Anderson who provides Carlson's third nodal point. He argues that her popularly-pitched *United States* (1980) did two things: it combined 'the two hitherto quite disparate approaches to performance' and 'brought the concept of performance art for the first time to a wide general public' (Carlson 1996: 96–105).

THE QUESTION OF CRITIQUE

In *Performance Art: From Futurism to the Present* (1988), Goldberg updated her 1979 narrative simply by adding pages to cover further years. Contrast another book from the late 1970s and its subsequent reissue. Bonnie Marranca's *The Theatre of Images* (1977) – a collection of scripts by Richard Foreman, Robert Wilson and Lee Breuer with essays by Marranca – offers to make sense of an emergence, as avant-garde theatre developed from obscurity to make New York a leading centre (Marranca 1996: ix–x). She is centrally concerned with the relationships between the critical discourses and practices of theatre and of the visual arts. *The Theatre of Images* brought these together 'in a new understanding of performance'. A 'coherent history of performance ideas' depends on the integration of the two histories in 'a comprehensive view of the twentieth century' (Marranca 1996: 164).

Marranca's specifically *theatrical* focus is of significance. Precisely, this is 'theatre for a post-literate age' (Kostelanetz 1968: 33). The works make transformative appropriations from Western theatre: Foreman for instance radicalises Brechtian technique. But for the most part their use of space, time and language do not derive from theatre, but from television and the cinema (Marranca 1996: ix–x). Marranca identifies two kinds of critical distanciation in the work. First, the shift in aesthetic grounding provokes 'a crisis in the artist's choice of creative materials, and in his relationship to the art object'. Audiences are thereby made acutely aware of their process of reception. The works are 'about the making of art'. Second, whether the works are text-based or not, they are concerned fundamentally with composition, and this is for a purpose. The 'alternative modes of perception' engineered by the aural, visual and verbal imagery aid 'a critique of reality' (Marranca 1996: ix–x).

In the second edition of *The Theatre of Images*, published in 1996, Marranca looks back on the 'glorious period' of 1970s downtown New

York, where 'a genuine avant-garde community' of artists, critics, and audiences organically generated an 'expansive discourse' around performance. Foreman, Wilson and Breuer in particular had 'rethought the nature of theatre, representation, and spectatorship'. In literary studies, McHale (1987) distinguishes between modernism's 'epistemological dominant' and the 'ontological dominant' of postmodernism, marking a shift from concerns about truth to ones about being and foundation. While Marranca aligns the Theatre of Images with the latter, she identifies it as 'modernist'. In a 1939 essay, Walter Benjamin suggested that the essence of the modernist Brecht's theatre of distanciation was the principle of interruption. In 1977, Marranca writes that the Theatre of Images is 'timeless . . . abstract and presentational'. She observes that the tableaux of the Theatre of Images 'compel the spectator to analyze its specific placement in the artistic framework, stopping time by throwing a scene into relief'. In 1996, she links her trio specifically to the modernist avant garde, especially as it had developed in the visual arts and dance. Their theatre had 'called for an art-historical understanding and an openness to conceptual thinking'. What had gone missing since was 'a certain quality of imagination' (Marranca 1996: 159–60, xii–xiii).

In retrospect, Marranca develops a number of linked binaries of opposition. One of these is modernism versus postmodernism. Where McHale maps a shift in the 'dominant', Marranca maps a simple decadence. The Theatre of Images had generated 'the last formalist, avant-garde theatre vocabulary', which 'emphasized the experience of the mind, the value of structure'; postmodern production since has merely celebrated 'pastiche', thriving on a 'general tolerance of mediocrity' and an arts culture of 'unrelenting hype'. To map the cause of this decline, Marranca invokes the triumph of 'theory' over 'art': right and left alike have stifled art with ideological agendas. The 1970s emphasis on a 'politics of consciousness' has been displaced by a 'social agenda'. 'Pedagogy' has triumphed over 'experience'; 'Foucault' over 'Duchamp' (Marranca 1996: 161–2).

The ideological agendas Marranca finds so stifling include feminism, queer and postcolonial theory. But she also turns to another agenda that might also be termed ideological, and sets the frame in which the first set operates, in her analysis, to the detriment of art: the agenda of accessibility. The 1970s were glorious because the avant-garde arts community was 'a subculture, positioning itself against the exigencies of the marketplace and populist demands, revelling in its freedom to embrace complexity'. But a break point was reached when in 1985 Laurie Anderson launched her work into the rock music business, was welcomed there and set a ball rolling. The result has been government attacks on artistic freedom and the decline of much Performance to the level of the TV talk show. The 'imagining of an entire other world, different from the empirical world, with its own language' was lost. Carlson's point of synthesis reappears here as Marranca's moment of betrayal (Marranca 1996: 162–3).

Marranca, then, declares a break. The Theatre of Images was, apart from a few exceptions, 'the last manifestation' of American theatre's 'utopian, universal spirit'. Since then, 'formal preoccupations' have been drowned by the 'political-cultural tide'. As US theatre becomes again dominated by the word, the languages of 'image–movement–music–text–technology' find new life in 'installations, photography, and video' which are organising themselves as 'the future of performance'. Lyotard suggests that postmodernism does not so much succeed modernism as work through some of its own problematics. Marranca here figures the Theatre of Images as tackling ontological concerns through modernist techniques of defamiliarisation. And rather than map theatre/performance and modernism/postmodernism as equivalent binaries, she concerns herself with tracking this avant-garde mission of critique from one species of theatre to a possible future of performance (Marranca 1996: 164–5 *passim*).

FLUXUS AND SITUATIONISM: KEYS TO ANOTHER NARRATIVE

Let us now return to the European avant garde. What do Goldberg and Carlson draw on to construct their narratives? Can we identify some alternative extensions to their joint excursion into American Performance?

Carlson provides a model of continuity and discontinuity between the avant garde of the early twentieth century and later work. Both share an interest in breaking down the boundaries between the arts and between art and life; and both focus on the performer as the creator, and on process rather than product. But while in the 1920s, the performer was one part of the ensemble of matters of expression, later performance was to focus on the performer as an individual (Carlson 1996: 89–93 *passim*).

Goldberg traces the energy and basic principles of Futurism through Dada, Constructivism, Surrealism and beyond, finding both a line of influence and some frequently shared concerns: the mass audience; play and pleasure; treating life as the subject of art; and finding a way to live (Goldberg 1979: 6–7). The Second World War provided a turning point, by interrupting the dominance of Surrealism, which had made 'the vast realms of the mind' the primary material for art, but largely remained language-based. After the war, artists turned to 'the basic tenets of Dada and Futurism – chance, simultaneity and surprise' (Goldberg 1988: 96).

In addition to indirect influences, Goldberg and Carlson both trace a direct link with pre-war Europe through the 1930s emigration of artists fleeing Nazism. The key link here is the Dessau Bauhaus, which in 1921 became the first institution to provide a specific course on performance. There, Oskar Schlemmer conducted systematic investigations of space, and with others pointed the way towards Moholy-Nagy's dream of a 'theatre of totality' that would free spectators from passivity, allowing them to 'fuse with the action on the stage'. Schlemmer celebrated the Bauhaus as being based on imaginative play, improvisation and the grotesque, noting its probable debt to Dada: it recognised 'the origin, conditions, and laws of theatrical play' (Goldberg 1988: 102–20 citing Schlemmer). The appointment of ex-Bauhaus émigrés to Black Mountain College in the US from 1933 was directly to inspire the experiments there of Cage and Cunningham: 'a turning point' (Goldberg 1979: 7).

Carlson almost entirely brackets off the political aspects of the avant garde. Goldberg affords them passing mention. She figures the Italian Futurist Marinetti as 'utilising' the political turmoil against Austrian domination for his own artistic agenda, rather than seeing that agenda as part of the turmoil (Goldberg 1979: 10). Similarly, the drive to follow Futurism's influence through the century reduces the Soviet Blue Blouse to 'the ultimate realisation, on a grand scale, of Marinetti's variety theatre', while passing swiftly over its revolutionary purpose (Goldberg 1988: 46). Marinetti's proclamation that 'the time will come when life will no longer be a simple matter of bread and labour . . . but a *work of art*' (quoted by Goldberg 1979: 21) has a more substantial political moment in historical terms than Goldberg allows. Let us then join Goldberg and Carlson in pursuing the avant garde deriving from Futurism. But by now focusing on the political dimension, we shall find other historical extensions to the avant garde. This will help us to map contemporary Performance in relation to other cognate practices.

We begin with Stewart Home's *The Assault on Culture* (1991), which also traces a narrative hitherto mostly unwritten in English. His concern is with a loose formation of 'dissident clusters', an 'anti-Bolshevik communism' greatly informed since 1945 by Futurism and Dada. It corresponds broadly to the Russian term *samizdat*, a dissident tradition concerned with self-organisation, its adherents often performing actions and simultaneously documenting them (Home 1991: 102). Points on his narrative include COBRA, Lettrisme, the Situationists, Fluxus, the Dutch Provos, Yippies, Punk and Class War. Home provides us with another map and another narrative which both intersect and contrast with those for instance of Goldberg, Carlson, Schechner and, as we shall see, Kaye. The performances Home tracks range from disruptive interventions into the practices of art to varieties of anarchist political and cultural action. While these are pertinent to the inclusive category of 'performance', Fluxus and Situationism bring us closest to the currently dominant concerns of a school of performance studies that centres itself on the aesthetic genre Performance.

Fluxus

Many of the artists first associated with Fluxus, including Allan Kaprow and Dick Higgins, had attended Cage's course in musical composition at the New School for Social Research in 1958. Its effective founder, George Maciunas, attended parallel classes.

From his relatively formalist point of view, Nick Kaye (1994b: 32) properly foregrounds the ways in which Fluxus objects and events confuse the distinction between art object and use object, and implicate the viewer in the making of meaning. But from Home's perspective, of equal significance is the fact that Fluxus was conceived in 1961 as an alternative distribution system for new work. In 1978, composer Nam June Paik celebrated Maciunas' prescience. Marx had focused on workers gaining control of the system of production; but while many artists own and control their medium, they nevertheless remain subjected to and alienated by the distribution system of the art world. Maciunas' revolutionary aim was to free art from the market so as to render it performative in the everyday (Smith 1998: 18).

In the event, the distribution systems developed around Fluxus were limited and under-resourced. And, by a huge irony, its multiple editions, designed to challenge both the commoditisation of art and its claim to profundity through uniqueness, have since become expensive collectors' items (Smith 1998: 16–17). Fluxus split as early as 1964 on political grounds, partly because Maciunas tried to run Fluxus as a centralised organisation along Leninist lines, contradicting its supposed guiding principle of dispersal. But there is more to it than this. When Fluxus moved into Europe, it developed both an artistic focus in intermedial performance and a cultural agenda that adds up to a political orientation, 'a specific anti-institutional stance'. Yet when Maciunas tried to further this potential back in America he met opposition (Smith 1998: 8–12). Calls in 1963 for demonstrations and acts of sabotage against institutions of 'serious art' and in 1964 to picket a Stockhausen concert, on the basis that the composer was a creature of the establishment, alienated members such as George Brecht and Kaprow. Maciunas gave up the political agenda. Fluxus in America was destined to become defined along aesthetic rather than overtly political lines (Home 1991: 53–4).

Early Fluxus recapitulated and transformed the cultural radicalism of Dada and Futurism. For its diehards, its works and performances were intended 'gradually to lead to the elimination of the category of fine art altogether' (Smith 1998: 18). Home argues that, in 1964, Fluxus could still properly claim a radically performative, 'functionalist' view of art. The typical emphasis on a single isolated action – say the destruction of a musical instrument, or simple unrelated actions performed to a found performance score – 'presented . . . an iconoclastic insight into the nature of reality itself'. But he complains that the designation of Fluxus actions as 'performance art' merely makes them fodder for histories of art. These focus on the 'mysticism' of North American Fluxus rather than the more 'hard edged' European manifestations (Home 1991: 52, 56). There are signs since that this neglect is being repaired.

Maciunas in the 1960s 'continually tried to demonstrate that Fluxus was neither serious culture nor serious anti-culture, but something else entirely . . . not part of the existing cultural system, in either its modes of production or distribution' (Smith 1998: 18). Home indicates a further specific area of social performance within Fluxus' sights: the urban environment. In *Fantastic Architecture* (1969), for instance, Wolf Vostell bears witness to a demand for 'unconsumed' built environments, geared to new patterns of social behaviour (Home 1991: 58).

Situationism and Debord

The Situationist International (SI) is best known for its involvement in the proto-revolutionary events of May 1968 in Paris. Wollen sees this as one of a series of 'legendary moments which serve to celebrate the convergence of popular revolution with art in revolt' (Wollen 1993: 120). Placing it in his own narrative of *samizdat*, Home follows Guy Debord to claim that Situationism draws on both Dada and Surrealism, so as to dispel a lack in each. We shall spend some time here on Debord, one of the chief theoreticians of Situationism, not in order to inflate his significance, but because he raises a number of useful maps and narratives for us. The ground we traverse here may as yet be unfamiliar to most students of performance. But it will lead us to (and therefore contextualise) some more familiar terrain with respect to performance, representation and postmodernity.

Debord argues that Dada had attempted to negate art, and not to realise it; while the Surrealists had attempted to realise art but without negating it. Surrealist André Breton had argued that art and politics should pursue their own separate ends, until social revolution produced the conditions in which art would no longer be limited by historical contingencies. Individuals could nevertheless transform aspects of everyday life in the here and now, by making voluntary use of unconscious desires in a poeticisation of everyday life. But, in Freudian terms, the unconscious is repressed desire. Rather than liberate the unconscious into the everyday, Debord wanted to abolish the very condition of its existence. Desire should have its full and free expression in direct democracy: 'the poetic revolution must be the political revolution, and vice-versa'. Art was to disappear as a category and be integrated into the totality of life. Art was to be realised through its negation (Wollen 1993: 133–6; and see Home 1991: 102–4).

As Wollen demonstrates, Debord's *The Society of the Spectacle* ([1967] 1994) folds three elements together: the theoretical framework of the Marxist Georg Lukács's *History and Class Consciousness* ([1923] 1971), the direct-democracy model of council communism upheld by the French Trotskyist group *Socialisme ou barbarie*, and the Situationist analysis of culture and society. Let us briefly pursue each of these three.

Lukács' theory of 'reification' figures the commodity as the reified form of human labour in the era of capitalist mass production. The goods we buy conceal the labour that produced them. Debord adapts Lukács's model to figure contemporary alienation in the era of mass consumption. If in the 1920s the commodity masked the process of human labour, the subject in the advanced capitalism of the1960s is fundamentally alienated from a grasp on reality itself by the universal dominance both of commodities and of the practices of representation commodity culture requires and sustains. The spectacle of appearances blinds modern subjects to reality and so also blunts their agency (Wollen 1993: 126).

Socialism ou barbarie takes us to a concern with representation in another sense. At the heart of their politics was the model of council communism first developed by the Left Opposition soon after the Bolshevik Revolution of 1917. Rather than seize the state for the Party, who would then work on behalf of the proletariat towards the withering of the state, as Lenin prescribed, the workers should immediately abolish the state itself and install systems of direct democracy.

With regard to situations, the found situation is given as the sole frame for human action in Sartre's existentialist writings, both philosophical and dramatic. Debord diverts Sartre's existential emphasis through the prism of Marxist philosopher Henri Lefebvre's *Critique of Everyday Life* (1947), into a prospectus for the interventionist *construction* of situations. He develops rubrics for such performativity in the frames first of the interpersonal, then of the city (urbanism), and finally of the social and historical totality (Wollen 1993: 125–6).

Debord draws on Trotskyism to claim that in both East and West the contradiction between middle and working classes has been supplanted by the opposition between a dominant bureaucratic class and its drones. From Lukács he borrows a model of false consciousness. For Lukács, proletarians could begin to liberate themselves once they saw through ideology and gained consciousness of their already-scripted historic role in humanity's progress to socialism. For Debord, liberation would come in the West when people gained true consciousness of their alienation in and by the spectacle, and thus engaged with reality. And this was something that could be achieved immediately. Total liberation was possible now.

The involvement of SI in the events of May 1968 was conducted on this basis and understanding. They would not offer leadership, but perform disruptions of the spectacle so as to release the autonomous subjectivities of the oppressed, so that they might perform directly on and in reality. The revolt was suppressed. And ironically, Debord's attempt to animate the politics of the situation was overshadowed and supplanted by SI's spectacular cultural initiatives. SI declined thereafter and was dissolved in 1972.

WESTERN MARXISM AND AFTER

The idea that the disbanding of the SI brought to an end an epoch of interaction between avant-garde arts and radical politics that began with the Futurist Manifesto is widely shared. But, for Wollen, the end of the SI also marked 'the summation of Western Marxism'. This is a more precise formulation than the supposed end of Marxism altogether, thanks to poststructuralist and postmodern critique. While the main focus of classic Marxism was on history and economics, Western Marxism shifted its emphasis to philosophy and aesthetics. This led to much of the 'critical theory' which animated performance studies, and hence also some practice, in the mid-1980s. Some have regarded Western Marxism as a detour, provoked by the collapse of the revolutionary project in the West. But others see it as a continuation of a left-orientation within classical Marxism, the continuation of a tradition of direct democracy, an historical alternative to Leninism. In the West, these more 'vitalist and libertarian forms of activism' were progressively woven together with classical Marxism. Lukács' *History and Class Consciousness*, published in French translation in 1960, was one stopping point along the way (Wollen 1993: 123–4).

Wollen usefully distinguishes between two artistic currents that have been active in the West – the 'Western avant-gardism' of Surrealism and its successors on one hand, and the Bauhaus and Constructivism on the other. He summarises, 'whereas Breton wanted to take art and poetry into everyday life, the aim in the Soviet Union was to take art into production'. The 'Soviet' model – that adumbrates for instance much of Brecht – was well on the wane in the West by 1968. For Wollen, the double summation of the Western avant garde and Western Marxism emblematised by the SI makes May 1968 'both a curtain and a prologue, a turning point in a drama we are still blindly living'. The means to liberation and the end of alienation remain obscure (Wollen 1993: 124–30).

Nonetheless, the question of art, including aesthetic performance, as an ethical or political praxis of course remains on the agenda. By attending further to May 1968 we shall encounter the provenance of some familiar propositions about the terms on which resistant art can operate in a postmodern world. Students of performance learn early on, for instance, about Lyotard's declaration of the end of all grand narratives, one of the death blows to Marxism.

The events of May 1968 led to a major reappraisal of revolutionary politics in France and beyond; this in turn was a major influence on French poststructuralism. If the Situationists failed in their attempt to be the nursemaid of popular revolution, May 1968 brought aspects of their perspective home to theorists of the revolutionary left who had thought they might lead a more orderly one. Organised political opposition came to be conceived as being itself 'integrated within the structures it thinks it is opposing' because it duplicates 'the very relations of power it imagines itself capable of negating' (Plant 1992: 118). At the same time, the Situationists' insistence on multiplicity also unsettled their own theoretical model of there being a governing contradiction within capitalism, based in the bureaucracy and its spectacle. Thus, the notion of spontaneous and total revolt issuing in a unified society based in the real also became untenable. The totalisations of both the Situationists and the traditional left had been fundamentally challenged.

Plant (1992) finds traces of 'the line of imaginative dissent' from Dada to May 1968 not only in poststructuralism but also in the postmodern perspectives it ushered in. Focusing particularly on the Situationists, she finds the gestures of appropriation, *détournement* (semantic shift, diversion) and *dérive* (drift) continued in poststructuralist writing, and the same key emphases on play, pleasure, subversion, the everyday and desire. And here we meet some familiar names (Plant 1992: 111–12).

As Plant summarises, Lyotard had before 1968 already begun to view revolutionary theory as merely 'a moral critique of capitalism' based on utopian hope and 'faith in humanity'. By pursuing dialectical synthesis in history and true consciousness in the working class, revolutionary groups were in fact oppressing the already oppressed. These were abstract models imposed on and falsely representing people's properly various perspectives and desires. His engagement in the events of May 1968 as a member of the *mouvement du 22 mars* confirmed him in this. Lyotard is perhaps best known for his attack on 'grand narratives'. In *The Postmodern Condition* ([1979] 1989) he argues that theories depend on stories told about the world (of progress, or salvation, for instance) and have no other basis, except for their testing and development by critique. And since critique is also baseless, to conduct it is to engage in 'dogmatic or even paranoid relations of knowledge'. He evokes instead the 'hidden intensities, desires and assumptions' that 'interrupt the apparent rigour of theory'. A 'politics of desire' is necessary to subvert the codifications of both capitalism and the revolutionary left (Plant 1992: 112–15, citing Lyotard; and see Anderson 1998: 24–36 for a critique).

Foucault argued in similar vein, figuring power, knowledge and subjectivity in performative terms. His reflection on the May events led him to believe that the analysis of social relations as a totality 'must be superseded by the study of an enormously complex series of specific power relations'. Perhaps most famously, Foucault argued that power is everywhere. The point is not to try to locate and resist an oppressive origin of power, but to trace its myriad operations, which can be facilitative as well as oppressive. Knowledge is the product of discourse generated as an articulation of power, and is therefore always local, provisional and partial. Human subjectivity is itself produced; it too is an effect of discourse. Thus there can be no presumptions as to truth, in the sense of a knowable reality to be grasped by an independently knowing subject. Knowledge is performative: 'representation itself becomes a meaningless term' (Plant 1992: 116–19).

People are, however, still oppressed in the world. What then can be done? Foucault draws on Nietzsche's idea of 'a perpetual contest between reason and the raw events it circumscribes' to propose domination be resisted through counter-discourse, 'localised and specific forms of knowledge . . . pitted against the totalising theories which would claim them'. Accordingly, he helped in 1971 to establish the *Groupe d'Information sur les Prisons* to promote the perspective of people imprisoned due to the 1968 events. In his major writings, Foucault tracks the genealogies of discourses concerned with discipline and sexuality. As Plant observes, his method includes the use of moments from totalising theories, not to claim their authority, but as parts of an available 'tool-kit'. Breton spoke in similar terms. Lyotard specifically invokes the Situationist principle of *dérive*: 'Critique must be drifted out of. Better still: Drifting is in itself the end of all critique.' And he similarly identifies 'avant-garde' research as being 'functionally outside the system' (Plant 1992: 119–21, citing Foucault).

Deleuze and Guattari also intersect crucially with the events of May 1968, and continue now to be a major influence. As Massumi (1992) relates, their *Anti-Oedipus* ([1972] 1984) both conducts a radical attack on Western systems of thought and identity and proposes 'a new typology of cultural formations'. They argue that in Western metaphysics since Plato, thinking subjects, their concepts and the objects they apply these to have been presumed to be self-identical, to have an essence. This is sustained by the principle of negation, whereby the identity of something is maintained by its active differentiation from what it is not. The system works through representation, which is to say the principle of analogy between object and concept. The analogy is made possible by the prevention of concepts or objects as it were leaking into one another. This is achieved by the 'limitative distribution' of qualities (identified with *logos*, law), and a 'hierarchical ranking' according to 'the degree of perfection in relation to a supreme standard' (such as 'God'). Of especially local interest to us here are both the critique of representation and the identification of its performative nature. Deleuze and Guattari further identify Western metaphysics as 'state philosophy'. The unitary essences of subject, concept and objects reflect, embody and sustain the unity of the state. Even when the state is crumbling in the face of international capital, the structures and procedures of state philosophy continue to operate. Modern universities are based on the model of the University of Berlin, which was explicitly founded on these principles (Massumi 1992: 3–4).

Actively to displace this system, Deleuze and Guattari elaborate their arguments in another manner, embodied in *A Thousand Plateaus* ([1980] 1988). Here, performativity is foregrounded. Rather than presuming an interiority, their 'nomad thought' celebrates exteriority and promiscuously makes use of disparate sources on the principle of 'conductivity' rather than of 'restrictive analogy'. Nomad thought escapes the 'striations' or 'grids' of state philosophy, instead working in 'smooth' or 'open-ended' space, where thought can perhaps emulate the tunnelling of electrons, moving from one place to another without traversing distance. Concepts are acts, utterly contingent upon the circumstance. Meaning emerges from the agglomeration of heterogeneous elements into points of coincidence, or 'intensities' which, if sustained, may come to constitute a 'plateau', a sort of holding together they call 'consistency' or 'style'. Deleuze and Guattari's foregrounding of performativity in a given situation is embodied in their term 'pragmatics'. In terms of their life performances, Guattari worked from the mid-1950s at a radical psychiatric clinic, where the traditional hierarchical relationship between doctor and patient was given over to collective social critique. A philosopher, Deleuze performed critical subversions of 'great' philosophers and tracked links between supposedly minor figures. Both came to the events of May 1968, then, as part of the nomadic forces that were to help it erupt and shape its aftermath. Indeed, it arguably constitutes a plateau (Massumi 1992: 2–7 *passim*).

As Lane (2000) explores, the events of May 1968 hastened the development of Baudrillard too – who brought to the experience, for instance, a resistance to the abstract idea of progress promulgated by the French state from the 1950s. Baudrillard has famously championed the idea that in contemporary society there is no reality other than the *simulacrum*, or copy. While Plant (1992) finds hope for the future in the theorists we have just reviewed, Baudrillard for her marks the point at which poststructuralist and postmodern thought becomes historically pessimistic and thus reactionary. In *The Radical in Performance* (1999), Kershaw places Baudrillard as the antithesis to Brecht. However, Zurbrugg (1998: 172–4) suggests that the finest of Baudrillard's writings, as well as the finest Fluxus and Dada works, are 'best understood as a kind of highly serious joke' – a 'ground-clearing exercise' that moves beyond the 'self-deconstructing wordplay' of postmodern writing. Baudrillard in fact castigates the very idea of the 'postmodern'. The performativity of his writings is complex because his intention is radically uncertain.

As we have noted, Western Marxism developed a theory of capitalist culture mostly disengaged from the economic concerns of classical Marxism. And it typically concerned itself with questions of aesthetics and high art rather than culture more organically understood. In a celebration of Fredric Jameson's work from the 1980s, Perry Anderson takes us again to the situation post-1968. The progressive congealing of high modernism had removed Western Marxism's aesthetic ground. And the political tumult suggested that a return to questions of political transformation and economic analysis was now due. The work of Western Marxism was over. However, Anderson argues, Jameson's work can be seen both as a recuperation of that tradition and one of its highest achievements. Drawing on Ernest Mandel's economic analysis and synthesising perspectives from Western Marxism, Jameson has developed a Marxist specification of postmodernism as the cultural logic of late capitalism. And while in the era of modernism, art and economics operated at least superficially as separate realms of value, in the postmodern era of late capitalism, politics and economics are inseparable from the realm of aesthetic representation. But, though this is a significant turn for theory, the path to radical transformation is still not clear (Anderson 1998: 47–77).

7

THE RISE OF
PERFORMANCE STUDIES

THE FIRST PERFORMANCE STUDIES DEPARTMENT

Richard Schechner is central to the development of Performance Studies as a discipline that embraces a range of human activity including for instance play, games, sports, theatre and ritual. In 1980, New York University's Graduate Drama Program was renamed the Graduate Department of Performance Studies, with Schechner at its centre. In 1986, Phillip Zarrilli reflected on this 'institutional and programmatic recognition of the increasingly interdisciplinary nature' of both performance practice and the theorised study of performance, by seeing how some recent books might begin to define the field (Zarrilli 1986, I: 372).

The idea that everyday life could be described as performance, '*performance as a fact of culture*', was now widely accepted. In the light of Singer's idea of 'cultural performance', Theatre Studies could now be specified as just one important part of a 'nexus of cultural metacommentaries', being concerned with one particular species of '*performance as an act*'. The task of the Performance Studies researcher in general, including the theatre specialist, was to articulate both 'the "deep structure" of meaning' disclosed by instances of performance, and the 'processual means' of its coming to expression, whether it be for instance rite, festival or theatre (Zarrilli 1986, I: 372–3, original emphasis).

Zarrilli takes keywords in the titles of some books – 'Rehearsals', 'Towards', 'Between' – to signal three things: a 'transitional' or 'liminal' period in which the field of performance studies was defining itself; the inherent provisionalities of interdisciplinary work; and the strong emergence of 'praxis' – the active mediation between theory and practice – in the academy. Looking back on the series of conferences that led up to the establishment of Performance Studies, he remarks that Schechner's insistence on the rehearsal process had prompted the social scientists to shift their gaze from the finished cultural product. Performance Studies insists on process (Zarrilli 1986, I: 373).

Zarrilli finds Schechner unparalleled in 'his attempt to embrace performance at its widest limits' through both practical and theoretical means. Schechner's thought is 'processual': he writes in the same way he makes performances, 'never finally arriving'. But while his insights are of 'great cross-cultural, theoretical, and potentially practical importance', his 'quick cuts and turns' make weak links, and he is given to overstatement and inappropriate use of value-laden terminology (Zarrilli 1986, I: 375–6). In chapter 8 we note Schechner's critique of the Cambridge School's thesis that theatre derived from ritual. Schechner writes that the model has only persisted because it is self-repairing, being based mostly on supposition, easily compressed and generalised, and therefore also easily teachable (1988: 5). But Schechner's alternative model of an efficiency/entertainment braid is also of course all of these things. It also places Schechner's own performance work at one of its privileged points. And in allowing 'efficiency' to include profits on Broadway, Schechner evacuates the term he has established.

Zarrilli also writes that Schechner's 'highly reflexive' models often do not 'tell us how other performers in other less reflective cultures view their own process' (Zarrilli 1986, I: 376). He calls for an active dialectic between 'abstract model building' and an attempt to understand 'a culture's understanding of itself'. Zarrilli sums up by suggesting that a shift needs to be instituted in the American university curriculum, from educating 'theatre practitioners as craftspersons' to developing 'practitioner/ theorists who will be eternally "between" and in process' (Zarrilli 1986, 2: 496).

SCHECHNER AND THE ETHICS OF PERFORMANCE STUDIES

In the first true undergraduate primer in the field, *Performance Studies: An Introduction*, Schechner figures the emergence of the discipline as part of a paradigm shift in Western culture as a whole. Performance Studies results from 'dissatisfaction with the *status quo*' and an 'explosion of knowledge' due in part to the internet. It emerges at the crux of a change constituted by new modes of knowledge production and circulation, feeding and fed by new relations and ethics of knowledge production: 'The world no longer appeared as a book to be read but as a performance to participate in' (Schechner 2002: 19).

Schechner's claims for Performance Studies are both ethical and far-reaching: he wants it to be 'nothing less than . . . a necessary tool for living'. The introductory chapter ends with a student exercise asking how Performance Studies can make the world a better place. He elaborates four ways in which the idea of 'action' informs Performance Studies. It is the object of study, especially in the sense of cultural repertoires of behaviour: 'what people do in the activity of their doing it'. And performance studies practitioners variously undertake three forms of activity: artistic practice, typically integrated with other modes of apprehension of the objects of study; participant observation (often of the home culture); and social intervention as the proper outcome of their investigations. Schechner emphasises the ethical dimension (Schechner 2002: 1–21).

Performance Studies is concerned with 'anything that is framed, presented, highlighted, or displayed' and actively regards phenomena and objects not traditionally considered performances, in their performative aspect: for instance, how a painting interacts with viewers. Meanwhile, Performance Studies refuses the option of becoming a traditional academic discipline. As Barbara Kirstenblatt-Gimblett declared in 1999. Performance Studies takes its lead from 'the historical avant-garde and contemporary art, which have long questioned the boundaries between modalities and gone about blurring them, whether those boundaries mark off media, genres, or cultural traditions'. Dominant Western academic and artistic categories are inadequate to address either contemporary Western performance, or the arts of other cultures, which have 'always synthesised or otherwise integrated movement, sound, speech, narrative, and objects'. The core is 'embodied practice and event' or 'presence, liveness, agency' (Schechner 2002: 3, citing Kirstenblatt-Gimblett).

While globalisation promotes 'cultural sameness' Performance Studies promotes 'tensions and partialities'. It resists hierarchies of 'ideas, organisations, or people' and is 'sympathetic to the avant-garde, the marginal, the offbeat, the minoritarian, the subversive, the twisted, the queer, people of color, and the formerly colonized'. It works best 'amidst a dense web of connections'. It celebrates postmodern performativity, which blurs any distinction between illusion and reality: in sum, 'It is hard to imagine performance studies getting its act together, or even wanting to' (Schechner 2002: 2–19).

If these are dizzying claims, much of their substance can be demonstrated. But, in the vortex of enthusiasm, some things drift out of view.

Indeed, Schechner is in fact often *less* than conventionally attentive to a range of disciplinary perspectives that might enrich Performance Studies. For example, he notes the move from book-based to digitally-based text and communication, as in the mobile phone; and that commonly-consumed cultural products create and require 'multiple literacies' geared to the reading of bodies, musics and visual cultures. In this new context, 'writing, speaking, and just about everything else is being transformed into performances'. Performance Studies is 'a response to an increasingly performative world' (Schechner 2002: 4). But, by Schechner's own criteria, Caxton or the eighteenth-century woman reader of *Clarissa* are engaged in performatives, and in cultural situations, indeed, where the activities of printing and reading respectively were very much foregrounded as behaviours. It might be more useful to say, then, that new cultural technologies now again foreground the persistently performative nature both of communication and of cultural production and consumption, at least for academics.

Schechner also disavows the rhetorical aspects of his own 'performativity': that is, his capacity to make persuasive arguments. In 1973, Schechner outlined seven points of coincidence between theatre and the social sciences. He developed extended versions of this list into diagrammatic representations, a fan and a web, both of which gained wide circulation through *Performance Theory* (1977). Schechner writes in 2002 that the web version is to be understood as a dynamic system. It has no real centre: his own 'environmental theatre' is there as just one possible articulation. But considered, in Schechner's own terms, *as performance*, the web clearly does have Schechner himself at the centre. It does more than trace independently active connections between, say, 'performance in everyday life' and 'dialogic and body-oriented psychotherapies' (Schechner 2002: 11). It enacts the felt necessity of binding together, and from a specific centre, of elements that have selectively been gathered to it. The web is a double performative: an illocution that effaces itself as a rhetorical act (see Keyword: Performativity).

Schechner also imposes abstract structures on the genealogy of the discipline itself. He claims that Performance Studies is both richly determined and rooted in some persistent fundamentals of culture. The 'philosophical antecedents' of Performance Studies occur in 'ancient times, the Renaissance, and in the 1950s to 1970s, the period immediately before performance studies came into its own'. Each vigorously expresses the *theatrum mundi* (world as stage) idea (Schechner 2002: 7–8). There is here a clear echo of Schechner's entertainment-efficacy braid. Roughly the same historical points feature in each. Performance theory develops through a series of nodal points, coming to full flower in Schechner's own time, in a narrative of unfolding efficacy. But, for instance, almost every aspect of medieval life, from greeting through journeying to prayer, was ritualised; and the feudal synthesis in particular was based on a fundamentally performative principle of rights, duties and their appropriate actions. While these are not within the *theatrum mundi* frame, they constitute a conscious attention to performance. But including medieval culture would produce a cluster rather than a neat braid; and perhaps it has less of a glow about it than the ancients and the Renaissance. Schechner cannot of course be expected to attend to everything. But he seems here selectively to construct a pattern and a narrative to authenticate his own practice.

Schechner properly and generously insists that his is not the only narrative to have determined Performance Studies. Reading cultural artefacts like paintings and buildings as performances, for instance, was developed especially at Northwestern University. We have focused here on the ways in which Schechner narrates and maps the emergence of his own paradigm and practice because, while Performance Studies is indeed a very broad field, Schechner's voice promises to be the one announcing the field to undergraduates (see also chapter 10).

PERFORMANCE STUDIES AND ACADEMIC IMPERIALISM

Schechner's expansiveness signals a sincere radicalism, though arguably naïve. But some have regarded it less positively. In a keynote address to the Association for Theatre in Higher Education (ATHE) in 1992, Schechner announced, 'The new paradigm is performance, not theatre'. Theatre departments should become performance departments in order to realise their 'full potential role in the university and in American society'. Theatre Studies had developed since the late 1950s from an adjunct of Literature to a professional training ground in theatre arts. But students were typically 'neither professionally trained nor academically educated'. And work was scarce, even in the new media. Schechner identifies three linked key frameworks for the paradigm shift he proposes. First, theatre understood as the staging of written dramas would become 'the string quartet of the 21st century: a beloved but extremely limited genre, a subdivision of performance'. Second, multiculturalism is a false panacea. It masks abiding segregations of power: 'How many Americans can imagine as their president a black lesbian?' The focus should rather be on interculturalism, as an 'arena of struggle' where 'cultures collide'. Third is the understanding of performance as 'a broad spectrum of entertainments, arts, rituals, politics, economics, and person-to-person interactions', a tool for creative intervention into the intercultural arena. His central contention is an ethical one: that the 'cultural crisis' signalled by the gap between multiculturalism and interculturalism can be creatively met by a radical change in departmental 'goals and curricula' (Schechner 1992: 7–9).

The proposed change is expansive. From a narrow focus on Eurocentric drama, the focus must shift to 'how performances are used in politics, medicine, sports, religion, and everyday life'; to the theorisation of 'the four great realms of performance: entertainment, education, ritual and healing' and their interactions; to the varying relationships between authors, performers, directors and spectators; and to 'the whole range of performance activity' from training through warm-up to performance aftermath. It also signals a shift from a solely scholarly address, to include the 'seeing and doing' of performance genres from many cultures. Where the Western dramatic canon is taught, it needs to include the experimental productions of the 'classics' achieved in the last 40 years. And Performance Studies will be inclusive in three further respects. First, there will be dialogue with specialists from associated disciplines such as anthropology and history. Second, experts from the genres and cultures studied will teach, requiring the urgent recruitment of women and people of colour to faculties. Third is the recruitment of a diverse student population. In sum, 'the coloring of the professoriate, the coloring of the student body, and the coloring of the curriculum go hand in hand' (Schechner 1992: 9–10).

Schechner was here reformulating a position he had been developing since the early 1970s. So why make a fresh declaration now? Inside the ethical glove, some of his colleagues saw a hand grabbing for institutional power. In 1993, for instance, Schechner led a vigorous campaign to have performance studies recognised as a new focus group within ATHE. Reflecting on the ensuing squabble, Jill Dolan advised that

> The oppositional framing of the discourse of belonging to the new paradigm of performance studies . . . barely represses a desire to *be* the institution . . . I read the exhortations to 'join' the 'new paradigm' as a gathering of power – institutional and intellectual.
>
> (Dolan 1995: 32, original emphasis)

Rather than gestures of opposition or colonisation, 'rapprochement' was needed, a gesture to 'extend boundaries until they finally disappear'. Fundamentally, Dolan agrees with Schechner: 'disciplines matter because . . . they are about people and power and knowledge and what those intersecting vectors *do*', especially in the wider world. But for her, meanings matter more than paradigms: the leading agenda should be the clarification of function, not the categorisation of form. To fight over categories was merely to surrender to academic planners looking for 'internally conflicted programs to offer to the knife of budget cuts' (Dolan 1995: 32–4, original emphasis).

Dolan agreed that Theatre Studies needed to reassess itself in response to a variety of factors. Yet such change was already in train. The theoretical approaches and genres it addressed, once confined to the enforced enclave of feminist Theatre Studies, now had wide exposure. Schechner's declared agenda was already well covered. Meanwhile, a focus on 'performance' was no guarantee of radicalism, as recent 'disappointing, empty analyses detached from . . . grounding referent' had demonstrated (Dolan 1995:

28–31). In an earlier reflection, Dolan claims that Schechner had presented Performance Studies as being so 'radical as to presuppose an inclusion of the politically marginalised through a naturally democratic process'. She reads this as little different from the universalising gestures of humanism and modernism (Dolan 1993: 427–30).

Theatre Studies, meanwhile, still both privileged 'the humanist ideology of the aesthetic' and divided theory from practice. While media textuality in the everyday was 'multiple, contradictory, and open', university productions were typically 'closed, parsed . . . and coherent'. The aspiration was towards high art or supposedly 'real' theatre. Pre professional programmes ensured that the 'notorious anti-intellectualism' of American theatre was perpetuated in the academy. It was time to escape the founding frame of the discipline, and for Theatre Studies to become 'politically aligned'. Ironically for Dolan, since she was calling for the development of home grown Theatre Studies models, it was the importation of critical theory that had done most thus far to break the frame (Dolan 1993: 420–5).

We have foregrounded here one struggle over the development of the broad academic field of drama/theatre/performance, not to claim that it is the most important, but because it focuses sharply on two things: what definitional distinctions have been claimed between theatre and performance; and what is ethically and politically at stake in the performance of those namings. Questions of ethics occur not only within performances that are studied, but in the study of performance itself. They occur at all levels and all the time. For instance, a question was asked from the floor at a Performance Studies conference in Mainz in 2001. What were delegates actually *doing* in this act of conferring? And what did the various shapes of academic presentation actually do? It was observed, for instance, that several papers from US postgraduates took primary cultural materials, put them through the grinder of postmodern theory, and issued in statements of clarity. This performance of closure seemed out of kilter with the theory being invoked. The leader of a postgraduate programme quietly agreed that this might be the case, but these young people needed to get tenure, and this was how. Academic employability, then, puts pressure on the active problematisation of knowledge production in the academy. And a frame for this is what scholars now identify as the 'capitalist academy' (Martin 1998).

HISTORICISING THE EMERGENCE OF PERFORMANCE STUDIES: THE LIMINAL NORM

We have suggested that Schechner's account of the philosophical genealogy of Performance Studies is selective. In *Perform or Else* (2001), Jon McKenzie addresses processes of selectivity in the formation of Performance Studies as a practice and discourse in the twentieth century within a wider frame.

Reconsidering the feedback between theatre and anthropology in the 1960s and 1970s, McKenzie makes a crucial distinction. On the one hand, theatre became a *formal* model through which anthropologists and ethnographers might 'see' performance; it provided 'metaphors and tropes'. On the other, when ethnographic studies of performance, and in particular Turner's work on liminal rites of passage, were used by theatre scholars to theorise 'the social dimensions of theater and other emerging forms of performance', they performed as a *functional* model, by which the emergent Performance Studies would come to insist on 'the *transformational* potential of theater and other performative genres' (McKenzie 2001: 34–5, emphasis added).

From the 1960s, Turner developed van Gennep's observation that the practices by which traditional societies sustained and reproduced themselves were characterised by 'in-between' or 'liminal' states, after *limen*, the Latin word for threshold. Trance is a liminal state, between consciousness and unconsciousness, or between everyday reality and that of the gods. And boys taken from the village to a special place for initiation into manhood enter into a liminal space, poised between civilisation and the wild, childhood and adulthood. Turner went on to suggest that while liminality is woven into the very fabric of traditional societies, industrial societies reserve special places and occasions for liminal behaviour, for instance theatres and the dance party. Turner called these places and occasions 'liminoid' (Turner 1982).

McKenzie argues that while Turner attends to both the normative and transformational functions of liminality in traditional societies, Performance Studies selectively shaped itself around the transformational potential of performance as a liminal activity. Key here was Schechner's development of the notion of 'efficacy'. Liminal rites of passage became 'an *exemplar* of the entire field of objects' addressed and made by the discipline. Moreover, liminality became 'key to theorizing Performance Studies itself' in two ways. First, many Performance Studies scholars see themselves as operating 'in the interstices of academia as well as the margins of social structures', seeking transformations in both spheres through liminal processes: 'we have theorized our own activities as liminally efficacious'. Second, the narrative of formation of the discipline is often rendered as a 'breakthrough, a passage'. Thus, the liminal rite of passage becomes 'an *emblem* of the paradigm itself' (McKenzie 2001: 36–7).

Performance Studies gathers together a very wide range of objects of study. McKenzie foregrounds their conceptualisation as a field of study, coupled to the gathering of 'a community of practitioners and researchers' as itself being performative. The field of 'cultural performance' and the paradigm of Performance Studies 'co-create and co-legitimate one another'. Thus bound, the category 'cultural performance' becomes defined in narrow but self-legitimating terms (see chapter 8). The idea of the liminal as radical, and both the proper object and nature of Performance Studies, constitutes what McKenzie styles 'the liminal norm'. The fact of the liminal norm in Performance Studies has thus far tended to distract attention from normalising and conservative performances, and hence from their critique. Paradoxically, Performance Studies' sense of self-identity robs it of important opportunities to facilitate transformation (McKenzie 2001: 29–53).

McKenzie sees this 'passage to paradigm' of Performance Studies as symptomatic of a 'general movement' between 1955 and 1975 throughout cultural practice and research: 'an attempt to pass from product to process, from mediated expression to direct contact, from representation to presentation, from discourse to body, from absence to presence'. At the heart of the concept of cultural performance within Performance Studies, he identifies the libidinal and immanent body assumed and deployed by 1960s radicalism as a challenge to an alienated and repressive order: 'Performance Studies emerged as witness and participant of this performance'. The demonstration by critical theory that the body is always already bound up with the dominant refashioned both Performance and Performance Studies in the 1980s 'theory explosion', and situated performance as a key site of deconstructive and post-theory praxis. But the 'memory' of the transgressive body 'still haunts us' (McKenzie 2001:

39; and see Reinelt and Roach 1992). Back in the decade of the immanent body, Derrida was developing deconstruction, which was to inform later theory. Reflecting in 1967 on the persistence of a 'negative theology' or felt absence of a centre, even within poststructuralism, Derrida suggested that it may in fact be indestructible: 'a ghostly centre is calling us' (Benamou and Caramello 1977: 5).

A GENERAL THEORY OF PERFORMANCE

McKenzie tracks more than the co-legitimation of 'Performance Studies' and 'cultural performance'. He also investigates 'Performance Management' and 'Techno-performance', with their respective co-legitimating objects of study, 'organisational performance' and 'technological performance'. He makes a big claim: that 'performance will be to the twentieth and twenty-first centuries what discipline was to the eighteenth and nineteenth'.

His argument draws on Foucault and Lyotard (see chapter 6). Foucault held that power is everywhere. It is not necessarily repressive, but inhabits all human exchange and productivity, and is intimately bound up with knowledge. In *Discipline and Punish* (1979a), he develops an historical argument on this basis. The principal operations and understanding of power in the eighteenth and nineteenth centuries were based on the model of *discipline*. More precisely, he identifies 'the legal register of justice and the extra-legal register of discipline'. Foucault sets out to demonstrate that, while this combination is most patent in the penal code and the panopticon (Bentham's model for prisons, in which a single guard can observe all prisoners), it is the basis upon which normalising power was articulated in factories, schools, hospitals and beyond (McKenzie 2001:15–18, citing Foucault).

In *The Postmodern Condition* (1979), Lyotard develops Foucault's analysis and raises the issue of the *legitimation* of knowledge. In the modern era, this operated on the assumption that knowledge opposed power; truth challenged repression. But in the postmodern era, legitimation has become 'performative': 'knowledge and power are simply two sides of the same question: who decides what knowledge is, and who knows what needs to be decided?' Foucault's deconstruction of modern assumptions about power is itself, then, best seen as part of a wider and deeper shift in the actual practice of power, and hence our understanding of it (McKenzie 2001: 18, citing Lyotard).

McKenzie writes that performative subjects are 'fragmented rather than unified, decentered rather than centered, virtual as well as actual' and performative objects 'unstable rather than fixed, simulated rather than real'. They 'do not occupy a single "proper" place in our knowledge' (McKenzie 2001: 18). This is familiar territory: the supposed nature of the postmodern condition, and performance as a paradigm for it. But McKenzie has greater ambitions: to work up a 'unified theory' of performance (McKenzie 2001: 4). He argues that the shift from discipline to performance constitutes the emergence of a new 'onto-historical formation of power and knowledge': a fundamental change in our understanding of knowledge, agency and history, at the level of being.

In *A Thousand Plateaus* (1980), Deleuze and Guattari (see chapter 6) playfully appropriate the model of the 'stratum' from geology, to think through not only epochal change but also the nature of things. If Foucault says that power is everywhere, Deleuze and Guattari figure power less as a thing than as a delimitation, or specific aggregation of *force,* which in itself is boundless. They evoke a chaotic system of forces and intensities. The blind generativity of force, intensified as it gathers up through unwilled self-organisation into a reproductive network, comes to constitute power. A stratum might be thought of as an aggregation of forces and intensities that has gained some coherence through self-repair. Deleuze and Guattari posit three fundamental belts of strata subject to mutual exchange: the inorganic, organic and human. Borrowing from them, McKenzie proposes that he has identified the consolidation since the Second World War, in the United States and then world-wide through the process of globalisation, of a 'performance stratum'. *Perform or Else* is designed to 'initiate a stratoanalysis of performance' (McKenzie 2001: 173–6).

The performance stratum reveals itself at two principal levels, the first more historical in emphasis. The emergence of the performance stratum of power/knowledge in the United States is evidenced by the development of the three discursive/academic disciplines with which *Perform or Else* first concerns itself. McKenzie reminds us that as early as 1955, Herbert Marcuse had, in *Eros and Civilisation*, identified a 'performance principle' dominating economic and social activity in the post-industrial West. Freud wrote of the infant moving from the 'pleasure principle' of self-gratification to the 'reality principle' of social responsibilities. Marcuse posits the 'performance principle' as an historical version of the reality principle: capital tells its workers to 'get real' by facing up to the fact that they must perform to survive. Marcuse thus identifies a new way in which alienated labour – work done by one class but appropriated by another; the worker not owning or controlling the means of production – is justified and enforced (McKenzie 2001: 16–20).

McKenzie stresses that the performance stratum he identifies is to do with 'normalisation' every bit as much as change. Expropriation and domination remain key features of Western culture and globalisation; and 'performance' is the mode by which people are coaxed, coerced and duped into compliance with it. But by, for instance, making only selective readings of Lyotard or Butler (see Keyword: Performativity), or forgetting Marcuse, the 'liminal norm' obscures the normative and coercive nature of the performance stratum as a whole, and thereby the ways in which the paradigm of Performance Studies itself is part of it. Postmodern theory has progressively moved its attention from 'uniformity, conformity, and rationality' to the more amenable concerns of 'diversity, innovation, and intuition' (McKenzie 2001: 6).

The scope of *Perform or Else* (2001) is vast. McKenzie first sets out to make 'genealogical readings' of the performance paradigms he identifies. This leads to an epochal argument. Alongside that runs a more 'metaphysical' thread. For instance, McKenzie distinguishes between *performances* as 'territorialisations of flow and unformed matters into sensible bodies' and *performatives* as 'encodings of these bodies into articulable subjects and objects'. The vocabulary echoes Deleuze and Guattari; as does McKenzie's deconstruction of the very binary he proposes: categories are foregrounded as process (McKenzie 2001: 176–7). But McKenzie also has critical work to do. Again emulating Deleuze and Guattari, he figures the performance paradigms as 'blocks of normative and mutational discursives and embodied performance'. The close of the book deploys his wittily-termed strategy of 'parfumance', a disruptive drifting-through of 'pockets of iterability, self-referential holes . . . located not only at the limits of social formations but also at their very core'. It is a strategy of 'destratification', which 'erodes and breaks up the forms and processes of performance power/knowledge' (McKenzie 2001: 20–5).

When both subjects and objects are multiple and groundless, the performance of figuring things becomes a matter of endless play. *A Thousand Plateaus* (1980) is a fine early example of such a strategy.

McKenzie himself faces the problem of posing such a thing as a 'general theory', and solves it by suggesting that it is 'hard-wired to our future' (McKenzie 2001: 20). But let us, as we have with Schechner, suggest a rhetorical feature of his argument. He moves between various levels of social organisation, of historical process, and of being itself, finding 'performance' everywhere. He suggests for instance that we regard even 'the explosive expansion of disciplines over the last half century; and their dissemination in the process of globalisation as itself performative' (McKenzie 2001: 13). But to say that everything is performance is ultimately to say very little. And alongside McKenzie's declared performance of parfumance, and much less playful than the 'lecture-machine' (McKenzie 2001: 20) by which he simultaneously unfolds and defamiliarises his argument, there is the whiff of ritualisation in Catherine Bell's sense (see chapter 8). The substance of the argument is engendered – performed – as much by the force (or do we mean power?) of abstract repetition at different levels as anything else.

And, just as in Schechner, the very comprehensiveness of McKenzie's argument makes some things drift out of view. McKenzie writes about 'a qualitative mutation of what we call knowledge, the becoming-performative of knowledge itself' (McKenzie 2001: 14). But this *mise en abyme* (a figure like the play within the play) is not the sole property of postmodern thought. Marx insisted that how we can understand the world is fundamentally a matter of how we produce ourselves through our labour and its organisation at any one historical moment. Even though there are good challenges to Marx's residual suggestion of a 'real' eventually to be discovered, and to his promotion of 'grand narratives', notions of the performative basis of knowledge are not that new.

And, come to think of it, the habit of writing grand narratives dies hard.

8

PERFORMANCE STUDIES: SOME BASIC CONCEPTS

In this section we look in more detail at some key concepts underpinning performance theory. We begin with a distinction between 'aesthetic' and 'social' drama.

AESTHETIC AND SOCIAL DRAMA

This is not quite like the general distinction between aesthetic drama and social performance, where the latter refers to a range of everyday interactions. The more specific term 'social drama' is the name given by the anthropologist Victor Turner (1920–83) to a unit of social process which arises out of a conflict situation. He says it typically has four main phases:

> (1) *Breach* of regular norm-governed social relations; (2) *Crisis*, during which there is a tendency for the breach to widen. . . . (3) *Redressive action* ranging from personal advice and informal mediation or arbitration to formal juridical and legal machinery . . . to the performance of public ritual . . . (4) The final phase consists either of the *reintegration*

of the disturbed social group, or of the social recognition and legitimation of irreparable schism.

(Turner 1992: 74–5)

This notion of social drama was developed by Turner in 1974 from Arnold van Gennep's demonstration that all rites of passage, such as the rites accompanying changes of age or social status, follow a three-part structure: separation of the subject(s) from society, margin or in-between state, and reincorporation. Turner's intention, however, was that 'social drama' had much wider application, being a 'well-nigh universal processual form' (1982: 71). And as such it is the source of what Turner calls 'cultural genres'. We may have already noted that the phase of 'redress' can be instituted through a ritual performance; but the performances it generates and sustains may be much more varied than this, including 'both "high" and "folk", oral and literate' (1982: 74–5). Aesthetic drama, for example scripted plays, may thus be seen as one possible constituent of the redressive phase of social drama.

There are other methods, or outcomes, of redress, for instance juridical activity or informal arbitration. A range of activities which may initially seem to have little connection, such as a trial, a football match, a carnival, a tragic chorus, can thus be linked together as elements of redressive mechanisms. They are all behaviours designed to make something happen, to perform a function. So all the varied phenomena of the redressive process, including aesthetic works, can be regarded as performance, and hence become the proper domain of the performance analyst.

Turner developed his concept of social drama as an anthropologist. For him 'drama' was a useful word to describe some basic shapes of human behaviour. The performance theorist Richard Schechner utilised this concept as a maker of aesthetic performances. For the early 1970s avant-garde interest in the relations of fictionality and everyday life the anthropologist offered the possibility of situating aesthetic performance alongside a range of other human performances. This not only retrieved it from 'theatre', but it also held out the possibility of discovering its most fundamental defining characteristics.

But Turner was not the first anthropologist to influence the study of aesthetic drama. We have already encountered, in chapter 4, the Cambridge School's proposition that ancient Greek drama had its origins in a primal *ritual*. Alongside this, the work of other disciplines, such as social and cultural history, psychology, also tried to get closer to the roots of drama through an investigation of play. Let us now look at each of these topics in more detail.

RITUAL

In daily life, words such as 'ritual' and 'ceremony' slide through various meanings and applications, ending up as the opposite of themselves. For instance enquiries into the presumed fundamentals of human behaviour, evidenced, say, in religious activities, invoke ritual as a moment of deep investment and shared meanings for the participants. On the other hand, there is the usage in phrases such as 'empty ritual', 'mere ceremony', where to refer to something as ritual is to suggest that it is only behaviour learnt by rote, with no inherent meaning, and above all no real investment. 'Ritual' can thus indicate both deep commitment and empty formality.

Within Performance Studies the concept of 'ritual' has various functions. These have to do with: history (ideas about drama's origins); performance practice (ways of being true); analysis (categorising the performed).

The first of these we have already mentioned, namely that consideration of ritual seems to be able to take us close to the presumed origins of dramatic performance. The early twentieth-century Cambridge School of Anthropology proposed a 'primal ritual' which, although now completely vanished, gave rise to and underpinned, first, the sacred phallic dances and then the choric tragedies and comedies of ancient Greece. The problem with this theory, as Richard Schechner has pointed out, is that there is not only no evidence for this primal ritual but that it also seems barely relevant to the forms of drama that have flourished in the intervening centuries. This model, says Schechner, is too universalist. It also excludes all theatre and drama which do not derive from Athenian comedy and tragedy.

Suspicious of theories that have theatre evolving from ritual, Schechner argues that they are instead concurrent genres. Along with play, sport and music they are all 'the public performance activities of humans' (1988: 6). A major object of his attention in *Performance Theory* ([1977] 1988) is the specific interrelationship of theatre and ritual. Using contemporary or near-contemporary sources he aims to 'outline a process through which theater develops from ritual and, conversely, ritual develops from theater' (1988: 112). Given this two-directional process, and the interest in the 1960s art scene in staging 'rituals', the two genres seem to become blurred. So Schechner develops an approach which can separate them. He begins from an idea that in 'ecological ritual' performance is a way of achieving 'real results': 'paying debts, incurring new obligations' (p. 119). He represents the process diagrammatically as two sets of transformations. One set converts potentially dangerous encounters into 'aesthetic and social enactments'; the other changes one actuality into another (debts being paid etc.). The first set enables the second set to take place peacefully. In different processes the balance between the two sets can alter. A focus on the aesthetic enactment can lead towards a prioritising of 'entertainment'; a focus on change in actuality will prioritise the 'efficacy' of the process, what it actually makes happen. By observing whether the qualities in a performance relate more to entertainment or efficacy, that performance can be categorised as theatre or ritual. 'Efficacy' and 'entertainment' are not so much opposites as stages on a continuum. In some cultural moments the qualities are co-present, in others far distant. Therefore it becomes possible, according to Schechner, to map Western theatre history according to the relations between efficacy and entertainment (or indeed ritual and theatre). He represents these relations diagrammatically as a pair of interwoven lines, a 'braid'. The crossing points of the lines produce great drama, and there are two such. The first crossing, for anyone familiar with the orthodoxies of the English literary canon, is utterly unsurprising: the drama of the Elizabethan–Jacobean period. The lines then cross again in the late twentieth century, when Schechner himself was working. To this we shall return.

Now, however, we need to note that the reflections on ritual's relationship with theatre take us into a new area. Thinking about a situation in which public life is 'theatricalised' Schechner observes that the performer is asked to 'take off her traditional masks . . . to "tell the truth" in some absolute sense' (1988: 121). A critical theatre has to shake itself free of the falseness of social processes. The performers are enabled to do this through a process of preparation and rehearsal, which offer a frame 'protecting the time/space of the theater' (p. 183). This frame has an adjective, 'ritual': it is, says Schechner, in rehearsal/preparation 'that

I detect the fundamental ritual of theater' (p. 183). The examples he cites of such preparation are those of Aborigines, the Moscow Art Theatre, and his own company, The Performance Group. So while theatre and ritual are supposedly interrelated, ritual nevertheless has a privileged position as something fundamental. It is there in the process of 'ecological' performance and high art, both alike on the side of truth as against a theatricalised public life. Just at the point in the argument where theatre and ritual have been established as interrelated and drawn within the terms 'efficacy' and 'entertainment', two things happen. On the same page Schechner suggests: first, that a Broadway musical is more than entertainment, having its efficacy shown in the backers' money and box-office receipts; second, that ritual is a way of guaranteeing authenticity. While one term becomes assimilated to the dominant economy, the other acquires critical authority. Ritual retains a special status in relation to truth.

At least that is how it struck Victor Turner. He summarised Schechner's method as 'making, not faking', and said it was particularly appropriate to anthropological teaching. Rather than aiming at imitation the actor's role 'is truly "created" through the rehearsal process' (1982: 93). Turner's enthusiasm perhaps derived from the interest that characterised his own approach to ritual. He insisted on the primary importance of the physical body, as opposed, for example, to the social body. (In doing so he departed from the work of the anthropologist Mary Douglas who argued that the 'social body' 'constrains the way the physical body is perceived' (1996: 69).) In the creation of role, a performance dramatises the relationship between the personal body of the performer and the symbolic arrangements of the social body. This emphasis on the body, in whatever relationship of social and personal, thus offers ritual as a model for that particular art of the body which is performance.

In putting it that way we run into a third function of 'ritual' within Performance Studies. It suggests a mode of analysis of the performed. At the start of this section, we looked at the basic scheme that is offered by Turner's 'social dramas'. In the previous paragraph, we defined performance as an art of the body, in which analysis might focus on the interplay of personal and social bodies. The pursuit of that sort of analysis takes us then into new territories. For, when Schechner opposes a theatricalised public to an unmasked performer, fiction to truth, ritual falls tidily into place against the everyday. But many analysts of society and culture argue that within the everyday there is a constant interplay of personal and social bodies.

Taken up by, for example, sociologists of football 'violence' and historians of royal pageantry 'ritual' extends the range of what might be considered to be performance. In doing so, a crucial aspect emerges: ritual is not any fixed thing, it has no intrinsic features. Instead it is, as Catherine Bell argues, an activity of differentiation (between, say, personal and social), a site of negotiation, a process of legitimation: 'intrinsic to ritualization are strategies for differentiating itself – to various degrees and in various ways – from other ways of acting within any particular culture'. An essential element is 'the circular production of a ritualized body which in turn produces ritualized practices'. In 'ritualisation' there is a repetition of a basic binary opposition or series of oppositions at various levels of a text or textual system; the effect is that a key opposition is naturalised and appears to derive from some transcendent principle. It is 'designed to do what it does without bringing what it is doing across the threshold of systematic thinking' (Bell 1992: 90–102 *passim*).

If ritual is an activity, then, in the view of, say, Mary Douglas, it is one in which the personal and social bodies mutually constitute one another. This is very different from Schechner's idea of taking off masks in order to reveal a 'truth'. Furthermore, Douglas suggests that ritual has no necessary precedence in shaping a society in which it figures. It is one of a series of activities. This view clearly contrasts with the Cambridge School's search for a primal ritual which would explain subsequent forms of drama (and it is reiterated by Rozik (2002) when he argues that theatre could never have originated in ritual because while theatre is a medium ritual is a mode of action). But Douglas's view also contrasts with Schechner's diagram of the 'braid', the weaving in and out of entertainment and efficacy through the history of performance. Their relative positions might vary, but the opposition between them remains constant, universal. Slipping out from under this universalised model there is a category that has been marked as fundamental: ritual.

Why, despite all his attempts to put it on a continuum with theatre, does ritual acquire this fundamental status? Schechner's book *Performance Theory* appeared in 1977. At this period he was exploring modes of performance that showed their own process. And he was not alone: the fashion for 'Happenings' from the 1950s through into the mid- to late 1960s saw the invention of numerous ceremonial events which sought to upstage theatricalised life with that which was both incomprehensible and inadequately fictional. We noted (see p. 59) that the early to mid-1970s saw an interest, in the work of Brook, Grotowski, Kott, Esslin, in the origins and primal, ritual, qualities of drama. This was the second time at which, according to Schechner's 'braid', efficacy and entertainment crossed together. The workshop process of his Performance Group is offered as an analogy to the ritual process described by Turner. What Turner himself tells us, however, is that he was introduced to 'underground' performance by Schechner in the 1970s, and that this had a profound influence on his theories. So we could say that the ritual process invoked by Schechner is, in a major respect, a process that has been brought into being, in a very 1970s way, *by* Schechner.

To describe the attitude to 'ritual' of Schechner and his peers we need to return to Catherine Bell. Commenting on the cultural readings, the analyses of ritual related to cultural 'meaning', done by anthropologists, she notes how there is an invocation of the practised as against the philosophical, the lived as against the conceptual, the personal perhaps against the social. In other words, a division is sustained between action and thought. The construction of this binary is itself a process of ritual-isation, a marking of difference, here between the ritual observer and the ritual action. This has wider effect: the 'domination [of the theorising subject] is maintained by virtue of the implicit structuring of the thought-action dichotomy in its various forms'. That domination is, in turn, rhetorically silenced, naturalised, precisely through ritualisation (Bell 1992: 54). We should thus be aware of the extent to which commentaries on ritual, by Schechner and others, are themselves part of a process of ritualisation that works to construct the status of the commentator.

PLAY

The word 'play' has been associated with dramatic performance for a very long time. In the fifteenth century *Tretise of Miraclis Pleyinge* the word 'pleying' is a synonym for performing; it still exists in contemporary usage in the more specialised sense of 'playing a part'. But in the *Tretise* it is something more than a mere technical word. Playing has a pejorative status: it is regressive, against reason, blurs categories, is wasteful. Playing is not working.

These associations with the word remain fairly constant. What changes is the value of play's qualities. In Clive Barker's *Theatre Games* (1977) play is associated with the release of actors' inhibitions. It operates by reaching back to a time lived before formal (actor) training and intellectual abstraction. Reaching back rather than regression, the informal rather than the wasteful: play's qualities gain a positive charge in relation to productive adult work.

An attempt to account for the change in the value of play can lead to a very generalised narrative of social change. This sort of narrative was most famously formulated by the Dutch sociologist Johann Huizinga. In *Homo Ludens* ([1938] 1949) Huizinga maps the relations of play and non-play in cultural formations. For him play is rooted in ritual and is 'productive of culture', which includes religion, science, law, war and politics. It is productive because it permits 'innate' human needs for rhythm, harmony, change (Huizinga 1949: 75). In saying this Huizinga is building on the position formulated in 1795 by the German dramatist Friedrich Schiller. In *The Aesthetic Education of Man* Schiller develops an elegantly dialectical argument that the play impulse reconciles the two opposed impulses that constitute humanity: the sense impulse (which responds to the outside world) and the form impulse (which imposes self on the outside world). These can be said to have 'life' and 'shape' as their objectives, so that the play impulse has as objective 'living shape'. This concept denotes what is called Beauty, and is central to what makes humanity complete: 'it is only the union of reality with form, of contingency with necessity, of passivity with freedom, that fulfils the conception of humanity' (Schiller 1989: 77). Huizinga's more generalised sociological model rearranges this so that the conflict is not between internal, and dialectical, human impulses but between the human being and an external thing called society: in 'highly organised' society religion, science, and the rest lose touch with play. In these cases the poet is particularly valuable, for 'the function of the poet still remains fixed in the play-sphere where it was born' (Huizinga 1949: 119). Poetry's special place is where the child, animal, savage and seer belong, 'beyond seriousness'.

Huizinga's work came under criticism from the French ethnologist Roger Caillois in *Man, Play and Games* (1958, trans. 1961). He attacked the idea that play produces anything: 'Play is an occasion of pure waste: waste of time, energy, ingenuity, skill, and often of money' (1961: 5–6). Play is 'free and voluntary activity', separated from the rest of life, but nevertheless there are 'precise limits'. Play is rule-bound: the laws of ordinary life are replaced 'in this fixed space and for this given time, by precise, arbitrary, unexceptionable rules that must be accepted as such' (p. 7). Furthermore there are varying qualities of play, varying sorts of engagement and pleasure. These differences are apparent in different sorts of game and it is through an exploration of the various opportunities for, and changing status of, these games in different cultures that Caillois narrates his own history of society.

For Caillois's social history it is not so much play as game which is the crucial concept. What emerges from his discussion of games, however, is a tendency to focus on rules of interaction between participants. And in this move he seems to dissolve the category of play, which for example Schechner distinguishes from games and their rules. But Caillois argues that it is only by understanding the place of rules that one can understand the pleasure: 'The game consists of the need to find or continue at once a response *which is free within the limits set by the rules*. This latitude of the player, this margin accorded to his action is essential to the game and partly explains the pleasure which it excites' (1961: 8, original emphasis). This sort of analysis can in turn lead into a more far-reaching sociological interest in the forms taken by negotiations of human relationships, which are designed to limit risk. Such risk-limitation conventions are known as 'frames' in the work of the sociologist Erving Goffman. In a different discipline, that of rhetoric, Geoffrey Bateson suggests a similar risk-reduction strategy in the form of the 'subjunctive': if this were to happen, we would act like this. Bateson is in fact trying to define a quality of play itself, but the category of the subjunctive works rather like a frame in its capacity both to promote, and render more secure, a real-life interaction. As Bateson says, 'the messages or signals exchanged in play are in a certain sense untrue or not meant', and further 'that which is denoted by these signals is nonexistent' (1972: 183). This – how shall we call it? – subjunctivity is most clearly seen at work in theatre games and in role-play scenarios.

Whereas theatre games and role play may be means to an end, however, the sociological interest in frame can also lead to a much more utopian version of play. Focusing mainly on children, Brian Sutton-Smith, following Huizinga, and indeed Schiller, says: 'play is in the first place a reframing of activity. To play with something is to open it up for consideration and for choice. Play opens up thought. As it proceeds it constitutes new thought or new combinations of thought.' Presented in these terms, play – and playing – become a force for change: 'play is the envisagement of possibility. Play is adaptive potentation' (Sutton-Smith 1979: 315, 316).

The social histories of play trace a gradual shift away, however, from the wilder sorts of play (Caillois's vertiginous, risky 'ilinx', for example) as society became more complex, more rule-bound; as it grew up. In this narrative play is a state associated with that which is not fully socialised: the primitive, that which is 'outside' a dominant order, the childish. But let us pause, for the two previous sentences have blurred together two rather different ideas: to say that games have changed their rules or become more complex is not to say the same thing as suggesting that there is a basic state which can be called 'play'. One describes a changing set of human interactions, the other looks for an essential quality.

This quality lurks somewhere deeper than the everyday. Sutton-Smith suggests some forms of play 'do not seek to imitate everyday frames, but to reveal the many other aspects of feelings and relationships that the ordinary frames deny' (1979: 318). Play does not happen within a frame; it is itself a form of 'frame creation'. In Mihaly Csikszentmihalyi's concept of 'flow' play is like a state of mind. He developed the concept from interviews with people whose activities have few extrinsic rewards, such as rock climbers or dancers. Their engagement with their activity apparently shows the following features: concentration, non-contradictory goal, immediate feedback, warped time sense, loss of ego. 'In the flow state, action follows upon action according to an internal logic. It seems to need no conscious intervention by the actor . . . play is the flow of experience *par excellence*' (1975: 36). The goal is the activity itself. A problem emerges here, though, in that this play can look indistinguishable from work. The rock climber and dancer, wholly concentrated on their more or less risky activity, are exerting themselves physically and mentally, utilising technique and invention, focused on getting to an end: the successful climb, the achieved performance. Play here looks like work which is not work or, to use a different vocabulary, work which is not alienated.

So even as play flows into something that looks like a version of work, we realise that play is difficult to pin down unless it is set in relation to something else. This is the move that Victor Turner makes when he prises play free from neural accounts of it. He says play does not fit in anywhere, 'is recaclitrant to localization . . . a joker in the neuroanthropological act' (1992: 167). 'Joker' triggers other words: free-wheeling, metamessages, *bricoleur*. And then he comes clean: 'You may have guessed that play is, for me, a liminal or liminoid mode, essentially interstitial, betwixt-and-between' (p. 168) (see p. 110, this volume). Now we enter his familiar territory, with a coherent model of relationships: the liminal as against the everyday. This is why he does not want to locate it in any fixed place in the brain: 'Its flickering knowledge of all experience possible to the nervous system and its detachment from that system's localizations enables it to perform the liminal function of ludic recombination of familiar elements in unfamiliar and often quite arbitrary patterns' (1992: 170).

While definitions of play in itself end up faced with something jokey and flickering and slippery, we can move onto more secure ground if we concentrate on the context within which play is being defined. Turner's thoughts on play are a version of his theory of liminality, which in turn derives from his study of tribal cultures. Barker's thoughts on play, by contrast, fit into the (counter-) cultural context of western Europe in the early 1970s. So, too Csikszentmihalyi's final chapter (1975), the 'politics of enjoyment', celebrates the value of 'non-instrumental' behaviour for creativity and pleasure. Indeed so much of the work on play seems to date from this decade, although one of the earliest treatments of drama games, by Viola Spolin, was published in 1963, and based on work that Spolin attributes to the inspiration of Neva L. Boyd in the field of 'creative group play' (Boyd was a sociologist at Northwestern University 1927–41). The widespread student protests of the late 1960s and early 1970s were a concrete instance of the feeling that the education system is itself a repressive force, training people to take up circumscribed positions according to the designs of a dominant order. Political opposition to the dominant espoused a call to 'de-school' society, as in Ivan Illich's book of that name. From within the area of performance at this time one of the most eloquent activists for this de-schooling position was Albert Hunt. In *Hopes for Great Happenings* (1976) he argued that 'By demonstrating the importance of play, the theatre is also demonstrating an alternative way of looking at social processes' (p. 124). Hunt was picking up on a mode of dramatic production that went back, through Barker, to the work of Joan Littlewood, whose use of games and improvisation functioned to strip away an actor's learnt, habitual techniques. Playing leads here to a mode of performing that is the antithesis of acting.

This is clearly not the same thing as the 'pleying' of miracles, where what was condemned as playing was the very business of imitation. Nor perhaps is it the same as postmodern performance practices which tend to set play against mimesis (see Keyword). But in turn these various practices bump up against the sociological argument that not only is everyday life an ongoing series of unscripted performances but that these performances are also, in order to be effective, mimetic.

The various attempts to define and discriminate between various sorts of performance all derive from the most paradoxical, and bewildering, of play's relationships. For while the relationship between play and work is relatively easy to pin down in the specific arrangements of a particular society, the relationship between play and play will not stay still. For inextricably tangled up in the word 'play' are both of its original meanings: imitating an action and escaping from the everyday.

THEATRE ANTHROPOLOGY

Our accounts of ritual and play suggest that anthropology is far from being the only discipline that offers to explain the roots of drama. And, further, when it attempts to do so, it begins to alter within itself. Yet by the 1980s anthropology had acquired such a crucial status in the study of theatre and drama that it spawned a new disciplinary entity, theatre anthropology. And by way of affirming its own identity the creature needed to deny its parentage. Thus in an explanatory note on the International School of Theatre Anthropology (ISTA) Eugenio Barba insists that 'the term "anthropology" is not being used in the sense of cultural anthropology but that ISTA's work is a new field of study applied to the human being in an organised performance situation'. The behaviour in such a situation is 'according to principles which are different from those used in daily life.' Theatre anthropology 'is not the study of the performative phenomena in those cultures which are traditionally studied by anthropologists. Nor should Theatre Anthropology be confused with anthropology of performance' (Barba and Saverese 1991: 7).

The first task of theatre anthropology is to search out those elements of performance which are common to all performers regardless of time and place. These 'recurrent principles' as Barba calls them will be evident in physiology operating in a mode which is beyond the everyday, and hence culturally coded, behaviour of ordinary life. His concentration on the 'extra-daily' and his project of exploring across cultures have enabled Barba to make new insights into the productivity of the performing body. By moving between Oriental and Occidental performing modes, and between acting and dance, his analysis breaks free of assumptions shaped by convention and genre. It is a method that goes some way towards accounting for the sense of a performer's 'presence', finding terms to define that effect of a 'decided body' for which no language exists. Thus the study of the organisation of musculature, balance of the body and deployment of energy accounts for apparently ineffable phenomena by grounding them in physicality: charisma as biological mechanics.

Barba stresses that, when it locates these recurrent principles, theatre anthropology will not have discovered a science of the theatre or universal laws. It will merely have isolated good 'bits of advice'. Now for all the caution about 'universal laws' these bits of advice relate to principles which remain 'common' despite place and time, as it were transcultural. And it becomes clear that Barba's project is to identify a biology which is outside or deeper than culture. By way of precedent for the project he cites an early version of anthropology: 'the study of human beings' behaviour, not only on the socio-cultural level, but also on the physiological level' (1991: 8). So when he defines his theatre anthropology against cultural anthropology, the opposition is not so much to anthropology itself as to the cultural.

Thus in Barba's hands theatre anthropology seems to be pulling in two directions. First, it is tending towards what we might call an ethnography of performances, a description of performance modes, illustrations juxtaposed to define, say, the 'fictive body'. But second it is interested in the formulation not perhaps of universal laws, but of – equally universal? – bits of advice that pertain to the physiology of all performance activity, where the body is understood as a biological organism separable from culture.

There seems to be a convergence between anthropology and aesthetic drama. We can see this foreshadowed earlier on. Victor Turner had at first used the word 'drama' in relation to a specific social process arising from a conflict situation. In 1977 Schechner likened 'social drama' to the sort of thing written by Shakespeare or Ibsen, but also placed it alongside Erving Goffman's use of dramatic metaphors to describe a range of social interactions (see pp. 45, 50). There was a feeling that all social process, all interaction, was like drama, a drama with rules, roles, masks, illusions. From here, in a work that charts the growth of his 'lively interest' in modern drama, published in 1982, the year before his death, Turner argued that social drama is a 'well-nigh universal processual form, and represents a perpetual challenge to all aspirations to perfection in social and political organization' (1982: 71). Picking up from Schechner, he says this nearly universal human mode imitates the shape of drama, understood specifically as aesthetic drama: 'a social drama, as I have analyzed its form, closely corresponds to Aristotle's description of tragedy in the *Poetics*' (p. 72).

Turner justifies this step by asserting that 'there is an interdependent, perhaps dialectic, relationship between social dramas and genres of cultural performance in perhaps all societies'. His argument here is heading towards the introduction and quotation of a model which illustrates this relationship in terms of a braid, a horizontal figure eight where social drama and stage drama loop in and out of one another. The model is Schechner's, and while Turner is not uncritical of it he seems to absorb from Schechner the idea that social drama and aesthetic drama converge, 'so that the processual form of social dramas is implicit in aesthetic dramas . . . while the *rhetoric* of social dramas – and hence the shape of the argument – is drawn from cultural performances' (1982: 90).

This convergence of anthropology and aesthetic drama was not confined to Turner. In his essay on 'Liminality' (1990) Colin Turnbull states that there are 'many points of correspondence between the anthropological process and the theatrical process' (1990: 75), in particular his own performance as anthropologist. This matters because Turnbull feels that anthropology needs a new technique to get closer to 'that central subjective essence that lies deep within any culture', the human element that is more than social systems (p. 51): we should note that the idea here recalls the 1970s experiments of Grotowski and Brook (see p. 59). Within this frame Turnbull's own 'performance' required total participation. It is something more than acting, for 'through such performance a transformation takes place, not a mere transition' (1990: 73). Most other anthropologists, he says, are not able to deal with the 'sacrifice of inner self and the willingness to become something else' (p. 76). But his own anthropological performance has improved precisely because he, like Turner, has spotted, and acted upon, the links between anthropology and theatre. And, also like Turner, his reference point for his understanding of performance is once again Richard Schechner.

A particular version of performance practice appears to be kept in place by this convergence of anthropology and theatre. The theory of that practice invokes Turner's or Turnbull's anthropology as a way of giving 'scientific' authority to its generalisations about human performative behaviour. But, as we have seen, by that stage the anthropology of Turner and Turnbull had already absorbed Schechner's performance theories. That absorption then produced a particular version of anthropology, where Turnbull can be interested in something human which is more than social systems. So theatre's convergence with anthropology is something of an institutional *coup de théâtre*: disavowing itself as an art of masks and roles it transforms into the master discourse of human essence.

CULTURAL PERFORMANCE

This is not, of course, the whole story. Now lost behind the current romance between theatre and anthropology is a previous meeting between the two, where, perhaps significantly, there was no performance theorist in evidence.

When Milton Singer was doing an anthropological analysis of Indian civilisation in the early 1950s his Indian friends advised him that he should watch religious rites and ceremonies. They thought of their culture, he says, 'as encapsulated in these discrete performances, which they could exhibit to visitors and to themselves. The performances became for me the elementary constituents of the culture and the ultimate units of observation' (1972: 71). They are clear units in that each performance has 'a definitely limited time span, a beginning and an end, an organized program of activity, a set of performers, an audience, and a place and occasion of performance' (p. 71). Yet in each observable performance 'the more abstract generalizations about Hinduism' could be exemplified. So it became apparent that analysis of specific performances 'might lead to more abstract structures within a comprehensive cultural system' (1959:

145). The name Singer therefore gave to these 'instances of cultural organization', such things as weddings, recitations, dances, plays, temple festivities, was 'cultural performance'.

Singer's concept of cultural performance, born in 1955, initiated a particular analytic method:

> Through analysis and comparison of these cultural performances and their constituents. . . . it is possible to construct the structure and organization of particular kinds of performances. Then by tracing the linkages among these structures and organizations it is possible to arrive at the more comprehensive and abstract constructs of cultural structure, cultural value system, and a Great Tradition.
>
> (Singer 1959: 145)

The mention of tradition here deliberately recalls Singer's colleague, Robert Redfield, and his description of civilisation, developed between 1951 and 1957, as a 'structure of tradition' (Redfield 1962: 392–3). By this Redfield meant the 'total structure of formed relationships for the communication of the tradition that is that civilization'. 'Civilization' may be thought of as 'kinds of people in persisting forms of relationship, so we may think of it as kinds of things thought and done, with characteristic forms for communicating this substance from generation to generation' (in Singer 1959: x). Cultural performance comprises both a persisting form of relationships and a characteristic form of communication.

Redfield's views were expounded in a lecture delivered in 1958; they were quoted by Singer in *Traditional India*, published in 1959. But since that time 'cultural performance' has been obscured by a different form of anthropologically influenced performance analysis. When Turner referred to Singer's concept he suggested that 'cultural performance' could be made more useful as an idea by stressing its reflexive nature, its capacity to make a critique of the daily life out of which it grew. Such a reflexive engagement with process contrasts with – and is, for Turner, more modern than – Singer's engagement with structure (for another account of Turner's concept of cultural performance, see Ley 1999: 166 ff.). Thus the phrase 'cultural performance' has become somewhat narrowed in application: Clifford Geertz, for example, uses it simply to describe 'full-blown ceremonies' (1975: 113). But Singer's type of analytic practice has remained potent. For, while in the late 1950s Redfield was developing his idea of civilisation as the kinds of ideas thought and done, on the other side of the Atlantic Raymond Williams had begun thinking about a model for social and cultural analysis that was to remain potent throughout his life, 'structure of feeling' (see p. 32).

Williams, working within literary studies, had a major influence on the analysis of drama and culture. But in the early 1980s a new anthropologically based approach demonstrated its potency in dealing with a culture's performances. Mervyn James's seminal essay 'Ritual, Drama and the Social Body in the Late Medieval Town' (1983) is an analysis of the medieval processions and cycle plays performed for the religious feast of Corpus Christi:

> the Corpus Christi cycle, by the nature of its structure, gathered together the different occupational guild groupings into a visibly presented unity. There then, once again, was presented as in the Corpus Christi procession, the wholeness of the social body and of its mythological world outlook.
>
> (p. 16)

Although this sounds similar to Singer's views on Hindu ceremony in Madras, James has arrived by a different route. For him 'the theme of Corpus Christi is society seen in terms of body' , and the concept of body provided the mythological apparatus within which ideas of society could be negotiated (p. 4). The idea that 'the human experience of body tends to sustain a particular view of society' is derived, says James, from Mary Douglas's book *Natural Symbols* ([1970] 1996). And, while Douglas does not discuss performances, James realises and demonstrates the productivity for performance analysis in particular of an approach which links together both belief systems and the experience of the 'human psychosomatic self' (1983: 6). The use of Douglas's work for performance analysis, despite its being underdeveloped, is potentially as important a step as any we have noted so far, for Douglas's work is materially based in that which is also pre-eminently the performer's medium, the body. And Douglas's insistence that the body shapes and is shaped by its belief systems then acts as something of a corrective to Barba's – or Grotowski's or Brook's – attempt to reach a physiology which lies deeper than culture.

Turner, however, has not disappeared yet. James invokes his notion of 'communitas', an essential human bond, to summarise the specific efficacy of Corpus Christi: 'the emphasis was placed not on the structural aspects of urban society, but instead (to quote Victor Turner again) on the "essential and generic human bond". The stress, in the first place, is on the creation of wholeness' (James 1983: 19). Despite the mention of Turner, however, the overall analysis feels more like Singer. And something curious happens: Turner's stress on a human bond that pre-exists society is, on its own, heading towards essentialism, but James uses it to describe a fictional effect of performance, a performance created out of all those material particular elements with which an analyst of cultural performance is concerned. For all his stress on 'process' Turner looks essentialist and abstracting alongside the more materialist cultural analysis. And, rather than replacing it, his views have been materially re-worked by – and found a place *within* the concept of cultural performance.

9

POSTMODERNISM AND PERFORMANCE

In 1977 Michel Benamou represented a gathering perspective when he wrote that performance was 'the unifying mode of the postmodern'. He identified three basic ways in which various senses of performance characterise postmodernity: the dramatisation of life by the media, the theatrical playfulness of art, and a focus on performance in the sense of technological efficiency. In post-industrial culture at large, where services and information rather than material products dominate, performance in the sense of process prevails. And while some modernist artists took refuge in ancient myth and symbol to compensate for the death of god, the postmodern artist instead follows Nietzsche to find affirmation in the free play of the will. Criticism, too, recognises itself as a performance, and so also plays (Benamou 1977: 3–4).

The poststructuralist understanding of 'truth' as an effect of performance, rather than an absolute given, was notably developed by Lyotard. In *The Postmodern Condition: A Report on Knowledge* (1979), he suggested that Western thought has grounded its truths in 'grand narratives' such as Marxism, Christianity and Freudianism. But these stories are without foundation and so have no intrinsic authority. He further suggested that this 'condition' of knowledge was now generally apparent, and that this defines the 'postmodern condition'. To live postmodernity is to live the performative nature of 'truths' (see chapter 6).

In *Postmodernism and Performance* (1994b), Nick Kaye takes a closer focus, and specifies the aeshetic genre Performance as a postmodern phenomenon. So 'performance' figures twice. It is first the *generic* term that defines the field of Performance, and especially here 'art performance' (see p. 183). And second, it is an *operational* term: the argument concerns live art's postmodern performativity, its rhetorical strategies.

Kaye reviews attempts to define postmodern art. Jencks (1987), for instance, has identified 'double coding' and Hutcheon (1988) 'parody' as key tropes. But for Kaye these are paradoxical enterprises. For him, 'the postmodern' designates 'a calling into question of the languages, styles and figures through which it is seen'. It is a way of doing art, rather than a sort of art. If modernism is characterised by 'a projection towards foundation', postmodernism 'occurs as a disruption of this very claim to meaning'. The performativity of postmodern art is precisely this resistance. To be more definite about it would be to deny its actual nature. Postmodernism is an ephemeral effect; it cannot be abstracted from the texts and events which conduct it (Kaye 1994b: 4–23 *passim*).

Kaye maps the way in which frustrations with the modernist work of art led to challenges to the authority of the artwork within the work itself. These performative strategies of deligitimation can, and were, said to be theatrical. And they ultimately also led to Performance as a new field of practice.

MINIMALISM, THEATRICALITY AND THE AUTHORITY OF ART

During the twentieth century, a major understanding of art turned in on itself. In the late 1960s minimalist art led various groups of sculptors, painters and other artists into theatre and performance. They shared a concern, which was exercised in much of the new work, about the nature and status of the work of art. At the same time, late 1960s minimalism provoked a 'seminal' defence of modernist art by critic Michael Fried. Fried was provoked precisely by the 'theatricality' of the new minimalism. It threatened the modernist ideal of the work of art as being 'self-contained and self-determining' (Kaye 1994b: 24).

From around 1965–6, minimalists had begun to make objects that seemed 'to offer themselves as irreducible "facts"'. They were simply there, 'a sheer physical presence'. They did not represent or symbolise anything; and there was no suggestion of an interrelation between their constituent parts. In some ways this was a logical extension of the principle of modernist art as defined by art theorist Clement Greenberg between 1939 and 1965. Greenberg argued that art had changed its function after the secularisation of the eighteenth-century Enlightenment, whereby rationalist thought radically challenged religious 'truth' and the transcendence of a godhead. After this, each art had no higher purpose than to become true to itself, to project itself towards its own 'formal essence'. Paintings were not about subjects but about colour and form; or paint; or, ultimately, flatness and its delimitation. Modernist art simply made this 'projection toward the absolute' explicit rather than implicit. Greenberg conceives the modernist artwork as being self-legitimating, totally self-contained and timeless, independent of the circumstances of its being witnessed. It achieves 'self-foundation'. Such works do not address the spectator, one enters into their presence; they are framed off from the rest of the world. But, as Kaye demonstrates, the new minimalist works presented themselves as if that 'frame' had gone missing. Paradoxically, the pursuit of an entirely self-contained work of art – pure 'objecthood' – had eventuated in works that begged the question about the status of those objects in the world. And that, according to Fried in a 1967 essay, was a species of theatricality: they were interacting with the onlooker, inviting them to reflect on their activity of looking. And while the modernist work is suspended from time, these pieces emphasised duration, as does theatre. It was as if the absolute had collapsed in on itself, turned inside out. We might call it a moment of immanent deconstruction. If these works were modernist, suggests Kaye, then the modernist work had now lost its meaning, 'its possession of its own definition' (Kaye 1994b: 33–4).

In the 1967 essay, 'Art and objecthood' Fried builds on Greenberg's arguments to defend the self-foundation of modern art from being thus undermined. There was 'a war going on between theatre and modernist painting'. Fried argued further that quality and value only had meaning within each individual art: 'What lies *between* the arts is theatre'. Walter Pater (1839–94) had said that literature achieves the ideal of art at the moment when it approaches the condition of music – because then matter and form cannot be distinguished from each other (Pater 1889). Fried scathingly turns this famous formulation around to declare, 'Art degenerates as it approaches the condition of theatre' (Kaye 1994b: 25–8; citations from Fried are Kaye's). What Fried resisted here was to become a cornerstone for many artists in future decades. They experimented across formal boundaries. And the idea of 'intermedia' connotes not simply working across formal boundaries but working in the gaps between, dissolving the idea of a boundary itself.

PREMONITIONS OF POSTMODERN PERFORMANCE

It is roughly from this point in the 1960s, in cross-over work by some minimalists and other artists, that art performance in Carroll's sense emerges. But Kaye traces the roots back further. He uses Fried's reaction to minimalism in 1967 as a lens through which to view earlier departures from the self-contained artwork, the emergence of a postmodern performativity in art. For instance, Robert Rauschenberg's simple *White Paintings* (1951–2) had been lit so that the shadow of the viewer fell on the painting. His subsequent 'combines', assemblages of disparate found materials, refused any sense of 'formal closure' and instead insisted on the activity of the spectator. And Jasper Johns began in the 1950s to make frontal paintings of flags and numerals. They presented formal ironies: were these representations in the sense of artistic interpretation? Or mere reproductions like a snapshot photograph? The endless and unsettling circulation between the senses of reproduction and representation insists on the sheer presence of the painting, and the activity of the viewer. The situation is both 'theatrical' and without closure (Kaye 1994b: 29).

The key works in Kaye's narrative that bring us directly into the sphere of Performance are associated with Fluxus (1961–) (see chapter 6). In a 1966 book, *Assemblages, Environments & Happenings*, Allan Kaprow reflected on his own work and that of others, in which the drive is towards the dissolution of the artwork as a coherent whole. The fashioned environments are temporary and subject to decay. Happenings are distributed across time, space and persons; are for doing not seeing; and blur the line between art and the rest of life. Works such as Claus Oldenberg's *Store* (1961) and George Brecht's *The Case* (1959) confused the line between art object and use object. Brecht's first exhibition in 1959 was tilted *toward events: an arrangement*. He presented 'games and loose assemblages of often rearrangeable objects or even unsigned objects presented variously within and outside of the formal circumstances of the gallery' (see Keyword: Aleatory). The work is not within the artist's control and there are no properties internal to the art object. Kaprow's actions are, in his own words, 'not-quite-art, not-quite-life'. Such art-making performs 'moves toward a "work", and yet, simultaneously, a set of strategies which serve to stave off a closure and so identification of what this work might be' (Kaye 1994b: 30–40).

Kaye summarises: 'the emergence of strategies which look specifically toward *performance* can be read as a final move towards an unravelling of the discrete or bounded "work of art"' (Kaye 1994b: 32). The effect is to 'make visible that which the work depends upon but which it cannot contain, to trip up and make apparent the move towards the "event" of its definition' (Kaye 1994b: 44). As well as establishing a position on the borderline between art and the rest of life, such work also demands attention to the transactions and negotiations common to all arts experience. It reveals the ways in which supposedly self-legitimating art itself depends on the spectator, for whom it indeed performs.

Reviewing the work of Foreman, Kirby and Wilson in the 1970s and 1980s, where the new strategies of Performance engage with the theatrical apparatus, Kaye identifies 'a fundamental opposition to the desire for *depth*, for the discovery of a "centre" from whose vantage point the various elements . . . may be understood'. Closure is made a perpetual lure never to be grasped by a 'play of prompts, of indications or traces which displace one another'. The idea that any meaning can 'belong' to the work is refused: the very process of its becoming is foregrounded as being the spectator's work. The performances thus force attention to process, to the 'event' occurring between spectator and presentation (Kaye 1994b: 69–70).

In one of many summations, Kaye writes that 'one might speak . . . of a moment which is both "theatrical" or "performative" and properly *postmodern*'; that 'the condition of "performance" may be read, in itself, as tending to foster . . . postmodern contingencies and instabilities' (Kaye 1994b: 23).

UNDECIDABILITY, AVANT GARDES AND THE RECUPERATION OF MODERNISM

In *Staging Femininities*, Geraldine Harris remarks that the only full-length accounts of postmodern feminist performance available at her time of writing were by art historians and theorists (Harris 1999: 6). While this marks a previous negligence by even feminist Theatre Studies, it also confirms a lineage: Performance/live art emerges principally from fine art practice. Accordingly, we shall spend some time here with fine art theory and criticism that has explicated Performance.

In *The Object of Performance* (1989) art theorist Henry M. Sayre divides 1980s paintings that declared themselves 'postmodern' into two sorts: those actually based in 'pluralism' and those generating an active 'undecidability'. He cites Hal Foster's opposition, in *The Anti-Aesthetic* (1983), to the regular conflation of 'pluralism' and 'postmodernism'. 'Pluralism' implies that 'all positions in culture are now open and equal'. This may suggest a productive openness. But Foster insists this is 'simply the inverse of the fatalistic belief that . . . we live under a "total system" without hope of redress' (Foster in Sayre 1989: xii). In contrast, Derrida's notion of 'undecidability' designates the impossibility of resolution, an active tension between different positions of possible closure. This 'condition of contingency, multiplicity, and polyvocality' is what 'properly' pertains to postmodernism. 'Pluralism' or 'indeterminacy' implies equivalence between various aesthetic choices: 'anything goes' as Foster nicely puts it, or what we might call closure through negligence. Pluralism is intrinsic to the work and is just another species of formalism, whereas undecidability foregrounds the ethics of perception: the socially meaningful relationships between people, the art they make, and what it implies (Sayre 1989: xii–xiv).

On this basis, Sayre posits 'a distinct and definable avant-garde' in American art and literature since 1970 that might be called 'postmodern'. He argues that while it opposes the modernist formalism associated with Greenberg, it derives from a different modernism, one grounded in Dada and Futurism. The postmodern avant garde strips the idea of 'modernism' itself of its assumed univocality, its consistency as a period style. And performance, 'styleless, diverse, and conspicuously unprogrammatic', has been one of the chief means to make this challenge (Sayre 1989: xi–xii).

Sayre argues that if Performance had been integral to the New York art scene from the moment of Kaprow's *Happenings* in 1959, it was the counter-cultural, protest and feminist actions in California and New York of the late 1960s that made performance 'a recognisable art form'. In this context, not only was performance a potent means of making political art, especially against the Vietnam War; it also militated against the art establishment as part of the official culture. Sayre thus identifies Performance as being 'intensely political in orientation' from what he maps as its true point of inception (Sayre 1989: 13–14). Relative to Kaye's ultimately rather formalist treatment (in that he foregrounds undecidability as an abstracted operational principle), Sayre's attention to historical conditions is welcome. But there is something of a sleight of hand here: Sayre is indulging in proof of essence by origin, and a selective origin at that.

FORMALISM, FEMINISM AND PERFORMANCE

One sculptor who made his way into performance in the 1960s was Robert Morris. He made a celebrated piece called *Site* in 1964 with Carolee Schneeman. The title is an evident pun. The work proceeds as a construction site, where ideas about the ways in which painting organises sight are mobilised. *Site* is a refunctioning of the realist oil painting *Olympia* (1863) by Edouard Manet (1832–83). Now, the subject matter of *Olympia* is a courtesan, lying naked on a couch, looking out from the canvas to engage the spectator's eyes. Sayre cites art historian T.J. Clark's demonstration in 1985 that the painting sets up a critical undecidability. In French bourgeois culture, the courtesan 'was what could be *represented* of prostitution' in art, and, for this to happen, she had to be divorced from ordinary prostitutes. Oil paintings represented female sexuality within the confines of idealised classical beauty; while common prostitutes represented themselves as sexual commodities in the streets; and courtesans plied their trade in private, beyond patent representation. The classically named Olympia gazes out from the painting to implicate the (presumed male) viewer in this set of contradictions.

Then, and especially now, *Olympia* of course also raises questions about the simultaneous exploitation and idealisation of women by men. Sayre demonstrates that while *Site* disrupts the authority of the artwork as a finished expression beyond process, it also cancels the critical work that

Manet's painting does. In his formalist challenge to Manet, Morris appropriates Schneeman into his own work as a passive object – as Schneeman herself later reflected, as 'Cunt Mascot'. Schneeman's own trajectory from expressionist painting into Performance was driven as much by resistance to male artists' objectification of women as to formalism. She called the gallery and academic art system 'the Art Stud Club'. Nothing much seemed to have changed.

In chapter 6, we refer to a perceived split between the more directly political Performance tradition that issued out of Fluxus in Europe and what grew after the mid-1960s in America. Here, we witness a radical split in the same period between formalist art made by some men and a more directly political performance-based art made by feminists. In one of the introductory essays to *Framing Feminism* (1987), art historian Griselda Pollock provides us with a political definition of Performance.

Pollock summarises arguments made by Mary Kelly in 1977 for the development of a 'feminist problematic in art': feminism needs to think in terms of 'feminist art practices' rather than 'feminist art'. The latter is a product of the bourgeois problematic, by which she means the underpinning ideological field, where 'art' and 'artist' carry assumptions about the separation of art from work and craft, male artists from female subjects, and the unique vision of the artist. Rather than attempt a feminist 'content' in 'art', women artists needed to develop 'tactical activities' and 'strategically developed practices of representation' geared to 'a radically different order of knowledge'. The theoretical grounding for this was a feminist problematic. Performance was one of the new areas of art practice with the flexibility and power to dislocate the dominant and build 'a new multiplicity of powers and knowledges for the diverse communities of the oppressed'. Pollock is adamant that the goal of feminism is not to be incorporated into 'the pluralism popularly labelled Post-modernism' (Pollock 1987: 80–1; see also above and chapter 5).

THREE SYSTEMS OF UNDECIDABILITY

In *Staging Femininities* (1999), Geraldine Harris develops an extended theorisation of the work of three British women performance artists, Rose English, Annie Sprinkle and Bobby Baker. Her necessarily complex argument is neatly summed up in the simple assertion that a piece by Rose

English is not only 'worth taking as seriously as Derrida' but is also funny. Appropriating the principle of 'undecidability' from Sayre (1989), Harris suggests that contemporary Performance, feminism and postmodernism all operate in this way: all resist definition (Harris 1999: 6).

She accords with Auslander's observation in 1997 that 'female performance art always potentially carries some sense of "political" message because, in being "authored" by "women", it inevitably imputes a critique of the politics of representation' (p. 22; Auslander 1987: 21). There is an implicit circulation between woman as subject and woman as object.

Harris, however, further identifies a strategic circulation. She suggests that at the heart of this work is a 'double gesture'. The term derives from Irigaray, and it relates to both the 'positionality' and 'strategic essentialism' discussed in chapter 5. The enactment of the double gesture simultaneously invokes essentialist categories and deconstructs them, in a manner which refuses either gesture final authority. While 'positionality' and 'strategic essentialism' suggest a diachronic situation (one articulated across time), Irigaray's formulation is synchronic, and hence of immense rhetorical power. Carried over from feminist praxis at large into these performances, it is 'the main means of negotiating the tricky terrain between theory and practice' (Harris 1999: 19).

An important underpinning for Harris's explication is her consideration of the complex relationships between feminism and postmodernism. Again, 'undecidability' emerges as the key term. Both 'offer critiques of humanist rationalism, scientific objectivity, historical truth and the transparency of language'. But while championing multiplicity, both paradoxically nevertheless tend to be regarded as 'easily identifiable, singular, transcultural phenomena'; and each has an equally paradoxical tendency towards metanarrative. A 'play between multiplicity and singularity' applies to both feminism and postmodernism.

Meanwhile, a possible 'aporia' between the two discursive practices is opened by the pressure exerted by postmodernism on the category of 'sex'. This is a similar problematic to the one we explored with Case (1990) in chapter 5. But this opposition can itself be seen in gendered terms. Postmodernist theory might be seen as tending towards the masculine, abstract and universal; and feminism as either properly concrete or marginally particular, according to contrasting, arguably gendered, points of view (Harris 1999: 10–13).

Another way of figuring that play between singularity and multiplicity in postmodernism is what Harris describes as a 'flux' between (singular) modernism and (multiple) postmodernism. She suggests that feminist postmodern theorists readily regard this pragmatically. Feminism is perhaps best seen, she suggests, as an 'enabling' discourse for both post-structuralism and postmodernism; and feminism has in fact contributed most at the points of conflict (Harris 1999: 17–18).

PRACTICE, CRITICISM AND THE BODY

Let us return to Fried's argument, but now with a specific focus on the body. He deals critically with work by artists who had reservations about illusionism in painting and the internal 'relationality' in both painting and sculpture, the way in which the work depends on the relationships between its internal parts. Several specifically sought 'wholeness'. Sculptor Robert Morris stressed that the object itself is only one term in this 'new aesthetic'. A strong gestalt or structure of repetition, as well as the scale of the work in relation to the beholder, produces a 'public mode' for the interaction and a 'more extended situation'. Fried calls the artists 'literalist' because he thinks they pursue wholeness merely at the level of the support, say canvas in a frame, rather than in artistic form. And their 'espousal of objecthood' is theatrical because it is concerned with 'the actual circum-stances' in which the beholder encounters the work. The experience is of 'an object *in a situation*' that '*includes the beholder*'. The public mode and extended situation construct the beholder as the subject of the situation; and the work, even though it is the centre of attention, becomes their object. And this is the essence of theatre (Fried 1967: 116–27, original emphasis).

Fried cites Judd's charge that relational modernist work is 'anthro-pomorphic'. Its elements make 'gestures' akin to human ones. When we talk for instance about the 'sweep' of a line, we invoke the sweep of an arm, and might even use one. Fried counters that there is nothing wrong with anthropomorphism as such. Anthony Caro's sculptures, for instance, do not imitate gestures, but embody 'the *efficacy* of gesture'. The work is 'possessed by a knowledge of the human body', how it engenders meaning. Fried then develops Greenberg's criticism of literalist work to suggest that it is itself anthropomorphic, but in a dishonest and theatrical way. It draws attention to itself by means of its large size and its posturing as non-art, achieving a kind of '*stage* presence' it can 'hide behind'. Further, the manufactured situation explicitly includes 'the beholder's *body*'. The situation for the beholder is like 'being distanced, or crowded, by the silent presence of another person'. They have the 'disquieting' sense of being in the presence of 'a surrogate person'. It is

> as if the work in question has been *waiting* for him.
> . . .
> [It] is incomplete without him, and it will not leave him alone. Finally, in being unitary, holistic and symmetrical, the new work in fact mimics the human form. And since it feels artistically 'hollow', it suggests it has an 'inside' as a person does.
>
> (Fried 1967: 119–40, original emphasis)

We have three modes of the body here. For Fried, Caro abstracts the *essential* human body and the modernism he champions cannot bear the *literal* presence of the human body. And the literalist work, according to him, manufactures an *ersatz* human presence that *implicates* the body of the spectator in the sense that it depends on their physical presence in order to mean anything.

If Fried's own modernism seems inseparable from disgust with the literal body, the work he resists remains principally perspectival rather than carnal. It is still looked on from a distance. The work is, precisely, transitional: it maintains a modernist contemplative coolness. In the next section, we trace a different mode of the body, in body art.

Reviewing *The Object of Performance*, Performance documenter and art academic Kristine Stiles accused Sayre of constructing another 'formalist tower' analogous to the one he supposedly challenges. His argument rests upon a series of binary divisions: modernism/postmodernism; formalism/anti-formalism; undecidability/indeterminacy; Fried/Derrida. He artificially aligns presence with formalist modernism and antiformalist absence with postmodernism; and precisely misses the radicalism of the way in which Cage and his generation engaged with 'indeterminacy'. Such formalism, she charges, ignores the 'broad intertextuality of events, influences, nationalities, gender and race' of Performance, its commitment to internationalism and political change. Of key importance to this project was the body. It placed 'the individual body in a discourse with the social body' the body as 'autonomous material object' with 'a collective history in which people have responsibility'. The body is the principal 'ethical and pedagogical element' of Performance (Stiles 1990: 35–43).

Rather than construct formalist distinctions, criticism should

> engage the question of how the body has become a formal *medium* and how that medium has replaced traditional theatrical narrative texts as a visual and conceptual transit for the embattled role of representation, figuration and narration, in general, throughout modernism into our own period. [Crucially,] performance art needs to be examined as a concrete social practice . . . in which the presence of the body in real events provides a paradigm for social action, not only for individuals but for the collective body.
>
> (Stiles 1990: 41–7, emphasis added)

THE BODY AND POSTMODERNITY

Carroll (1986) aligns the 'art performance' that developed in fine art with resistance to Greenbergian formalism, and the 'performance art' that developed in experimental theatre with Artaud. Things are not always so simple. Consider again Carolee Schneeman. In *Body Art/Performing the Subject* (1998), Amelia Jones points out that by 1963 Schneeman was already posing a radical challenge to the 'Art Stud Club' while still working within the terms of abstract expressionism, 'several years before the development of a cohesive feminist movement in the visual arts'. Schneeman is a touchstone for Jones, as is Artaud.

Directly quoting Artaud, Jones describes body art as 'passionate and convulsive'. It begins to realise Artaud's call in *The Theatre of Cruelty* (1938) for 'a direct theatrical enactment of subjects in relation to one another'. It has been the major road to a 'radicalisation of cultural expression' in the twentieth century. And as rhyme, she cites Carolee Schneeman's description of her own work as having 'a visual-kinaesthetic dimensionality; a visceral necessity drawn by the senses to the fingers of the eye' (Jones 1998: 1–2).

A plausible narrative runs that while in the 1960s counter-culture the body was naïvely deemed to be a resource of unalienated humanity, the 'return' to the body in the 1990s was predicated upon the deconstructionist understanding of the 'body in discourse' developed in the 'Theory' decade of the 1980s. Some aspects of Schneeman's work in the 1960s might, indeed, fit with such a chronology. But while 'Artaudian' in this sense, it might also be argued to be 'deconstructionist' before its time. Schneeman uses her body to make radical interventions into regimes of representation. Jones writes that in Schneeman's work, the female subject appears as 'a deeply constituted (and never fully coherent) subjectivity in the phenomenological sense, dialectically articulated in relation to others in a continually negotiated exchange of desires and identifications' (Jones 1998: 3).

Body art made by feminist and other 'nonnormative' artists 'performs', says Jones, the split and dispersed subjectivity of postmodernity at its point of emergence. Performances of body art 'exacerbate, perform and/or negotiate' the dislocations of social and private life in the late capitalist West. These 'instantiations' of the postmodern subject actively engage the wider social reality. Jones also crucially argues that body art has insisted on the *eroticised* intersubjective relation of artistic production and reception, denied by modernist and masculinist art practice and theory, thereby opening up a space for progressive political work around difference. If Performance implicates both artist and spectator in the work, body art specifically implicates the 'body/self' in all its charged particularities in that transaction (Jones 1998: 1–19).

Rebecca Schneider challenges a similarly established map, writing that Elinor Fuchs' distinction in 1989 between the 'sacred' body of 1960s feminist performance and the anti-essentialist 'sacrilegious' work of the 1980s is in fact 'by no means neat' (Schneider 1997: 131). In *The Explicit Body in Performance* (1997), Schneider explores 'the explosive literality' of much feminist Performance since the 1960s. While by no means positing an 'originary, true or redemptive' body, explicit body artists have 'deployed the material body to collide literal renderings against Symbolic Orders of meaning'. Habitual perceptions and assumptions that 'buttress sociocultural assumptions about relations between subject and object' are disrupted. The 'sedimented layers of signification' that inform, articulate and surround the socialised body' are unfolded (Schneider 1997: 2–3; 126–52).

Schneider maps the explicit body in Performance in relation to the avant garde, commodity capitalism and postmodern criticism. The avant garde appropriated the primitive for its shock value, associating it with sex and excretion. But discourses such as psychoanalysis and practices like fine art readily absorbed this notion of the primitive and its attendant shock, as for instance in Freud's notion of the unconscious and paintings by Picasso. Clearly, that first shock effect was predicated on, while it also sometimes challenged, deep ideological assumptions about gender and race. Schneider argues that while the association of 'savagery' with physicality 'ghosts contemporary explicit body works', it is now 'the primitivized, or sexualized herself who (re)performs her primitivization' She 're-plays her primitivization across her body . . . to expose the cultural foundations of shock' (Schneider 1997: 4–5).

Of central concern to Schneider is 'the link between ways of seeing the body and ways of structuring desire according to the logic of commodity capitalism'. Desire, like commodities, she writes, 'is produced'. There is of course a Foucauldian echo here. But there is also one of Marx, and Lukács and Debord (see chapter 6) For 'the secret of circulating, insatiable desire is the labor that goes into its construction'. Commodity culture both depends on our experience of a repeated lack and *produces* that lack. Commodity culture informs us: it shapes not only our environment but our very bodies and minds. In order to keep us spending, late capitalism especially installs Woman as the emblem of that which can never be reached. In doing so, it calls on 'the legacies of perspectival ways of seeing' in which Woman acts as a figure for the 'Real' that Western civilisation has fetishised from Plato to postmodernism. Shockingly, the explicit body artist enacts 'a ribald refusal to vanish'. Perspectival vision and commodity fetishism are 'played back across *the body as stage*' so as to suggest that 'these social theatrics might be differently scripted, differently dramatized, differently real-ized'. Much of the work enacts 'a confrontational satiability (both of pleasure and pain), and a refusal of the logic of infinite loss' (Schneider 1997: 5–7).

There is a challenge here to the discourses of lack (Lacan) and deferral (Derrida) in poststructuralist thought. Further, as Schneider reports, there has been a postmodern assumption that 'the avant-garde, and its "bad boy" hope in the political promise of transgression, died sometime in the 1960s'. A *locus classicus* for the teaching of performance theory has for instance been Auslander's citing of Hal Foster's prescription for a postmodern politics of resistance from within – since there is no longer any believable external point of purchase from which to operate a transgressive politics. But, as others before her, Schneider finds 'cause for suspicion'. How is it that the idea of the avant garde and its attendant shock 'should die just as women, artists of color, and gay and lesbian artists began to make critically incisive political art' on their own terms? The political right certainly regard this as transgressive. The issue is not so much 'the abandoning of transgression' as asking who does the abandoning. Funny how 'postmodern theorists' are 'generally male' (Schneider 1997: 3–4).

In a gesture that might connote both Turner's 'social drama' and the feminist narrative of patriarchy we touched on in chapter 5, Schneider concludes:

> Significantly for feminist inquiry, the drama of Western cultural loss and misrecognition has been played out across the stage of the body and its ultimate disavowal. It is a drama based on the tired mandate that coagulates the bodily as the literal detail, the literal as terrifyingly finite, the penetrated, the feminized.
>
> (Schneider 1997: 183)

DEFINING FIELDS: ART VERSUS PERFORMANCE

Jones has a properly disciplinary imperative: body art has a 'particular potential . . . to destabilize the structures of conventional art history and criticism'. These are still inclined to versions of Greenbergian formalism and Kantian 'disinterestedness' based upon a 'masculinist and racist ideology of individualism'. She wants to disrupt the narrow focus of visual arts criticism on linguistic and visual paradigms, which has occluded the body (Jones 1998: 3–5). This recovery of the 'repressed phenomenological dimension' of French poststructuralism is informed by Simone de Beauvoir's *The Second Sex* ([1949] 1997). De Beauvoir was as much an influence on Judith Butler as was Derrida; and as subversive of masculinist assumptions in her realm as Schneeman was to be in hers. Jones's project 'to re-embody the subject of making and viewing art' (1998: 11) is clearly just as pertinent to the development of a critical vocabulary for Performance Studies.

It seems extraordinary that Stiles could still complain in 1990 of the 'uniform neglect and marginalisation' of Performance in the art academy (Stiles 1990: 39). Perhaps this motivates Jones to insist on a distinction between body art and Performance. She argues that while body art can be seen as just one part of Performance, it properly designates 'a complex extension of portraiture' embracing documentary mediation, whilst 'performance art' itself is confined to the 'theatrical'. But this is surely too nice a distinction. It denies the breadth of 'performance'. Jones even uses 'proscenium' as a synonym for 'theatrical'. Rather than divide work between disciplinary domains, she would do better to describe body art as occupying a position embraced by both 'art' and 'performance' discourses, practitioners and institutions. Similarly, Jones contrasts the way in which body art 'provides for the *possibility* for radical engagements' rather than presume 'redemptive' and 'utopian' aims as Performance does (Jones 1998: 13–14). But here, again, she orders material and history into neat boxes that obscure rather than reveal the (we want to say 'real') shape of things.

By contrast, we should be attentive to the ragged edges that surround maps and narratives. The useful activities of gathering cultural materials into fields and stories inevitably obscure some things from view. Battcock, for instance, reminds us that many artists moved into Performance either because they simply felt they had exploited the limits of their exisiting medium; or because this novelty promised more opportunities in a flagging art market (Battcock and Nickas 1984: xiv–xviii).

RADICALISM, NARCISSISM AND PERFORMING THEORY

Let us consider various aspects of the ways in which artists and writers situate themselves in their work. Jones reviews the performativity of images which construct the female body artist as public figure, forcing the viewer 'to engage deeply with this particularized subject who so dramatically stages her work and/as herself'. This 'radical narcissism' generates a destabilising circulation between her status as object of the normative gaze and authorial subject of the work (Jones 1998: 5–9).

Jones, like many feminist critics and others, foregrounds the way in which she herself is 'performing' criticism. Her interpretations are to be understood as partial and invested, designed to put issues into productive play. Through these strategic engagements, she intends to perform 'interpretation-as-exchange'. She also situates her own work within art historian Thierry de Duve's notion of the 'paradoxical performative', by which postmodern critical work 'performs' the postmodernity of works erstwhile considered modernist, by declaring them such (Jones 1998: 1–10).

Meanwhile, Stiles (1990) accuses Sayre of conducting a different kind of performance. His book is a commodity in the service of his academic career. It constructs an imperialist grand narrative of American high art and narcissistically constructs Sayre himself as its guardian and seer, especially in its final self-consciously 'performative' chapter. But dividing the radical sheep from the opportunist goats can be a complex business. Jones's *Body Art* (1998) is the first in a series of three books culminating with the hefty coffee-table picture-book, *The Artist's Body* (2000). Is the insistence on the specificity of body art as fine art rather than Performance not so much a matter of refining the object of radical critique as a means to capture the art-book market?

10

RECENT MAPPINGS OF DRAMA–THEATRE–PERFORMANCE

In this chapter, we look at the terms that govern this book: drama, theatre, performance, together with some associated ones: score, script and text. The list is not exhaustive; we by no means aim to provide an authoritative map; nor do we provide definitions. Rather, we are concerned to explore some of the ways in which these various words have been deployed and mapped together, to what effect and in what circumstances in recent decades. The chapter falls into three sections.

PERFORMANCE VERSUS THEATRE

Are performance and theatre opposed terms? Consider first the making of shows. We saw in chapter 6 how Performance emerged partly from resistance to traditional text-based theatre, often with Artaud as figurehead. Derrida's appropriation of Artaud's assault on the 'theological stage', while a critique of a Western metaphysics of presence, has sometimes been banalised as a justification for an anti-theatrical animus in Performance (see Keyword: Presence and representation).

Consider academic disciplines. We saw in chapter 7 how Schechner declared a 'paradigm shift' in 1992, from theatre to performance. This had two rationales: Theatre Studies lacked the scope to engage with increasingly 'performative' as well as 'intercultural' Western societies, or performances beyond; and it addressed a redundant form. Meanwhile, Zarrilli mapped Theatre Studies as one part of the new paradigm of performance.

Auslander (1997) is persuaded that the relationship is one of 'continuity rather than rupture'. According to historian of science Thomas S. Kuhn, a new paradigm not only replaces but invalidates previous ones. Auslander argues that the paradigm of 'theatre' is not invalidated, but rather remains 'deeply engrained' in both the practice and discourse of Western performance. Better to think in terms of 'articulation' of the theatre paradigm, its 'application and extension to new areas of research'. Auslander cites Blau (1987: 164–5): 'theater is the repressed in performance', and Diamond (1996: 4): 'it is *theater* which haunts all performance whether or not it occurs in the theatre'. In a characteristic twist, Auslander suggests that this is so 'perhaps especially, when it is a kind of performance that is overtly antitheatrical'. Nevertheless, 'the project of political art must be reconceptualised in postmodernist terms'; the models of political theatre derived from the modernist avant garde no longer serve. And the aim is resistance rather than transgression (Auslander 1997: 1–7).

Kershaw (1999) also argues for the displacement of theatre by performance, but according to specific understandings of each term. Since the 1960s, the theatre building has become 'not so much the empty space of the creative artist, nor a democratic institution of free speech, but rather a kind of social engine that helps to drive an unfair system of privilege'. In Foucauldian terms, it is a 'disciplinary system' that ensnares its audience into an unconscious acceptance of a repressive *status quo*. Kershaw identifies three interlocking aspects to this: the training of the audience into consumerism; the shaping of social formations along lines of class, gender, race and other differences through cultural policy; and a 'spatial indoctrination' whereby the different participating groups (audience, actors, etc.) are arranged hierarchically. Theatre now participates fully in the postmodern cultural ethos of late capitalism, especially the consumerism of 'shopping malls, heritage sites and other tourist venues', and a supposed 'new pluralism' that 'masks a deadening cultural conformity' (Kershaw 1999: 31–3).

While the principles of equality and mutuality are absent from the disciplinary forms of theatre, Kershaw identifies 'an explosion of performance beyond theatre' rooted in the 1960s counter-culture that has aimed both to increase the realm of creative freedom and to 'reinvent the socio-political role of performance'. Significantly, Kershaw's list embraces new 'theatre' genres as well as 'performance' ones: it includes for instance community theatre, black theatre, performance art and physical theatre (Kershaw 1999: 58–60).

This is an argument about cultural forms and institutions rather than genres. Kershaw resists genealogies that draw a straight line between contemporary Performance and the historical avant garde. And he warns that claims for postmodernism as a break from the essentialisms of modernism are themselves trapped into a quest for essence: they risk replicating modernism's rhetoric of pure originality. Meanwhile, postmodernist claims to productive marginality risk leaving the dominant intact (Kershaw 1999: 60–1).

Kershaw sees radical contemporary performance practice as he defines it as being set on an historical cusp, between the modern and postmodern, the irrecoverable optimistic rationalism of Brecht and the unacceptable pessimism of Baudrillard: though he wittily allows that the cusp may just be a postmodern fiction. The practices he celebrates are 'articulated to their local and global socio-cultural contexts in ways that are different *in kind* to those that were created by the modernist avant-garde theatre movements or figured by most post-modern cultural critics'. The key pragmatic features are *self-created* circumstances, in *fresh* types of venue that are *beyond* existing theatres. Kershaw is interested in practitioners who are 'culturally representative' and 'socially formative' rather than either avant garde or marginal. The fundamental question is the contribution the practice makes to democratic processes. This is to be realised not as totalising transformations but as local instances of 'autonomous subjectivity' summoned forth by the performance situation (Kershaw 1999: 61–2). There are echoes here of de Lauretis and the feminist subject.

DRAMA, THEATRE, PERFORMANCE . . . SCRIPT AND TEXT

Schechner: drama/script, theatre/performance

In a 1973 essay republished in *Performance Theory*, Schechner asserts that 'the phenomena called either/all "drama", "theatre", "performance"' are universals of human culture from the earliest time. But Western cultures have concentrated their attention on the drama. He then introduces a fourth term, 'script', as being antecedent to drama: drama is 'a specialized kind of script'. He reflects on Palaeolithic cave paintings, which he presumes without evidence were associated with religious rites. A script must have pre-existed each enactment of a rite, and persisted from one to the next. The efficacy of the rite coincided with the dancing of the script. Drama developed as 'a specialized form of scripting' long after the invention of writing and its articulation with power. Scripts are 'patterns of doing, not modes of thinking'. He suggests that the shadow of the script is in Aristotle's conception of action. But, with the Greek drama, the doing moved from the concrete to the abstract, from actual movement to 'movement in the lives of people'. Western theatre since has merely sought for new ways to present any one drama. This inverts 'the ancient relationship between doing and script'. However, popular entertainments in the West, traditional theatres elsewhere, and the Western avant garde have 'refocused attention on the doing aspects of the script' and so brought the natures of theatre and performance into fresh view (Schechner 1988: 69–71).

Schechner offers two models to help think about the four terms under consideration. First is a stacked set of four discs of diminishing size, the largest, performance, on the bottom:

> The drama is the domain of the author, the composer, scenarist, shaman; the script is the domain of the teacher, guru, master; the theatre is the domain of the performers; the performance is the domain of the audience.
>
> (Schechner 1988: 71)

Or, Schechner suggests, we might model in a complementary way: oppositional dyads of 'drama–script' and 'theater–performance'. Cultures emphasise one or the other, drama–script being the least common. There are internal distinctions. While the drama is independent of its carriers, the script must be known by its transmitters. While the theatre is 'concrete and immediate', the performance embraces a 'whole constellation of events, most of them passing unnoticed' (Schechner 1988: 71–3).

In relation to the first model, Schechner figures performance and theoretical work after Stanislavsky as constituting 'an increasing attention to the *seams* that apparently weld one disc to the others'. For instance, Brecht's *Verfremdungs-effekt* reveals 'the script as of different conceptual order than the theater event containing it'; Richard Foreman and Robert Wilson 'explore the disjunctions between script and drama'; and Schechner's recent production with The Performance Group of Sam Shepard's *The Tooth of Crime* effected a 'dissociation between drama–script and theater–performance, as well as a further dissociation between theater and performance' (Schechner 1988: 73–6, original emphasis).

Here is evidence of Schechner's aptitude for fashioning abstract models that return us productively to the real. But let us take a closer look, following Schechner's own account of *Tooth*. Shepard wrote to say that he disliked what he had heard of the production. Plays are written because 'a writer receives a vision which can't be translated in any other way'; and Shepard's constant hope is for his plays to 'come to life in the way I vision them' (Shepard in Schechner 1988: 76).

Thus prompted, Schechner declares some assumptions. First, 'plays "present" themselves to their authors as scenes'; this is coexistent with playwriting. Second, this 'scening process' becomes redundant 'once the play takes shape as dialog'; Classical and Elizabethan dramas persist precisely because they are 'unencumbered by didiscalia [such as stage directions]'. Third, 'the original vision' is 'tied to the original matrix, and decays with it' while 'the drama' is 'that which can be passed on through successive sociocultural transformations' (Schechner 1988: 76–7).

We thus have a fifth term, 'vision' to be mapped, and it seems to point in two directions. For Shepard it is originary and thus to be respected; for Schechner it is culturally symptomatic and hence subject to being transcended. Our own observation is that while Schechner's production opens up metatheatrical seams, his response to Shepard effects a closure. While Shepard's use of 'vision' slips between the two senses of 'inspiration' and 'stage imagination', Schechner follows Aristotle to precipitate out dialogue-as-action as the soul of the drama, but now with the notion of *script* as guarantee. This allows him to open up a separation between Shepard and the act of authorship, occupying the latter position himself, as performance-auteur. Schechner is here both shaman and guru. While Shepard regards his drama as a script for a theatrical event, Schechner treats it simultaneously as a found object and the bearer of a transhistorical deep action.

Schechner invokes the distinction between drama and script; and hence the triviality of didiscalia. In an earlier essay, he challenges the notion that theatre develops from ritual, a claim that in the twentieth century acted as a guarantee of theatre's fundamental significance. Schechner argues instead that we think of ritual and theatre in horizontal relation: each is a human universal; neither precedes or underpins the other (see p. 119) Yet he seems to be in pursuit of a guarantee all the same. Here then we might invoke Derrida, specifically his deconstruction of the hierarchised binary spoken/written. In the ritual repetition of binaries – doing/thinking, oral/written, actual/abstract – script appears in Schechner's formulation as the 'spoken'. Derrida would surely challenge us to consider script as citation rather than origin.

Schechner's modelling both illuminates and obscures. Here, it obscures the cultural formation in which the production was done. Yet there is an historical 'seam' to be identified. On the one side is a dramaturgical practice relatively set adrift from the contexts of theatrical production (contrast, precisely, Shepard with Greek and Elizabethan playwrights). If didiscalia are historically less present in some dramas, it is usually because the playwright was writing within established stage conventions. Didiscalia enter as playwrights begin critically to address the theatrical apparatus itself, often to script a particular sort of performance event.

On the other side is Schechner's own bid for authorship. This overrides the theatrical inscription contained in the dramatic text. Schechner's assertion that the dramatic author's only proper realm is dialogue both forgets what stage authors have been and fails to ask what writing for performance might now be.

Vanden Heuvel: theatre, difference and indeterminacy

Twenty years after Schechner's formulations, in 1991, Vanden Heuvel reviews the terms 'drama', theatre' and 'performance' in the light of what he sees as the subsequent failure of Performance to differentiate itself fundamentally from its precursors. Let us track the way he sets up the terms of his argument.

He first considers drama as 'theatrical expression that is constituted primarily as a literary artifact . . . and empowered as a text'. The powers of such dramas to move, pleasure or distance spectators in performance are 'mainly textual, rooted in literary conventions of narrative, language, scene, character, and semiosis'. The category of drama Vanden Heuvel here addresses is what Barthes calls the 'readable' text, one which presents itself as a transparent medium to an ordered and knowable reality and constructs its reader as a unified subject. Its theatrical manifestation is what Derrida after Artaud called the 'theological stage'. It constructs a sense of authorial mastery and integrity and is wedded to coherent forms characterised by a stability of character, language and plot. In a larger frame, it is one instance of Derridean *écriture*, the general 'cognitive activity of imposing structure and meaning on reality'. In a more historical dimension, it is an instance of 'textualisation', 'the activity of fabricating master emplotments of history . . . or of constructing holistic integrative frames of reference between people, events and objects, or synthetic relationships between language, objects, and desire'. Textualisation, then, is an aspect of the humanist presumption of mastery over the world, which Nietzsche mocked for its naïvety (Vanden Heuvel 1991: 3–4) (see Keyword: Presence and representation).

Vanden Heuvel turns to 'performance'. It now designates *both* an established art form (Performance) *and* 'the privileged mechanism for deconstructing the theological stage and conventional dramatic semiosis' (the postmodern performative). Both are held to displace the power of text and author, to deconstruct Presence. He cites Schechner writing in 1982 that 'the beauty of "performance consciousness"' is that it is 'subjunctive, full of alternatives and potentiality'. Through strategies of indeterminacy and resistance to settled form ('*Gestell*'), its processual mode supposedly 'breaks down the illusion of rational control and power over meaning'. Performance, then, is said to constitute what Foucault termed an episteme, a 'system of cognitive activities' cognate to poststructuralism (Vanden Heuvel 1991: 5–6).

Vanden Heuvel argues, however, that there is a paradox. He follows others from the mid-late 1980s, including Blau, to argue that, whenever Performance privileges 'the spontaneous and physical activity of performing as an autonomous form of artistic expression', it merely 'substitutes one authoritarian locus of power for its opposite'. The Presence of the author is simply replaced by that of the performer, as the one who now induces the response of the spectator, even if that is 'the *jouissance* [a term appropriated by Barthes, which literally means 'orgasmic joy'] of deconstructive dispersal'. If anything, the uniqueness of the event strengthens such authorial Presence. Indeed, while 'text does not mask its Presence . . . performance art uses a more subtle strategy to mystify its relationship to the spectator'. Freud became aware that people undergoing psychoanalysis sometimes 'project' their own fantasies onto the analyst. Vanden Heuvel suggests that the critique of 'textual imperialism' in theatre was simply projection on the part of Performance (Vanden Heuvel 1991: 11–12).

He then makes a counter-claim to the anti-theatrical prejudice uttered in the name of P/performance. Theatre in the 1990s is 'the privileged site of difference in a culture increasingly given to simplified dichotomies'. While the general culture flattens out difference, 'theatre has maintained itself as an arena where potentially conflictual, even antithetical, issues and value perceptions about the world . . . are transformed into interactive energies that can be made to sustain, rather than dominate, one another.' His particular focus in his book, then, is on the theatre space as a machine and frame for the interplay of the dramatic and the performative, exchanges between textualisation and indeterminacy (Vanden Heuvel 1991: 6). He is more optimistic about theatre than are Kershaw or Marranca.

Worthen: text, textuality and performance

One of the responses to Schechner's declaration of a 'paradigm shift' came from W.B. Worthen, who attempted a reformulation of the relationships between 'text' and 'performance'. In the immediate context, some found his intervention quaint and off the point. His focus is on 'performance' simply as the staging of the dramatic text; and his argument is based in literary poststructuralism. It must have felt like an icy draught from the past. But, for us, it takes us to what remain useful formulations around text and textuality.

Worthen aims, like Vanden Heuvel, to challenge some 'romantic' assumptions. He sees 'covertly inscribed' Authorial notions in claims for the liberating 'textuality' of performance. He identifies three interlocking ways in which we think of text: '(1) as a canonical vehicle of authorial intention; (2) as an intertext, the field of textuality; (3) as material object, the text in hand' (Worthen 1995: 14). And his key strategy is to invoke the 'epistemological slide' from traditional notions of the *work* to the more relativised notion of *text* identified by Barthes. While *work* implies a 'signified' to be 'approached through interpretation', *text* implies a field of signifiers in which meaning emerges through 'slippage and interplay between signifying formalities' and from which the sense of authorial mastery is absent. Text as opposed to work aligns with the principle of textuality (Worthen 1995: 14–15).

Worthen argues that Barthes' distinction between masterful work and playful text might be applied to anything corresponding to that third sense, of textual object: it could be a book, an aesthetic performance or social rite. He contends that there has been a rhetorical slippage from Barthes' sense of textuality as performat-*ive* to claims that perform-*ance*, as a textual *object*, is somehow necessarily the epitome of a liberating *textuality*. Having achieved a break from the straitjacket of supposed authorial intention, performance, thus conceived, claims superiority with respect to the written.

Claims for the superiority of stage performances of dramas over the written text are, however, apt paradoxically to deploy 'strategies of authorisation'. Literary 'authorisations' regard proper performance as expressive of authorial inscriptions in the written/printed text as work. Similarly performative 'authorisations' regard the written text as an 'enabling accident' through which the stage realises authorial intention. But this merely substitutes the stage text for the written as the repository of authorial truth (Worthen 1995: 15–16). There are echoes here of our comments on *The Tooth of Crime*, except that Schechner has Shepard join the 'enabling accident' that releases the authority of the deep human script.

We need to follow Worthen through one further turn of argument. It centres on the notion of 'textual condition'. Studies of Shakespearean texts in particular have demonstrated that any printed playtext is massively overdetermined shaped by multiple factors by stage and publishing practices. It will have been through many versions, due probably to several hands, having been both tested in performance and prepared for mere reading. Any idea that the printed playtext corresponds organically to an author's 'work' forgets the realities of publishing in the Renaissance. Jerome McGann argued in 1991 that this 'textual condition' is a characteristic of *all* texts: the text is not a thing but an event. At the point of reception, the event is open: the reader is free to play. But, as Foucault (1979b) maintains, a culture will license only certain readings. Guided by the ideological notion of the 'work', those focused on authors will regard the text as signifier for an absent author. In the same way, those focused on authority will regard the textuality of the stage as signifying the text, and, beyond it, work and author. Worthen reminds us that 'reading is as much a performance, a production of the text, as a stage performance is', and cites Judith Butler's idea that performance accomplishes 'the compelling illusion' of a motivating identity. Considering the facts of intertextuality and the provisionality of the textual object, Worthen suggests, 'the notion that there *is* a text to produce onstage is surprisingly resistant to change' (Worthen 1995: 16–18).

While accepting the assertion, we might also want to ask what implications this perspective has on how we understand cultural production and artistic agency. If the authorial vision (say Shepard's) is best understood as a gathering up of discourses and the text produced as fundamentally plural and unstable, this particular moment of textualisation (in Vanden Heuvel's sense) nevertheless produces a train of performances (in Worthen's). The 'motivating identity' is both an 'illusion' and a cultural fact. This might suggest that we need a sort of cultural reading that is cognate with the dialectical notion of 'positionality' (see chapter 5). We need a notion of agency that is both relativised and substantial.

DRAMA VERSUS THEATRE

We consider here two recent accounts concerned with dramatic texts that have not hitherto been valued by either the literary or the theatrical academy. Each argues that innovations at the level of the *dramatic* text in these non-canonical plays had a profound effect on the development of modernist *theatre*. Both are concerned with productive relationships between high modernism and the avant garde.

In *The Aesthetics of Disturbance*, David Graver argues that the principles of montage and collage allowed sections of the early twentieth-century avant-garde to maintain a disruptive distance from high modernism without falling into 'the needless repetition of bluntly self-destructive, anti-aesthetic gestures'. By deploying montage and collage, plays by Kokoschka and others insinuate 'anti-aesthetic, disturbing, self-consuming, and anarchistic elements' into what nevertheless remains an artwork. The aesthetic nature of the work becomes contaminated with 'critical discontent'. On the page, the plays simultaneously challenged three things: the conventions of bourgeois drama; the 'aesthetic stabilities' of modernism; and 'the simple shock and disdain of anti-art'. But the ways in which they were staged remained very conventional (Graver 1995: 210–13).

Graver identifies Brecht and Artaud as practitioners who began their careers within the avant-garde tradition, but responded to the limitations of the available performance styles to develop what Graver calls the principles of 'performative montage' (the Brechtian *lehrstück*) and 'experiential collage' (Artaud). And the basis of this theatrical innovation for each of them was a 'call for a new cultural practice' (Graver 1995: 214–21). Schechner's map of dramatic, theatrical and performance levels can help us grasp the sequence of Graver's historical account.

The stage and theatricality have been attacked since ancient times. Many pamphlets against playing were published in Renaissance London. Barish conducted a summary analysis of this tradition in *The Antitheatrical Prejudice* (1981). In *Stage Fright: Modernism, Anti-Theatricality and Drama*, Martin Puchner identifies a set of persistent concerns: immoral public display, arousal of the audience and deception. But what precisely underlies the anti-theatricality in that strand of modernism represented now so famously by Michael Fried (Puchner 2002: 1; and see chapter 9)?

His answer is that such modernism is founded on a fear of the mass. Fried's insistence on absorption in the gallery work of art and New Criticism's preference for reading over watching plays amount to just this.

In both cases theatricality is being resisted. These prescriptions, Puchner argues, are 'barriers against the possibility of the public role of art suggested by the theater'. And the contrasting 'triumphant theatricalism' of the avant garde of the early twentieth century, associated with various kinds of populist politics, is predicated on the same association (Puchner 2002: 9–11).

What interests Puchner is that both 'modernist anti-theatricalism' and 'avant-garde theatricalism' come to similar conclusions: an attack on existing theatre. His own point of arrival is the modernist theatre of Brecht, Beckett and Yeats. And the broad shape of his narrative is that these playwrights internalise both the modernist critique of theatricality and the avant garde's enthusiasm for it, to achieve 'a far-reaching reform of the dramatic form and of theatrical representation'. By becoming kept 'at arm's length' theatre becomes 'utterly transformed' (Puchner 2002: 2–12).

Puchner develops a genealogy of anti-theatricalism within modernism, looking in particular at the philosophers and thinkers Nietzsche, Adorno, and Brecht's friend Walter Benjamin. Nietzsche deplored Wagner's prescription for the *Gesamtkunstwerk* as the imposition of a 'theatocracy' over the other arts. An important factor for Benjamin was his concern about the Nazi 'aestheticisation of politics' which invoked Wagner's ideal of the *Volk* as mass audience. And there are particular concerns with the actor. In line with his fears over far-right mass politics, Benjamin celebrates cinema over theatre because, he argues, it robs the actor of 'aura' or special presence on stage. Adorno despised the 'primitive mimesis' or 'aping' of standard acting. Puchner puts this down to 'theatre's uneasy position between the performing and the mimetic arts'. While modernism requires the integration of mimesis into a complex work of art, the actor is not only sign-vehicle but also idiosyncratic bodily presence. This gets in the way of the modernist abstraction Adorno championed (Puchner 2002: 2–11; and compare Pontbriand, see pp. 231–2; and Schneider, see pp. 146–8).

The route Puchner takes to the modernist avant garde is through the 'closet drama' of the modernists Joyce, Mallarmé and Stein. The plays were designed to be read or be seen by only small invited audiences. These coteries resisted normative theatrical values. Borrowing terms from Plato, the emphasis was on *diegesis* (narrative) rather than *mimesis*. In consideration of, for instance, Brecht's call for the 'literarisation of the theatre

(Willett 1964: 43–7) or Beckett's severe hampering of the actor's mobility, Puchner dubs this fully-flowered modernist dramaturgy 'diegetic theatre'. Beckett, Brecht and Yeats each deploy 'narrative strategies' to 'channel, frame, control, and even interrupt what it perceives to be the unmediated theatricality of the stage and its actors' (Puchner 2002: 16–22).

But has the anti-theatrical impulse been dissipated by postmodern Performance? Puchner thinks not, and cites the Wooster Group as example (see Savran 1988). Their use of audio and visual technology to evacuate the sense of live theatre is, he argues, 'a continuation of the modernist impulse'. The contemporary mediatisation of the stage aligns, say, the Wooster Group with Benjamin's analysis of the destruction of aura through mechanical reproduction. Or better, Puchner suggests, the closet drama and the diegetic theatre can be seen as 'part of a history of mediatization' (Puchner 2002: 174–5).

Let us summarise this brief sampling of recent decades. We have encountered three ways in which drama, theatre and performance have been articulated in relation to one another. First, the contemporary primacy of performance over theatre as a *practice* has been argued according to different understandings of each term (consider Schechner and Kershaw); and has been challenged on various grounds (consider Vanden Heuvel; and also Dolan, see pp. 108–9). Second, Schechner usefully extends the conventional understanding of 'drama' as script for theatrical performance – as deployed in Graver's examination of pressure put on theatrical convention by innovations in dramatic texts – to develop models of drama, theatre and performance (along with script) as *dimensions* of any performance event. Third, Puchner develops a dialectical argument around the *quality* of 'theatricalism' resisted by high modernism – just as we have encountered the qualities of textuality (consider Barthes) and of performativity (see Keyword: Performativity and chapter 9). Further, we have frequently been concerned here with the modern/postmodern divide: Kershaw considers aesthetic performance at this provisional 'cusp', aligned rather lamely by some with the shift from theatre to performance; we, as others (see Kershaw 1999: 107–8), find the theoretical modelling of performance's champion Schechner modernist. So our three key terms serve as useful tools to distinguish different aspects of performance practice as well as different genres or paradigms; are laden with particular values in use; and shift and slide in meaning and value within the cultural process. The important work is not to arrive at supposedly secure definitions of the meanings and relationships, but instead to be aware of what is at stake each time one definition of drama, theatre or performance is made.

PART TWO

KEYWORDS

In this part of the book we offer genealogies of selected words that we think are most pertinent, or provocative, to an explication of the three terms drama, theatre and performance. To trace the genealogy of a word is to trace the shifting uses made of it in differing circumstances. Frequently, then, we shall be engaged with debates or negotiations around meaning; and with the changing historical and institutional circumstances that frame them.

ACTION

The most common contemporary use of the word 'action' in relation to a dramatic fiction is in the phrase 'action movie' or 'action-packed adventure'. 'Action' here suggests that which is visually busy, physically testing and risky, outside the everyday, often involving a close relationship between bodies and equipment or machine.

This notion of action seems far distant from the concept which the student of dramatic theory has to master: Aristotle defined tragedy as 'a representation of an action which is serious, complete, and of a certain magnitude'. This is not a word denoting what merely happens in a play. On action depends success or failure in life: 'while men do have certain qualities by virtue of their character it is in their actions that they achieve, or fail to achieve, happiness' (Halliwell 1987: 37). Two aspects of action are suggested here. First, plays provide a way of modelling the ways in which significant human events typically unfold in the real world (as we explore in the Keyword: Mimesis). Second, plays do this modelling through actions done on a stage rather than, say, through the recitation of verse, which is a different form of artistic creation (*poesis*).

For Aristotle character was a vehicle through which to investigate value-laden human action. It was philosophically subordinate to action. This relationship then altered after Aristotle. For example, in *Hamlet* it seems that the hero's psychology prevents him taking action. It is as if the play itself performs an historic shift in focus from an emphasis on ethical action to that on psychology. This rhymes with a seventeenth- and eighteenth-century interest in mind, alongside of which developed a notion of human will, seeing the human as an agent, able to deliberate and take choices, having responsibility for actions (Vernant and Vidal-Naquet 1990: 54).

Within such a framework the German philosopher Hegel radically redefined the category of action, or *Handlung*. Although he followed Aristotle in suggesting that action is the priority to which all other dramatic elements are subordinate, Hegel saw drama's crucial medium as dialogue. For in dialogue the characters can express themselves and so drive the action forward. This action has a specific quality. Not only is it to be distinguished from mere activity; the action is produced by character as an act of will. As Steve Giles puts it, for Hegel 'Action is realized volition, which is known to be such both regarding its inner origins and its final result. Only in this way can action count as *action*' (1981: 13).

Let us briefly note the contrast between Aristotle and Hegel. The contemporary French classical scholar Jean-Pierre Vernant observes that in the case of Aristotle, 'The idea of a free power of decision remains alien to his thought' (1996: 59). In Vernant's analysis, Greek religious thought saw crime – or criminal error, *hamartia* – as something which takes over an individual and spreads its effects beyond him or her. The 'defilement of crime' spreads beyond the individual, affecting relatives, the family lineage, polluting a whole town, moving through generations. Vernant concludes that where 'the action of the criminal is seen, in the outside world, as a daemonic power of defilement and, within himself, as an error of the mind, the entire category of action appears to be organized in a different way from our own' (p. 62). An individual who commits criminal error is caught up in the force that s/he unleashes. 'The action does not emanate from the agent as from its source; rather, it envelops him and carries him away, swallowing him up in a power that must perforce be beyond him since it extends, both spatially and temporally, far beyond his own person' (p. 63).

Aristotle's concept of action was taken up and re-worked in the mid-twentieth century by Suzanne Langer, a philosopher of aesthetics. In her work on tragedy in *Feeling and Form* (1953) she says that 'creating the characters is not something apart from building the plot, but is an integral portion of it. The agents are prime elements in the action, but the action is the play itself' (p. 352). From here she quotes Aristotle and goes on to gloss: 'All human happiness or misery takes the form of action; the end for which we live is a certain kind of activity, not a quality' (p. 352). In a play characters are included 'for the sake of the action'.

Langer's return to Aristotle seems to have two purposes. First, she wants to discard 'All this concern with the philosophical and ethical significance of the hero's sufferings' (p. 358), which distracts us from the properly 'artistic' significance and replaces it with discursive ideas. Her push towards a re-emphasis on the particular art of the artwork would appear to be influenced here by the mode of New Criticism that came to dominance in the mid-1940s. This assumed that each work was autonomous and required the act of close reading to engage with it (see pp. 28–9). From here, however, Langer makes a second move. The art of the artwork is no abstract thing but has its roots in the life process, with its unrepeatable stages of growth, maturity, decline. The form of tragedy, she says, 'reflects the basic structure of personal life' (p. 351).

That connection to fundamental life process is facilitated by Langer's key term. She does not talk of form so much as *rhythm*, which she derives from Francis Fergusson, who talks of 'genuine' tragedy exhibiting 'the tragic rhythm of action' (in Langer 1953: 354). This 'rhythm' of dramatic action makes drama 'a poetry of the theater' (p. 355), and not simply a superficial imitation of everyday life. The job of analysis is to show how the overall rhythm is constructed from various elements of the work.

Both Fergusson and Langer draw on the linked Aristotelian notions of *poesis* and *mimesis*, but in ways that are strongly conditioned by their own historical moment. When Langer notes that the rhythm is integral to a written text, and remains the same 'whether we read it or hear it read, enact it ourselves or see it performed' (p. 356), we hear the voice of New Criticism – just as when Aristotle treats spectacle as the least important element of tragedy, we understand that he never saw the plays acted. For Langer, the basic rhythm is unmarked by a change from the read to the embodied. It is the rhythm itself which is powerful: 'Tragic action has the rhythm of natural life and death, but it does not refer to or illustrate them; it abstracts their dynamic form' (p. 360). And here we detect a second voice from the early 1950s. Contemporary visual theory had an interest in the body's relation to form, as, say, in the work of Rudolph Arnheim (see Keyword: Kinaesthetic). Langer seems to be applying this visual theory to dramatic criticism.

To follow Langer's proposition that rhythm of action is the defining quality of drama, and the rubric for its analysis, we need to go forward to 1970 and the publication of Bernard Beckerman's *Dynamics of Drama*. Beginning with non-dramatic materials – daily tasks and then acrobatics – Beckerman argues that existence, and thus performance, are organised into units and segments of activity. These segments, in their content and their interrelation, work on an audience kinaesthetically through a process of accretion. 'Activity' can then be distinguished from action: actors, says Beckerman, 'generate the activity that, in turn, produces the theatrical tension. The sequence, or path, of theatrical tension is the action, the flow of which creates the illusion of inner life' (1970: 50). What has disappeared from here is Langer's sense of a rhythm connected into felt life. So too the Aristotelian priority given to action over character is slipping: action seems to work to create 'the illusion of inner life'.

Beckerman shares with Langer an opposition to a 'conceptual' approach to the analysis of drama. This is why he stresses drama's roots in activity, conceived as a set of physical motions. But his starting out from daily life and 'non-dramatic' performance has a second function. Much of the performed work around him in the late 1960s would have been not only 'non-Aristotelian' but also non-drama. His analysis of the segments of an acrobat's activity identifies how as a non-Aristotelian action it holds its audience's attention through a pattern of intensification and relaxation. Before the orthodoxies of 'Performance Studies' had begun to emerge, his model aims to embrace as performed activity rituals and acrobatics.

Beckerman's dissolution of the Aristotelian notion of action, both intentionally and unintentionally losing its precision, was part of a larger process. Looking back at it, Timothy Wiles concluded (1980) that in the new practices of drama, and specifically 'performance', the category of action has evaporated:

> Rejecting the formal and aesthetically completable concept of dramatic *action*, recent theoreticians have called for the centrality of *activity*; not, as Aristotle had it, 'what might happen,' a probable and universally applicable action, but 'what happens,' the fragmentary, contingent, time-bound, and unrepeatable activities which have the advantage of being real, not ideal.
>
> (p. 115, original emphasis)

We might remark nonetheless that Kaprow, say, was fascinated by the interplay in his scripted Happenings between mere activity and the appearance of art. The fact that it is offered as a deliberate creation, *poesis*, itself confers value, signals that *activities* in the everyday have a significance equal to any idealised sense of an abstract *action*. In the next generation, Richard Foreman eschewed dramatic action and focused hard on the creative moment itself, *poesis* as liminal moment – highly contingent *act*, yet significant human *activity*; one person and an audience making sense of things.

Alongside these revaluations of action alongside activity, another concept of action persisted. Let us recall Vernant's image of the human agent carried along by an action that is unleashed, and return to the action movie. Within an action movie the human is one part of the unleashed action; its other elements will be, say, cars, guns, urban streets – objects and spaces – music, sound effects, fast cuts between shots; a sense of a speeded-up sequence which starts moving with its own momentum. The same effect was also produced by the genre from which this sort of movie derives, melodrama and its characteristic suspense narratives.

Behind this idea of action movie seems to lie a specific application of the word. Soldiers are described as 'killed in action'. The use of a noun in this phrase obscures the idea that the action has been done by particular human agents. 'Action' here amounts to a set of activities which are more than the sum of their parts, something larger than human agency. Thus for example when soldiers are trained through repetitive drills they develop team spirit, which 'allows them to behave as a single organism' (de Landa 1998: 64). This illustration is taken from Manuel de Landa's account of self-organising processes as manifested in military history. Such a process is one 'in which order emerges out of chaos as a result of non-linear dynamics'. He names the process 'machinic phylum', and applies the term both to 'any population . . . whose global dynamics are governed by singularities' (defined earlier as transition points where 'order spontaneously emerges out of chaos' (p. 15)) and 'the integration of a collection of elements into an assemblage that is more than the sum of its parts' (p. 20). The effect of the machinic phylum is seen when a gaggle of men turn into a drilled troop, or a corps de ballet, or a chorus.

The concept of machinic phylum, derived from study of non-linear dynamics, takes us a further stage in the tracking of 'action'. Those stages might be summarised, roughly, as Aristotle's philosophical and ethical modelling followed by an Enlightenment emphasis on free will followed by an evaporation of the viability of both ethos and free will, which then leads to a notion of humans caught into self-organised machinic process.

ALEATORY

An aleatory event is one that is governed by chance. The introduction of planned uncertainty into performance practices is associated especially with the work of the composer John Cage (1912–92) in the early 1950s. His *Water Music* of 1952 required activities that would generate sounds that were unpredictable in range and quality: the performer had to pour water from one vessel to another, deal cards into the piano strings, slam shut the keyboard lid.

The philosophy underpinning these experiments was associated with Zen Buddhism, which privileges chance over structured organisation. But the aleatoric artwork also has roots in other artforms earlier in the same century. The Dadaist Tristan Tzara (1856–1963) used random selections from newspaper text to create poems. Jean Arp (1887–1968) assembled collages by dropping small pieces of paper and fixing them where they fell. In a deliberately polemical gesture towards dominant ideas of art and beauty in a stifling bourgeois society, Dadaism's use of aleatory techniques was designed to mock the values placed on individual creativity, structure, organisation and control. The aleatory work is thus a claim to freedom from tradition, received formulas and consciousness. It is a work scripted, we might say, to perform the role of chance in performance.

In 1959 such activities acquired a name from the title of a work created by one of Cage's pupils, Allan Kaprow's *18 Happenings in 6 Parts*. Monologues consisted of randomly organised lists of words and phrases. Verbal text was released from the constraints of syntactical structure and operated instead as pure sound. In this respect Happenings are 'non-verbal'. They enact their distance from the orderly communication system that is maintained by the observance of language rules. Their structure seems designed not to communicate but to inhibit information. Michael Kirby designates this structure 'compartmental', meaning that the Happening consists of self-contained units, which in *18 Happenings* were, literally, three separate rooms. Another difference between Happenings and 'traditional' theatre is that in the latter 'the performer always functions within (and creates) a matrix of time, place, and character' (Kirby 1985: 5). In the Happening, performance is 'nonmatrixed': to explain this concept, Kirby instances the situation of stage-hands changing the set in the interval of a show, on stage but not performing. A sporting event is also, he says, nonmatrixed. Coming chronologically after Brecht's attempt to show the actor alongside the character, 'a new category exists in drama, making no use of time, place, or character, and no use of the performer's comments' (p. 7).

Attempting a 'taxonomy' of Happenings, Darko Suvin begins with the 'Event', a scene with one activity such as a children's game. Events are linked to music and dance 'since they deal with the rhythmic use of a *delimited time-duration*' (1970: 126). Next are 'Aleatoric scenes'. These he relates to music where the structure derives from a combination of authorial choice (Cage's requirement for the water vessels) and chance. Discussing Happenings, the next category, he notes either a desire to escape into nature or 'to convert the urban American environment into a new naivety without physically challenging it' (p. 128). They work by a process of (attempted) sensory re-education and thus have about them a utopian urge. When the techniques of Happenings are matrixed in space and plot (as in Kenneth Brown's *The Brig*) they develop as Action Theatre.

Writing in 1970 in *The Drama Review*, at a time when the journal was interested in Happenings, Suvin was arguing against those like Richard Schechner who approved of Happenings because they interfered with modes of perception. Viewing this as a merely formalist approach, Suvin argued that the emphasis on the aleatory was an ideological construction connected with a specific historical moment. The major period of Happenings was the mid-1950s to mid-1960s. Suvin describes it as a time when the internal 'stagnation' of the United States broke down 'in an inconclusive flurry of shocked recognition of America's papered-over contradictions . . . The New York *bohème* lacked available or persuasive foreign models, lacked strong native workers' or Socialist movements, and was subjected to new and more pervasive methods of mass persuasion based on the lure of prosperity' (1970: 141). Thus Happenings 'very rarely – and this is a clear weakness - focus their attention on political or economic relationships of any kind: Happenings are more than a little socially inbred' (p. 140). At the same time we should note that Happenings also coincided with the work being done by philosophers of perception, such as Arnheim and Polanyi (see Keyword: Kinaesthetic), who were interested in different sorts of knowledge, and the role of the body within them.

The picture of the Happening makers as 'an isolated little group catering mainly to each other' (p. 141) needs extension and qualification, however. It could describe most emergent artistic groups in an age of mass communications. In Britain there were Happenings at the end of the 1960s, associated with the counter-culture that also embraced the student protest movement and the events of May 1968 in Paris. In the same period the more radical elements associated with Fluxus made important, albeit abortive, attempts to integrate aleatory art practice with political praxis. The aleatory here is potentially a political instrument.

In the 1990s in Britain, although no-one speaks of Happenings, there are shows incorporating aleatory elements. The live chat show, especially where the presenter talks to the audience, has about it an element of risk-taking on all sides. The event is apparently nonmatrixed (except that the celebrities have to maintain their celebrity personas) and the everyday is incorporated – from everyday objects through street interactions to the 'everyday' people in the audience. Here too there is, apparently, no political reference point. This is the aleatory now placed within mass entertainment. And the scripted framing of the aleatory is the basis also for 'reality TV' shows such as *Big Brother* (Channel 4), where chance human interactions determine not only the course of the drama, but also who will become a celebrity. Here, however, the audience are positioned as judges and executioners. They are invited to play with the sensation of being in control of the commodity apparatus. In reality TV, engagement with the aleatory positions, and ideologically consolidates, the viewer as consumer–god coupled with the promise that they, too, might be a celebrity.

These late instances of the aleatory have resolved a cynical hopelessness in the face of mass media and mass consumption into a sort of festive cynicism where anything goes, everybody knows everything, and nothing matters. Less concerned with unravelling traditional art, the 1990s aleatory delivers a savvy quiescence. In all cases, however, the aleatory may be said to be associated with freedom, or, perhaps more precisely, its image.

CATHARSIS

This word is very often used to explain the effect on an audience at the end of a tragedy, or indeed any serious play. In its common modern use, 'cathartic' can mean a therapeutic discharge of strong emotion, and from here it is often used simply to describe the experience of strong emotion. A 'cathartic' experience is thus merely an emotional one.

The end of a tragedy is commonly supposed to produce an emotional response in an audience in order to draw the emotion out of them, to get them to express the emotion in order to get rid of it, and then to be left calmer afterwards, emotionally purged.

This general sense of tragedy's operation has earned it some enemies. In Augusto Boal's account of Aristotelian theory, catharsis figures as a cultural safety valve because it leaves the audience drained and safely calm. The tragic effect reconciles an audience to situations about which they should feel – politically – the reverse of calm. But, as Milling and Ley point out, Boal is not actually engaging with what Aristotle wrote so much as with what he thinks he wrote. His conculsion 'depends on the invention of a missing emotion, which is not pity or fear, but which is mysteriously "*something directed against the laws*"' (Milling and Ley 2001: 154, original emphasis).

Since so much has been made of the term, and since it has been associated in such a defining way with Aristotle's version of tragedy and its political efficacy, it often comes as a surprise to note that Aristotle uses the word just once in his definition of tragedy: the defining quality of tragic action is that it is 'capable of eliciting pity and fear from its audience and of effecting a *katharsis* of such emotions' (Halliwell 1987: 89). The lack of explanation or clarification has generated pages of commentary and argument. And, as with mimesis, the word as used here cannot with any security be rendered into English. Stephen Halliwell thus advises caution:

> It had better be said at once that we do not really know what [Aristotle] meant in this context by *katharsis*. We can be moderately confident only that it offers a response to the Platonic view that tragedy arouses emotions which ought, for the sake of general psychological and moral well-being, to be kept in check (*Republic* 10, 603–5).
>
> (1987: 89–90)

Some commentators try to get closer by relating its use here to Aristotle's other uses. Most common among these, according to Jonathan Lear, is the meaning of menstruation. So when it occurs in the definition of tragedy it has something to do with a root meaning that involves the process of expelling matter from the body. This gives rise to further questions: what is being expelled? by what means? in the body of the audience or the body of the play? Attempting to take an even-handed and very cautious overview, Halliwell suggests

> it is possible to move towards a very tentative interpretation of *katharsis* as a powerful emotional experience which not only gives our natural feelings of pity and fear full play, but does so in a way which conduces to their rightful functioning as part of our understanding of, and response to, events in the human world.
>
> (1987: 90)

The debates that have raged both before and since Halliwell's formulation have seen catharsis defined as purgation, purification and education. In his own attempt to reach a definition Lear rejects these definitions and lists the constraints which need to be satisfied in order to get at Aristotle's meaning. These include an audience that knows itself to be at the theatre yet can conceive the possibility of the events happening to themselves, that feels pleasure as well as relief. Lear stresses that Aristotle is aware that the appropriate response to a mimesis – tragic pleasure and catharsis – 'would be thoroughly inappropriate to the real event'. Catharsis is able to seem like relief because it is experienced 'in an appropriately inappropriate environment' (Lear 1992: 334).

The constraints on the meaning listed by Lear take us some distance from those assumptions by Brecht and Boal that tragedy absorbs its audience into its own illusory space, or that it replaces real-life judgements with fictional ones. Another attempt to fix the meaning is that of Andrew Ford at a conference on performance and performativity in 1993. Contextualising the *Poetics* with *Politics*, he argues that Aristotle proposes catharsis as available for those who do not have an educated response to tragedy (for Aristotle presumes that the form is mainly destined for an educated audience).

The work of defining catharsis is imbued by a political concern with appropriate civil behaviour, together with a radical uncertainty about the operation of public emotion. As much as Aristotle, Boal is concerned with the emotional response proper to enacted fictions. This is perhaps no surprise, for what remains constant through the debates is that at base discussions of catharsis involve discussions about artificially induced emotion in a public setting. Aristotle himself was writing after the age of tragedy (fifth century BCE) and was thus dislocated from commonly held tragic values. He was attempting to explain a lost public emotion within a very different social context. And it is that sense of cultural discontinuity which gives the edge to the most urgent discussions of catharsis.

For one such famous discussion we can look to the English Renaissance. This is the period at which, according to Stephen Orgel (1995), the word catharsis came to pre-eminence in discussions by self-conscious theorists of dramatic art. To many of them the contemporary drama represented chaos of form, produced in conditions that, in new commercial theatres, seemed to exemplify the absence of proper order and decorum. So they looked instead for their reference point back to theoretical writing of the classical age, when cultural production may seem, in hindsight, more orderly. The key figure here was Aristotle together with the other figure who influenced much Renaissance thinking, the Roman poet and theorist Horace.

Horace's view of poetry was that it both instructed and delighted; indeed, it was good at instruction because it created delight. This idea forcibly links pleasure to function. It is another instance of how serious art engages with the business of emotion management. Thus instructional delight joined useful purging as a way of explaining the effects of plays. Each had particular appeal in a society which was concerned about the popular emergence and social impact of an art that was clearly capable of pushing large numbers of people into emotional excitement.

The value in discussing catharsis seemed to derive from its capacity for defining an abstract relationship between artwork and society, and, within that, the proper government of civil emotion. If antipathy to emotional release in the Renaissance links to a concern with ungoverned social gatherings, then in the later seventeenth century and beyond, with the development of a civil and 'rational' bourgeois society, catharsis was at first rejected and then emotionally redefined. The turn towards emotional redefinition is seen in Lessing, who defined a tragedy as a 'poem which excites pity': the pitying state ends as the play ends, to be followed only afterwards by fear (in Carlson 1994: 168). And for Goethe the key element of catharsis was reconciliation and harmony, to be achieved between the parties on stage rather than in the audience. Catharsis thus seems to mutate: from a purging of pity and fear, through a stress on pity and fear in relation to education, to a main emphasis on the creation rather than purging of pity, with fear as a subsidiary element. Alongside this mutation of the concept the social place of early-modern theatre-going was also changing: the activity was becoming more dominated by the personnel and norms of the gentry. The eighteenth century gave birth to an urban 'civil society'. So we could suggest that the theatrical emphasis on fear declines because it has a less important place in civil society's view of its own way of doing things.

The interest in catharsis that came from dramatic theory was boosted and disseminated more widely with developments in the exploration of human psychology. In the mid-nineteenth century German scholars assumed that the cathartic process was the expulsion of pathological emotion, something which has its own psychic history beyond the response to dramatic text. The famous case is the commentary on Aristotle by the German philologist Jacob Bernays (1824–81): he interpreted Aristotle's idea of catharsis as medical rather than moral in application. Freud knew and admired the work of Bernays, to whom he had a family connection through his wife. With Breuer Freud developed a treatment for hysterics, described in the case history of Anna O, which they called the 'cathartic method'.

In the Renaissance catharsis gathered resonance from the need for management of public emotion. After the nineteenth century it acquired overtones from a medical model that, in its popularised form, works by unpicking the mechanism of repression through the 'talking cure', thereby releasing that which had been so damagingly contained. Less to do with social engineering, catharsis becomes a term of personal therapy. And such therapy is often self-chosen, as a way of coping with personal crisis. It is a short step, as the term gets popularised, until catharsis becomes associated with experience, not purging, of high emotion.

CHARACTER, MASK, PERSON

In dominant Western theatre, the fictional individuals presented by a playscript are usually referred to as 'characters' in the play. The work of actors is assumed to be the production of 'characterisation' of the individual they are responsible for and the discovery of the 'motivation' for its behaviour, leading to an outcome in which, thanks to their efforts, the written text 'comes alive'.

It its earliest uses 'character' had, by contrast, little to do with individuality and interiority. It was associated instead with a minor literary genre, the 'character sketch'. The genre reached far back, to the ancient Greek writer Theophrastus. His work was translated into English at the turn of the sixteenth and seventeenth centuries. But, as Jean-Christophe Agnew notes, the Greek model in which 'characters' were 'personifications of moral vices and virtues' mutated into something more typical of England in the early seventeenth century. 'Characters' became popular as prose distillations of recognisably topical social types (the sea captain, the puritan, the brothel-keeper): 'Character books offered their audiences a witty, sociobotanical excursion . . . around contemporary English society' (Agnew 1986: 74–5). They appeared alongside pamphlet descriptions of low life and manuals evoking the protocols of polite conduct. Caught into this general discourse of social mapping, playtexts also incorporated 'characters' – entertainingly recognisable social types.

Even into the later eighteenth century a 'character' was still understood to be a distillation in words of a person's salient attributes, a prose epitome of that individual. Such a meaning remains in the somewhat old-fashioned job advertisement that requires persons of good 'character'. And it hangs on as the 'character reference', a reliable report on a person's qualities.

So even though, in the currently dominant practice and discourses of Western theatre, 'character' is tied up with notions of roundedness, depth and interiority, the word itself comes down to us with a sense of typification. Alongside it the plays of the early seventeenth century used a different word for fictional individuals. That word is familiar from the stock Latin phrase, *dramatis personae*. The activity of presenting the 'persons of the drama' led, in Andrew Gurr's opinion, to a theoretical coinage:

what the players were presenting on stage by the beginning of the century was distinctive enough to require a whole new term to describe it. This term, 'personation', is suggestive of a relatively new art of individual characterisation, an art distinct from the orator's display of passions or the academic actor's portrayal of the character-types.

(Gurr 1970: 73)

Although the word 'characterisation' is somewhat unspecific, the key point about the difference between personation and portrayal of 'character' is very clear.

The categorisations here do not necessarily suggest that any one of the activities is more 'realistic' than the others. Behind the English word 'person' the Latin *persona* retains the specific meaning of 'mask'. In early seventeenth-century commedia dell'arte the persona is a generic type: Pantalone, Il Dottore, Arlecchino. While s/he may not wear an actual mask, the actor's body is nevertheless trained to conform to the physical regime conventionally associated with the particular persona. For a mask is not simply worn, but is inhabited by the performer. It provides the chief frame for their performance. Further, we might say that the mask inhabits the performer, though in a different way. In the performing of commedia, for example, the mask works through the musculature on the psyche. The performer's brain is taken into the attitude of the mask, leaving behind the protocols and constraints of everyday existence (Webber *et al.* 1983).

By inhabiting a set of externally-given gestures and muscular shapes, the body may be said to be masked. And it is this sense of externality or mask which the political philosopher Thomas Hobbes (1588–1679) associated with the word 'person' in 1649. He pointed out the derivation from *persona*, which 'signifies the *disguise*, or *outward appearance* of a man, counterfeited on the Stage, and sometimes more particularly that part of it, which disguiseth the face, as a Mask or Visard' (Hobbes 1976: 217). From here he goes on to say that there is a similarity between person and actor: 'a *Person*, is the same that an *Actor* is, both on the Stage and in common Conversation; and to *Personate*, is to *Act*, or *Represent* himselfe, or an other' (p. 217). Hobbes is here assuming a continuity between stage and 'common conversation', since in all dealings between persons each party deliberately presents an outward appearance, adopts a 'mask'. Thus about 300 years before Goffman formulated his ideas of 'face' and presentation of self in everyday life, Hobbes, at a founding moment of market society, suggests the idea of everyday performance.

In its English form persona loses its connection with mask. It begins gradually to drift towards a sense of the 'private person': something deeper than a social exterior, unique and natural. This attention to a private self gained special force in the early years of the nineteenth century. Radical thinkers distanced themselves politically from a repressive and corrupting social order. What mattered was not simply the 'Romantic' poet's private response but the effort to free one's head of learnt illusions. In the shift of emphasis towards the authoritative reality of what is inner, external appearance became associated with falseness. The mask, as Hobbes had already suggested, was a cover, something to hide behind. Arriving at this meaning, mask became a trivialised concept, a long way removed from masked performing.

That drive to look 'inside', which presumes, of course, that there *is* an inside to look into, is usually connected with the work of the Russian theatre director Stanislavsky (1863–1938). As Joseph Roach says, 'His name became associated with the doctrine of "affective memory" whereby the actor, following in a tradition founded by Diderot and developed by Talma and Lewis, subjectively revived his own past emotions in the circumstances demanded by the role' (Roach 1993: 197). In Roach's account both Diderot and Stanislavsky are the major figures who address an abiding problem of acting, that of how to produce passion to order even while sustaining spontaneity. Each used current scientific thinking in developing their own ideas. So for Stanislavsky the interrelation of body and mind, explored in contemporary science, was the key to the development of his system for training actors: 'The bond between body and soul is indivisible. . . . In every physical act there is a psychological element and a physical one in every psychological act' (in Roach 1993: 205). Taken together, Stanislavsky's three books *An Actor Prepares, Building a Character*, and *Creating a Role*, published in English with large intervals between, suggest that the work of physical characterisation proceeds alongside the development of psychological, and indeed 'subconscious', techniques. Through his system of training, his 'psycho-technique', Stanislavsky suggested an actor can 'reach the spiritual life of a role reflexively through its physical life' (Roach 1993: 209). Through the conscious, the subconscious could be accessed. When the actor's training concentrates on techniques to stimulate subconscious reflex, the concept of character, even though it is something to be 'built', becomes thoroughly organic and privatised.

It is precisely this effect that the German dramatist and theorist Bertolt Brecht (1898–1956) objected to when he warned against the 'complete fusion' of actor with role which makes it seem so 'natural, so impossible to conceive any other way' that the audience accept it as it stands. For Brecht, where the project is to change human nature, the actor must instead attempt to 'shed light' on the human being 'at that point where he seems capable of being changed by society's intervention' (Brecht 1964: 235). This required both a different attitude by actors to the work of characterisation and a different concept of character itself. The actor was asked not to tidy away the inconsistencies in a character but instead to demonstrate its contradictions, its instability and capacity for change. While 'empathy, or self-identification with the character' may be a useful rehearsal tool, it is, says Brecht, just one method of 'observation'. The task is not to falsify coherence: 'The coherence of the character is in fact shown by the way in which its individual qualities contradict one another' (pp. 195–6).

Brecht's minority opposition to a persisting mode of loosely Stanislavskian characterisation was restated in 1965 by his follower, the US critic Eric Bentley. Questioning the value placed on individualised characters, he argues that the effect on an audience comes from that which is representative, generalisable, not that which is particular and individual. He derives this position from the observation that 'the original cast of characters in the drama of life' is the family, and that drama is later replayed 'with more and more people cast for the same few parts' (Bentley 1965: 36). From here he moves on to emphasise the importance, and prevalence, of dramatic types, who are presented through action. Within the category of types, however, the minor fixed characters are separate from those major types which can become archetypes: 'If the traditional fixed characters typify smaller things – groups and their foibles and eccentricities – the archetypal character typifies larger things and characteristics that are more than idiosyncrasies' (1965: 49). An analysis of the prevalence of types then reveals the extent to which drama functions as myth.

Writing well before poststructuralist thinking took hold of performance theory, Bentley suggests that dramatic character is less a fixed entity than a relationship, a force-field even, between play and audience. Shakespeare is less interested in 'attributing qualities to people than in providing a demonstration that they are alive'. Thus: 'We identify ourselves with a Shakespeare character less in the sense of: "I am this man, I have these traits of character" than in the sense of: "Becoming this man, I know what it is to be alive"' (1965: 61). This is both a restatement of the Aristotelian idea that character is a function of action and, in a world that had digested its psychoanalysis, a reformulation of character as that which is unfixed.

Similarly J.L. Styan separated the activities of the dramatic agents from the overall impression created by these activities, the 'character'. Using both Bentley and Styan, Bernard Beckerman distinguished between 'character-made' and 'character-in-the-making':

> The character-made is an afterimage, 'a product' in Styan's phrase, which can be handled imaginatively or critically after the play is over. It is this afterimage that is often detached from the circumstances of the drama for the purpose of either contemplation or explication. As long as we realize that the entity we discuss is not identical with the character-in-the-making, no real harm is done. . . . The character-in-the-making, with which analysis is concerned, can never be considered an entity. Instead it is a series of behavioral possibilities. Although the actor is concerned with the Impression he produces, he cannot achieve character impression directly but must leave to the spectator the coalescing of an image from presented activity.

In summary, 'character is the interpretation we attach to an individual's activity' (Beckerman 1970: 210, 213). As we note elsewhere (see Keyword: Kinaesthetic), Beckerman was much influenced by contemporary work on perception. Gestalt philosophy from earlier in the century underpins his idea, as too that of Styan in *Drama, Stage and Audience* (1971), that it is the spectator who resolves all the different behavioral possibilities into a cognitively graspable summary impression. In thus appropriating insights from visual theory, Beckerman in 1970 anticipates the later emphasis on the provisionality of the performer's work. The performer, he suggests, can only produce a set of 'behavioral possibilities'. The coherent overview which is called 'character' is only available outside the performance.

Another version of character as abstract summary is proposed by Manfred Pfister's use of the word 'figure'. This proposition comes within an attempt to develop a theory of drama which is not, like all other theories including Aristotle's, tied down to historically specific sorts of drama. 'Figure' appeals to Pfister because it 'hints at something deliberately artificial' and 'evokes the impression of functionality rather than individual autonomy' ([1988] 1993: 161). This prevents it being thought about as a 'real' person. He defines it as 'the sum of the structural functions it fulfils' and 'the sum of the contrasts and correspondences linking it with the other figures in the text' (p. 163). The problem here, however, is that because Pfister is looking for a transhistorical formulation he has abstracted 'figure' (and character and person) from relationships with those other historically very specific persons, the actors who show the character and the spectators who interpret it. Some would argue that these transactional relationships are crucial to the power of 'character'.

DEFAMILIARISATION AND ALIENATION

Brecht, Marxism and feminism

The persistent misapprehension that Brecht wanted to alienate his audiences and was therefore humourless relates to some confused translation, whereby both the German *Entfremdung* and *Verfremdung* are frequently rendered as 'alienation'. While Brecht himself used the terms interchangeably for a time, the latter is best understood as 'distancing', 'estrangement' or '*defamiliarisation*'. In Brecht's Marxist framework, both human labour and humanity itself are *alienated*, in the sense that they are prevented from self-realisation, becoming what they could best become. Making the obvious strange is a political technique designed to help the oppressed recognise the form of their oppression, and so overcome it. If Brecht set his face against the *Gesamtkunstwerk* of Wagner (in which all elements were to be integrated into the whole), the two men held in common a sense (though not the same sense) that humanity was alienated, and that art could help overcome this. But while Wagner prescribed aesthetic immersion in myth, Brecht promoted critical enquiry. Defamiliarisation techniques in the theatre – *Verfremdungs-effekt* – are designed to overcome alienation – *Entfremdung* – in life.

Brecht provides a stage fable to demonstrate this. In scene 13 of *The Mother* (1930), revolutionary activist Pelagea Vlassova infiltrates a queue of women waiting to donate copper to the Russian Tsarist military in the First World War. A sign declares that these donations will help the nation by shortening the war. Vlassova argues as if innocently that more bullets will surely lengthen the war; and later, bitterly, that the working class on each side are killing each other for the boss class. The sign hides, or inverts reality. This is what Larrain (1979: 27–31) identifies as a 'negative' definition of *ideology*. The scene shows how ideology works; and how defamiliarisation first identifies and then inverts or pierces through ideology to reveal what it conceals. In a 1939 essay, Walter Benjamin writes that the task of Brecht's epic theatre is 'to represent conditions', not through 'reproduction' like Naturalism but by uncovering them, by '*mak(ing) them strange*': and this is done by 'interrupting them' (Benjamin [1939] 1973a: 18, original emphasis).

Rather than fable, it would be more accurate to call the scene an extended *gestus*. More than a story, it shows the shape of some typical conditions. Consider the scene as a gestus of ideology: the women queue up blindly, misled by the sign. So it is also a gestus for defamiliarisation: Vlassova interrupts the queue, reveals the truth behind the sign, and divides the women along class lines. Further, it provides a gestus or model of the activist: Vlassova succeeds until she blows her cover by becoming angry. Her behaviour and its consequences are something for audience and actors alike to consider. They learn two things: important questions about techniques of political agitation; and the habit of looking at the whole of life through defamiliarising eyes. Third and fundamentally: Vlassova interrupts the queue to reveal to the women that they have real choices that can change themselves and the world. And the activists in the audience and on stage can also change things.

Willett usefully renders the German *gestus* as 'both gesture and gist'. Bodily relations and the shape of human interactions are made diagrammatic; human behaviour is scrutinised (1977: 173). Fundamental here is the technique of *demonstration*: the performer ostends the act of representation, standing 'beside' the character. The gestus operates at two levels simultaneously: the Brechtian actor gests the material; and adopts the gestus of demonstration in the playhouse. In fact, the actor's single body generates three persons at once. There is the character, the actor who demonstrates, and the person who takes on the social role of acting. Brechtian theatre depends both on the abstraction of reality and on the concrete reality of the people on stage and in the auditorium. Meanwhile, Brecht's *separation of the elements* itself is a *V-effekt*. In revealing the means of theatrical production, it foregrounds the rhetorical functioning of the stage, its performativity as a representational apparatus.

Elin Diamond notes the Brechtian basis of Mulvey's (1975) critique of the male gaze within the cinematic apparatus. In a developing argument first published in 1988, Diamond calls for an intertextual reading of Brechtian and feminist theory on the basis of some grounding principles in each. For feminism, these can be summed up as 'an engaged analysis of sex and gender in material social relations and in discursive and representational structures . . . which involve scopic pleasure and the body'. Her aim is to discover, through the development of a '*gestic feminist criticism*', 'the specificity of theatre' (Diamond 1997: 44).

The key engagement is between Brecht's *Verfremdungs-effekt* and feminist gender critique. Butler, de Lauretis and others have demonstrated that while it appears natural, the gendered body is a construction (see chapter 5). In gender, Diamond recognises 'a perfect illustration of ideology at work' and in many feminist art practices that challenge this construction, a version of Brechtian defamiliarisation: 'by foregrounding the expectation of resemblance, the ideology of gender is exposed'. And, when gender is defamiliarised, 'the spectator is able to see . . . a sign system as a sign system'. This, then, is the same territory as Vlassova and the copper queue. But in the case of gender, as Butler in particular insists, these 'illusionistic trappings' are '*nevertheless* inseparable from, embedded, in the body's habitus' (Diamond 1997: 46–7, original emphasis).

A developed strategy in feminist and queer theatre and Performance is to foreground the historical person who takes on the role of actor as part of the gestus. The performer's body is itself part of the critical, deconstructive gestic text. Diamond uses the Brechtian principle of *historicisation* to elaborate her remarks on defamiliarisation. This insists not only that the elements of the fable be regarded as strange by performer and spectator alike, but also that both thereby come to see their *own* situation in this way – that is, historically produced. In the theatre, the feminist spectator can take pleasure in a shared defamiliarisation of the sex/gender system that inscribes both her own body and that on stage. On this basis, a play of productive difference can emerge (Diamond 1997: 49–54).

The Prague School and Russian Formalism

One inspiration for Brecht's concept of *Verfremdungs-effekt* was his meeting the Russian Formalist Viktor Shklovsky in 1935. Shklovsky and others asked what it was that made literature literature. The notion of *priem ostranenie* ('making strange') refers to the way in which literature reveals words and constructions as things in themselves. The Prague School of semioticians (see p. 236) adopted and developed the notion of *ostranenie* as *aktualisace* ('foregrounding'). This refers to the way in which an unexpected linguistic usage brings it to conscious concern. In their pioneering development of theatre semiotics, Keir Elam reports, they 'conceived of the performance structure as a dynamic *hierarchy* of elements'. Fixity of attention on, say, the actor renders other matters of expression on stage transparent. They operate only in their function as sign-vehicles. But the foregrounding of another element will disrupt this automatisation (Elam 1980: 17, original emphasis).

Elam suggests that theatre and Performance are characterised by a fundamental defamiliarisation: 'the general connotative marker "theatricality" attaches itself to the entire performance and to its every element'. The audience are aware that theatre is bracketed off from the rest of life, and read it as a text. 'Theatrical semiosis invariably, and above all, connotes *itself* (Elam 1980: 12).

Elam argues that in formal terms, the split between actor as transparent sign vehicle and physical/social presence we have identified in the gestus is a condition of all theatre. Brecht and those who emulate him drive 'a dramaturgical wedge between the two functions' and so render the actor 'opaque'. It 'put(s) on show the very process of semiotization involved in the performance' (Elam 1980: 9). Diamond writes in similar terms about 'challenges (to) the mimetic property of acting', or in semiotic terms its 'iconicity'. Iconicity (the mechanism of resemblance) is not so much refused as revealed (Diamond 1997: 45–6).

Postmodern Brechts

In a study of Pina Bausch, Norbert Servos quotes Brecht: 'a theatre that takes everything from the Gestus cannot ignore dance. The very elegance of a movement and the grace of movement defamiliarises' (Servos 1984: 21). Bausch's dance theatre is fully within the remit of postmodernism. But she also can be seen as an heir to Brecht. Her performers arrest reality by repeating gestures of abjection, hope and dependency. The repetition acts as an estranging device: it foregrounds attitudes of body/mind. But it is also gestic: it embodies *routine*, our schooled submission to orders of gender, age and class. As Birringer writes, the performers work 'from inside out' in order to lay bare the deep interpellations (see p. 79) we all carry within our culturally-inscribed bodies, our habitus (Birringer 1993: 163–5). As Servos remarks, 'the body is no longer a means to an end. It has itself become the subject of performance' (Servos 1984: 23).

While Brecht despised Naturalism for dealing only with superficial appearances, it emerged principally as a movement to reveal the truths of bourgeois culture. It offered a supposedly objective slice of life: some proponents spoke in terms of scientific truth. In this respect, it shares with Brechtian epic a conception of *irony*. Both Naturalism and Brechtianism as usually understood operate within the remit of Althusser's science/ ideology binary. It is often argued that both Marxism and Brecht are certain that there is indeed an ultimate objective truth to be known; the gist of Brecht's mature plays seems at the surface to be that sufficient scepticism will reveal the truth that ideology hides. Nevertheless, the complexity of the gestus that Diamond recovers for feminism, and the principle of *literarisation* of Brecht's dramaturgy as a whole, namely the insistence on narrating and declaring that you are doing so, arguably comprise what we might retrospectively call a 'deconstructive' potential.

Some of the more banal mappings of the 'modern' against the 'postmodern' suggest that the latter has undone the 'unified subject' presumed by modernism. But Counsell reminds us that Brecht is broadly aligned with the Frankfurt School of Marxists and other proponents of 'critical reason'. This major current within modernism foregrounded the untenability of the humanist view of perception as based in a transparent reality perceived by a unified subject (Counsell 1996: 107–10). Epic theatre insists to the audience that they are witnessing 'a construction of events as viewed from the position of an acknowledged, and subjective, "demonstrator"' (Counsell 1996: 104–5). A counter view is that the performance gestus of the Brechtian actor is an act of authority: the actor appears as a representative of a theological principle elsewhere, the Party, Marxism, that is in possession of a truth already known and guaranteed.

In *Postmodern Brecht*, Elizabeth Wright conducts an examination of Brecht in relation to the modern/postmodern binary. She cites Lyotard's suggestion that in postmodernist art, 'everything is subject to a V-effect and so the concept becomes redundant'. The very 'uncanniness of the concrete' in postmodernity flattens the gesture of irony (1989: 96).

Sartre and undecidability

In 1960, Sartre argued in a Sorbonne lecture that the epic was only one means of theatrical defamiliarisation. While also a Marxist, his own situation differed from Brecht's. His theatrical milieu was bourgeois. From the 1940s, he developed another form of aesthetic distancing. It accords with his philosophy of *existentialism* and the idea that human subjectivity is fundamentally unstable and ambiguous, caught in internal contradiction. The existentialist subject is at every moment faced with concrete choice. But in acts of *'bad faith'* we tend to invent stories about ourselves and the world, and seek to become objects for others, to excuse our passivity. Sartre's play *Huis clos* (1944) is a fable to that effect. But the audience are not simply treated to a parable of existentialism that they can quietly absorb. The aim of Sartre's stage is to destabilise the subject in the auditorium. One means to this is a sort of 'double gesture' on the part of the actor, who *simultaneously* identifies with and estranges the character. This undecidability produces a kind of nausea in the spectator, designed to lead to critical self-reflection (see e.g. Goldthorpe 1984).

EMBODIMENT

Although a play can be read on the page as a coherent script, its performance is pre-eminently an activity of bodies. The silent character who vanishes from attention in a written script can, as a physical entity, become highly important. The script is a set of instructions for, and sometimes a record of, a physical event. Drama in this most elementary sense is a medium of bodies, its performances are embodied events.

The body that does the performing is, however, more than a natural tool, a means of giving body to the writing. The human body always carries the effects of the society in which it grew and was educated. The clothing of seventeenth-century aristocratic bodies produced them as tall and stiff, with the neck enclosed in a high collar or ruff and the abdomen held in a tightly-laced corset. In this respect an 'upper-class bearing' is a body trained to inhabit and demonstrate its class position through its physical organisation. As the French sociologist Pierre Bourdieu puts it, 'the *sense of honour* is nothing other than the cultivated disposition, inscribed in the body schema and in the schemes of thought, which enables each agent to engender all the practices consistent with the logic of challenge and riposte' (1998: 15). That 'cultivated disposition' controls the range of activities by which the body interacts with the world around it. Bending down is, literally, out of order.

The term that is given to the body's learnt bearing and its assumed range of techniques is *habitus*. The word was early used in this sense in 1934 by Marcel Mauss (1992), an ethnologist teaching in Paris. In his essay 'Techniques of the Body' he begins by noting how in his own lifetime techniques of swimming, and teaching swimming, have changed: breaststroke has been replaced by crawl. Similarly he notes how, in the war, British soldiers could not dig with French spades. Where physical techniques for carrying out elementary activities differ between generations and national cultures, the 'habits' of the body derive from something larger than personal attitude or habit.

Mauss's argument was consolidated with the publication in 1939 of Norbert Elias's *The Civilizing Process*. By attending to the history, for example, of table manners, Elias (1897–1990) showed how the body became regulated, and how taboos around some of its functions developed, through the evolution of elementary and everyday practices. Such practices are carried out, said Mauss, by actions 'assembled for the individual not by himself alone but by all his education, by the whole society to which he belongs, in the place he occupies' (1992: 462). Actions do not so much express individual intention as social education of the body. The gesture with which a person sits down to eat tells of her class.

To phrase it thus is to invoke, alongside Mauss and Elias, a third person who was thinking about the body and social value in the 1930s. Working with his actors on ways of making apparent the social and economic structures underpinning individual interactions, Bertolt Brecht (1898–1956) developed his concept of *gestus* (see Keyword: Defamiliarisation and alienation). The *gestus* shows a moment of interaction as the interaction of socially educated bodies, where, as it were, class speaks louder than personality.

But even without being foregrounded in *gestus* *habitus* is a feature of each body, part of the body's own script. It is present when the body enacts a written script. Furthermore it has its own range of effects on an audience. Mauss notes how in the early 1930s young women in Paris had begun to walk like Americans, imitated from movies. This is a particular instance of bodily education, in which a child or adult 'imitates actions that have succeeded, which he has seen successfully performed by people in whom he has confidence and who have authority over him' (Mauss 1992: 459). The person performing the 'authorised' action has prestige. The imitative action thus functions as ideological transmission, whereby social values are imprinted on individuals through their bodies. The imitators take up a position, as it were, psychologically and biologically towards what they imitate. They are, to put it briefly, moved.

While all bodies display their social education, bodies on stage also display their theatrical education. Performers are often explicitly trained in muscular disciplines. Dance in particular offers many examples of how externally imposed regimes are internalised and thoroughly inhabited. But even without explicit training the actor makes assumptions about the proper way of moving and standing on the stage. These assumptions derive both from a conscious sense of theatrical genre and from an unconscious assimilation of what 'works'. The melodrama performer cultivated a different stage body from that of the naturalist performer. A technique for acting Pinter may not be 'proper' for a musical.

The body in the performance is both socially and theatrically produced. Bernard Beckerman gives it a name that he has borrowed from costume design, *silhouette*. The actor's silhouette is first and foremost what Mauss and Bourdieu would have termed *habitus*, a learnt mode of behaviour. As Beckerman put it: 'Each historical period and each social class within each period seems to have a characteristic stance, a stance that is the product of some prevailing image of man in the world.' Alongside that, every theatrical tradition also has its silhouette: 'Partly a consequence of theatrical practice, partly a response to the fashions of the day, the theatrical silhouette serves as a basis for the performer as he searches for the silhouette of the individual character' (Beckerman 1970: 228). A performance then gives us two sets of bodies – the body scripted by society and the body scripted by theatrical practice and value. Within these terms even the bodies of a form such as live art will be loaded with social and theatrical *habitus*.

A brief overview of the ways in which the performing body carries cultural 'script' is given by the performance theorist Patrice Pavis. He borrows three definitions of culture, that it is a 'shaping', artificial and transmitted by 'social heredity'. He then applies these to performance and in particular the performing body, suggesting that it shows the 'inscription of culture', that the performing person 'takes on the value of a sign or artefact', and that actor-dancers have 'interiorised' and pass on 'an ensemble of rules of behaviour'. From here he moves on to discuss interculturalism, and argues that this is most effective 'when it is accepted as *inter-corporeal* work . . . the greater its concern with the exchange of corporeal techniques, the more political and historical it becomes' (Pavis 1996: 3–4, 15). By contrast Eugenio Barba used the exchange of corporeal techniques, from different performing traditions, to try to discover the basic mechanisms of gesture and balance which would be generalisable across cultures. It is a conscious effort to take bodies out of, abstract them from, their specific cultures. This bringing-together of different performing cultures is less a political project than what Barba calls a theatre anthropological one (see p. 127).

Talk of the body's script and abstracted techniques should not, however, lead us entirely away from where we started. The bodies in the performance are physical entities, with specific height, width, reach and rhythm. Some theatrical modes deliberately make bodies higher, as with ancient Greek tragedy, or slower, as with Noh performance, than the norms assumed for bodies in their cultures. Many sorts of actor training seek to educate into the body a sense of deliberateness in all its actions, such that even the most instinctive gesture is offered for view. That sense of deliberateness also comes from the fact that the actor's body occupies a space specially provided for it or made to open up for it. So for an audience they are in the presence of a form practised by bodies which are both like them in their physical arrangements and unlike them in their apparent deliberateness and spatial coherence.

This complex physical proximity ensures that an audience does a lot more than simply 'read' the show. As we explore in the Keyword Phenomenology, the activity of watching is an ongoing process of physical adjustment and response to other physically present bodies.

EMPATHY

The word 'empathy' occurs in discussions of audience response. Its meaning is kept in place by two sets of oppositions. The first one distinguishes it from a response which is similar but more familiar, 'sympathy'. The second opposition, perhaps best known to students of drama, sets the word against its opposite, 'alienation'.

To sympathise is to feel *for* someone: they remain distressed but outside oneself. To empathise is to feel *with* someone: one is imaginatively not outside but in their shoes. Thus, as Augusto Boal puts it: 'Without acting, we feel that we are acting. We love and hate when the character loves and hates' (Boal 1979: 34). Put this way, when we feel we are doing something we are not, the mechanism of empathy seems to be associated with illusion. Empathy is thus a 'terrible weapon' (p. 113), because it destroys the ability to distinguish fiction from reality. Its manner of operation bypasses the consciousness, so that the spectator unthinkingly incorporates the fiction, an 'Esthetic osmosis' (p. 113). Emotion is not combined with understanding. Empathy is thus the opposite of a response which is encouraged to feel for distress, while seeking to understand how that distress comes about. That response, within Theatre Studies, is associated with Brecht and his so called 'alienation' techniques (see Keyword: Defamiliarisation and alienation).

For Brecht, as much as for Boal, empathy was associated with an Aristotelian theatre: he defined 'non-aristotelian drama' as 'a type of drama not depending on empathy, mimesis'. Non-aristotelian dramaturgy 'does not make use of the "identification" of the spectator with the play' (1964: 50, 78). It is, however – and despite Boal's rhetoric – not clear that Aristotle is the place where it all starts (Milling and Ley 2001 identify Boal's misreadings: see Keyword: Catharsis). For Aristotle identification with a character only happens as a result of spectators thinking themselves to be like that character. As Jonathan Lear puts it, 'we cannot identify with the very bad or with the gods: it is precisely because we are so distant from such beings that our emotions must retain a similar distance from theirs. That is why, for Aristotle, there is no important distinction to be made between our feeling our fear and our feeling Oedipus's fear. The very possibility of our imaginatively feeling Oedipus's fear is grounded in the recognition that we are like him: that is, it is grounded in the possibility of our fearing for ourselves' (Lear 1992: 332). So, by this account, the ability of empathy to play its illusory tricks is limited.

Aristotle's suggestion that recognition of similarity precedes identification is the reverse of what is now commonly understood as empathy: a mechanism which produces identification irrespective of similarity. The shift towards that concept was enabled by the mid- to late-eighteenth-century culture of 'feeling'. Late in the century the writer Thomas Holcroft (1745–1809), among others, suggested that the experience and expression of this sympathy can break down learnt prejudices and lead towards the good man's beneficent fellow feeling (see also Hazlitt 1991; see p. 25): sympathy as ideological tool. From here, eighteenth-century interests in sensibility and feeling, and then early nineteenth-century interests in cognition, fantasy and the separate life of the mind, gave way in the late nineteenth century to a more self-consciously scientific discipline of psychology. The theory of empathy was developed by a psychologist who had interests in aesthetics, Theodor Lipps (1851–1914). In the theory he proposed in 1897, empathy (*Einfuhlung*) has two elements to it: perceivers respond to the characteristics or qualities of an object and simultaneously project their own characteristics or qualities into it. The process is both responsive and active; it receives the content of the object perceived and also reaches out towards it, embracing its distinctness. The implicit relationship between perception and physical response was taken up by visual art theorists and led towards the formulation of the idea of kinaesthetic response (see Keyword).

Doubt about the benefit of the process of empathy was, however, expressed in the writings on psychology of Wilhem Dilthey (1833–1911). For him an empathetic projection of the spectator's own concerns into, for example, characters on stage can hinder the understanding of them. Such projection was, however, encouraged by new realist modes of acting and scenography and the darkened auditorium. These brought into being a new assumption about the proper viewing relationship in the theatre. When Boal assumes that empathy reaches back unchanged to Aristotle, he ignores a history of changing assumptions about what people do in theatres. If for Boal empathy depoliticises spectator response, for Holcroft 'sympathy' undoes dominant assumptions. Similarly, in 1993, Elin Diamond argues for 'the radical power of identification to override the constraints of identity and thus it can have useful political effects, seen in identifications with those who may be culturally, racially and sexually other to oneself (Diamond 1993: 90).

The shift from 'empathy' to 'identification' here is prompted by a new theoretical paradigm. Underlying Diamond's argument is the engagement with psychoanalysis done by feminists from about the mid-1980s onwards. Reviewing this work a decade later Diane Fuss notes that the mechanism of identification presents problems: 'Identification is both voluntary and involuntary, necessary and difficult, dangerous and effectual, naturalizing and denaturalizing.' The arrival at a sense of personal identity depends on a series of identifications; Fuss quotes Sedgwick: 'to identify as must always include multiple processes of identification *with*'. Further, as Butler argues, identifications are never brought to closure and are inevitably failed identifications. How identifications are going to function cannot be known in advance; they are 'mobile, elastic and volatile'. Fuss suggests therefore that a politics of identity has to 'come to terms with the complicated and meaningful ways that identity is continually compromised, imperilled, one might even say *embarrassed* by identification' (Fuss 1995: 6–10). That thing we call 'empathy' in the theatre is clearly not only part of these processes, but is more imponderable and necessary than we usually allow for.

INTERCULTURALISM

In 1973 the English director Peter Brook took a company of actors to Africa. The project was to find a new language of theatre, a language that would be understood by people of different races and cultures, a 'universal' language of the theatre.

This was, some would claim, an experiment in interculturalism, an attempt to play Western theatre in a way which would engage with African audiences. But the word 'interculturalism' was not then in common usage. Richard Schechner says that he began using it in the early to mid-1970s, in opposition to internationalism:

> I felt that the real exchange of importance to artists was not that among nations, which really suggests official exchanges . . . but the exchange among cultures, something which could be done by individuals or by non-official groupings, and it doesn't obey national boundaries.
>
> (1996: 42)

Schechner's view here might have been influenced by his own importation of theatrical forms, encountered on his trip to Asian countries in 1971–2, into his own productions. But the idea of the individual as a free agent, outside that which is officially national, is not unquestionable as an assumption. We shall, in due course, return to it.

Four years after Brook set off for Africa, on a different continent, and wholly unaware that the word 'interculturalism' existed, Rustom Bharucha saw in Calcutta the dance theatre of Chhau. It was this event that introduced him to interculturalism, not through the Chhau performance, however, but through the 'unofficial' performance, in front of the stage, of visiting Western interculturalists, presumably on the sort of tour that Schechner had made a few years earlier. What Bharucha saw was a double image: 'the Chhau dance on a makeshift stage, cut by the bodies and technology [the cameras] of the interculturalists' (Bharucha 2000: 20). And from that moment flowed questions: who were these people and why did they ignore all those sitting behind them? Did the Calcutta audience become alienated from the Chhau dance by their presence? Or, in the range of cultures across India, was the Calcutta audience anything more than strangers to this regional 'folk' form? In his consequent explorations of 'interculturalism', Bharucha had to question not only the terms of the exchanges between cultures but also his position as an 'individual' in relation to these exchanges.

Which brings us back to the assumptions made by both Brook and Schechner as to what they were doing. Immediately before Brook went to Africa he had been in Iran, working on a project called *Orghast* (1971). The aim was 'to see whether there are elements in the theatrical vocabulary that pass directly' to an audience, without being tangled with cultural references (Smith 1972: 248). He wanted to move beyond what he called state or individual cultures, each vitiated either by official blandness or individualism, and discover a form of culture that enables people to open up from their confinement within 'invisible limits'. This 'third culture' is achieved by establishing links between different cultures in such a way that individuals discover and discard superficial 'mannerisms' on the way to finding deep connections with one another (Brook 1996: 65–66). That project informed Brook's gathering together of performers from different cultures into his International Centre of Theatre Research, where the act of theatre is made 'inseparable from the need to establish new relations with different people'.

There is a problem, however, in that the gathering of various performers begins on a more or less equal footing, albeit shaped by the master's vision, while exploratory journeys to Africa or appropriations of Indian forms can perpetuate inequalities. Those inequalities are sustained by a cultural stereotyping which runs through the most apparently utopian theatrical project. For Brook, the journey to Africa was to a place 'where the intertwining between the real and the imaginary world is at its freest', for 'Africa has the energy, the power, the spiritual and imaginative qualities with a lack of formal structure which makes the free movement between awe and laughter open to us' (Smith 1972: 255). The list of nouns here recalls an attitude to Africa that was adopted by modernist artists in the early twentieth century. They saw the continent as having a primitive energy which could be tapped into, through borrowing its art forms, to reinvigorate the stale and deadly culture of the West. Half a century or so later, Brook restated this attitude as a utopian vision of how his sort of theatre would re-establish links between different people, and spread around the world. He likened it to the story of Cortez, spreading 'influence through a vast nation' (Smith 1972: 258). It is a pretty troubling analogy: what Cortez spread was Christianity, through the planned genocide of indigenous peoples. Thus Brook's celebration of African difference grates somewhat: 'Mature African actors simply have a different quality from white actors – a kind of effortless transparency, an organic presence beyond self, mind or body' – one might almost add, a lovely sense of rhythm (in Williams 1996: 72).

Brook's enthusiasm has been unpicked by Biodum Jeyifo to show how it congeals round two assumptions: 'a "spontaneously" new recreation of theatrical expressions which are strangely familiar and easily assimilated to received Western theatre traditions and paradigms' and 'an absolute first age of origination' (Jeyifo 1996: 152). These assumptions, says Jeyifo, fall into line with the orthodox discourse about African theatre, which has three basic theses:

> First, there is the thesis of the non-existence of indigenous 'native' traditions of drama or theatre in Africa . . . This thesis was later revised or modified to 'concede' that if Africa does indeed have indigenous theatrical traditions, they are nevertheless properly 'quasi-theatrical' or 'proto-dramatic'. The second thesis holds that compared with Europe and Asia, Africa does not possess well-developed theatrical traditions, especially in terms of the formalization of technique, style and aesthetic principles, and their historical transmission through successive ages and periods.

The third thesis follows from the impact of Western colonisation and 'asserts that what there are today of theatrical expressions on the continent are wholly, or pervasively derivative of Western sources, forms and traditions' (Jeyifo 1996: 153–4). Against this disocourse with its Eurocentric values there emerged an 'Afrocentric' counter-discourse. But, argues Jeyifo, this has been shaped by the values of what it opposes, in particular buying in to the idea that theatre develops from ritual to drama (see chapter 4), as may be exemplified in Kole Omotoso's work on drama in the English-speaking Caribbean (1982).

In Wole Soyinka's 1976 essay 'The Fourth Stage' the valorisation of the indigenous culture coexists with assumptions about value that are centred on Europe: Soyinka makes his case for the significance of the

Yoruba Mysteries partly by invoking Nietzsche and Greek myth (Soyinka 1988). The break came with the idea that one culture's criteria may be non-criteria for another. What follows, as Jeyifo says, is that 'African theatrical expressions and traditions which the critical orthodoxy of Western academicism had declared "quasi-theatrical" and "proto-dramatic" were reappraised in the light of different criteria and affirmed as valid indigenous traditions of theatrical performance' (Jeyifo 1996: 156).

If Brook's African trip provoked controversy, his adaptation of the Indian epic the *Mahabharata* (1985) led to even fiercer criticism. (See Carlson in Pavis 1996 for summary, and Bharucha 1993 for an eloquent riposte to Brook's orientalist appropriation and the Indian government's endorsement of it.) The critical, even journalistic, awareness of issues around intercultural exchange had developed fast since 1973. Brook's drive to find a theatre of the 'third culture', or a 'transcultural' theatre, made his work an obvious target. Less obvious perhaps is the other figure with whom we opened, Richard Schechner.

In *The Intercultural Performance Reader* Schechner describes inter-cultural activity as a form of shopping: 'People will wish to celebrate their cultural specificity, but increasingly that will be a choice rather than something you are simply born into automatically. "The culture of choice", which I talked about in one of my essays, is increasingly coming to be' (Schechner 1996: 49). Rustom Bharucha identifies this as a neo-liberal vision located 'within the comforts of a metropolis, where cultures can be readily consumed along with their cuisines' (Bharucha 2000: 43). He wonders how far India's low-caste *dalit* participates in this 'culture of choice'. And he asks whether ethnicities are so fluid they can be 'bartered'.

Bharucha's use of the word 'bartered' here is presumably a reference to the activities of Eugenio Barba and Odin Teatret. In their travels members of Odin, Barba says, were wary of situations where a theatre group's own project breaks the 'rules and taboos' of the communities it visits, for that 'violates the organism of the community'. They recognised that exploration of 'diversity' meant mutual exposure, where the theatre group's general behaviour was more important than its particular performances. Thus they were given performances in exchange for theirs, in a process of 'barter'. This idea of 'barter' is stated more clearly in a previous text. The group did not want 'to "teach" anything'. Thus when people asked them to perform, Odin asked what they would give in return: 'They had to find local people, not professionals, who were willing to "pay" us with song or dance' (Barba 1986: 175, 159). Put that way, the arrival of Odin seems to establish, by demand, a particular structure of inter-cultural engagement. Although Barba likens them to two tribes, he also concedes that one of the tribes is a gathering of people from different cultures who have chosen to work together whereas the other is locked into the culture with which it was born. Barter becomes an imposed system that produces false equivalence.

Whether around 'barter' or 'culture of choice' debates were moving fast, and they seem to have had effect when Schechner published *Performance Studies* (2002). He had absorbed previous criticism and was at pains to distinguish between a contestatory interculturalism and its opposite, the false synthesis of multiculturalism. For, as Bharucha puts it, multiculturalism 'is increasingly identified with the official cultural policies of western democracies like Australia, Canada, and Britain.' It is 'concerned with the cohabitation of different cultural and ethnic groups negotiating an ostensibly common framework of citizenship' (Bharucha 2000: 33). And thereby it works, as its opponents see it, to erase cultural specificity, dissolve class solidarity and depoliticise race as a category.

Yet while it may be positioned against the threat of multiculturalism, interculturalism itself is not without ambiguities and dangers. It can only really resist multiculturalism if, says Bharucha, its proponents reject certain myths and assumptions. One of these is the rhetoric of globalisation, with a 'liberalised' world economy dissolving national boundaries. Another is a version of interculturalism in which exchanges happen between people who are seen as simply 'human', everyone broadly similar in their funda-mental humanity.

Commenting on the 'interculturalist' drive towards discovering universal human values, Gilbert and Tomkins say that this is not only a-historical and a-cultural, but also 'neo-colonial'. They suggest that Western theatre makers such as Schechner, Barba and Brook mine '"exotic" – usually "third-world" – countries for theatrical raw materials, much in the way that multinational companies have been known to exploit materials and cheap labour from the developing world' (Gilbert and Tomkins 1996: 10). Gilbert and Tomkins define postcolonial performance as, by contrast, acts that respond to the experience of imperialism, whether directly or indirectly; acts performed for the continuation and/or regeneration of the colonised (and sometimes pre-contact) communities; acts performed with the awareness of, and sometimes the incorporation of, post-contact forms; and acts that interrogate the hegemony that underlies imperial representation.

(1996: 11)

From here they go on to survey a range of postcolonial work.

The word 'postcolonial' has perhaps an even shorter history of general usage than the word 'intercultural'. But that short history has been enough for a similar set of problems to emerge. As the editors of the 1995 *Post-colonial Studies Reader* say, 'post-colonial studies are based in the "historical fact" of European colonialism, and the diverse material effects to which this phenomenon gave rise'. Over a decade, however, a steadily more unfocused use of the term has made it less effective. Their *Reader* thus attempts 'to redress a process whereby "post-colonial theory" may itself mask and even perpetuate unequal economic and cultural relations. This happens when the bulk of the literary theory is seen to come out of the metropolitan centres' (Ashcroft *et al.* 1995: 2). A good example of the effects on 'theory' of a (Western) metropolitan location can be seen in Patrice Pavis's *Intercultural Performance Reader*, which emerged the next year. The contents list is divided into four parts, of which Part 2 is 'Intercultural performance from the Western point of view' and Part 3 is 'Intercultural performance from another point of view' – in other words, everything which is non-Western lumped together by virtue of its being, simply, non-Western. This third part has in it two essays on African (Nigerian) theatre and two on Maori theatre, as against two and a half pieces by and about Brook, two by and about Wilson, two by and about Barba, two by and about Grotowski. The rest are mainly North American/ European as well. The *Intercultural . . . Reader* seems thoroughly US/ eurocentric in its bias.

The last three books we have mentioned were all published in 1995–6. Although it appeared in the mid-1980s, alongside 'postmodernism', 'postcolonial' work tends to be a feature of the 1990s. It is as if, following the theory decade, the attempt was actively to look beyond the academy and its Western metropolitan centres. Nevertheless postcolonialism also became a highly publishable topic even while it perhaps lost its effectiveness. There remains, however, another way of thinking outside homogenised metropolitan and academic cultures. This is done through 'intraculturalism'.

In his survey of terms, Patrice Pavis defines intraculturalism's remit as: 'the traditions of a single nation, which are very often almost forgotten or deformed, and have to be reconstructed' (Pavis 1992: 20). There is a similar emphasis on working with the past in Brian Singleton's more recent article (Kennedy 2003: 'Interculturalism'), where he describes indigenous artists being 'permitted' to 'imagine and reconstruct their own cultural past for present consumption'. But these definitions, once again, are not without their difficulties. Bharucha suggests that it would be more useful to concentrate on '"regional" rather than "national" considerations', and, further, that the concept of 'dying' minor traditions allocates power and superiority to a healthy dominant national tradition: 'The task of any intracultural initiative in India is not to reconstruct "dying" traditions but to create new possibilities of interaction and exchange within and across a wealth of "living" traditions from vastly different time frames and cultural contexts.' Pavis's Eurocentric view has a homogenising thrust that is determined, claims Bharucha, by 'the industrialization and capitalist economy' assumed by European theatre cultures. By contrast 'we have in India a more differentiated gradation of cultures in tribal, rural, folk, ritual, *mofussil* (district town), urban, and metropolitan contexts' (Bharucha 2000: 62–3). But this generalisation about European theatre itself needs qualifying, since in their different projects Joan Littlewood, Charles Parker and 7:84, for example, have all used and explored a 'gradation of cultures' in Britain.

Pavis returned to the matter of inter- and intraculturalism in a lecture he gave in 1997. His general argument was about the state of the disciplines of Theatre and Performance Studies. In his analysis Theatre Studies was intellectually drifting. Its embrace of 'interculturalism' seemed to offer a coherent new direction. This was illusory: 'If the multi- and intercultural forms and the reflection on alterity have considerably altered our thinking about theatre and its analysis . . . they haven't delivered a brand new epistemological model.' Despite an apparent extension of the field, he identified a 'neglect of theory and methodology' (Pavis 2000: 83). The solution Pavis suggested is that theatre studies historicise itself, and that it do so through intraculturalism. For him this means not only an exploration of history, but specifically the Western tradition. The currently diffuse discipline of theatre studies should condense and contract itself 'with the principles of Western rationality and universality' (p. 85). Picking up much of the logic of the attack on 'interculturalism' mounted by Bharucha and others, Pavis thus redefines intraculturalism as a basis for something like a programme of cultural purification leading to disciplinary unity.

The problem with an intraculturalism conceived as relationship of past and present is that no historical participants can be present. The same agents assimilate different materials. They are not challenged as agents in the process. By contrast Bharucha tells a story of the deep impact on himself of an intracultural project. He staged *Peer Gynt/Gundegowda* (1995) in 'a contemporary Indian "company theatre"' (Bharucha 2000: 71). Of himself he says: 'it is neither possible to suspend an engagement with the diversities of specific communities, embodied in the cultural legacies that have been passed down through generations in the form of languages, songs, customs, preformance [sic] traditions, local knowledge, nor to avoid the creative risks and play involved in incorporating and inscribing differences that emerge across regional and linguistic boundaries' (p. 65). Here is a final, familiar, opposition within our account: theory and practice. While authors of the theoretical text may remain thoroughly in control of their chosen argument, and its 'correctness', the work of the creative performance practice leads to contradictions. We thus return whence we started, in the company of Peter Brook: the role of the individual in cultural exchanges. The contradictions in the creative process are felt, suggests Barucha, within the person.

His own particular point of difficulty and 'negotiation' in the *Peer Gynt/Gundegowda* project related to the critique of orientalism. It was pointed out to him how in one scene he was 'glossing over the political risks of Indian actors playing "orientals"'. Yet, in the production process, while the actors had been told of Said's concept of orientalism, 'they were more interested in playing with their *own* imaginary Orients. I realized, not without a sense of irony, that in criticizing orientalism, one does not have to suppress one's own fantasy of the Arabian Nights' (Bharucha 2000: 83–4).

The potency, then, of intercultural and intracultural performance practices may be to do with more than their questioning of assumptions about worldwide distributions of power and wealth. They also can provoke an exploration of our own cultural location, with all the contradictions, and acceptance, of its deepest fantasies.

KINAESTHETIC

The effect of an exciting movie is to have the audience 'on the edge of their seats'. In an exciting moment in a football game, when one team gets close to the other's goal, a seated crowd will usually rise to its feet, and sometimes breathe in unison. The similarity between both sets of excitement is that, as a consequence of what the eyes see, the audience's muscular state is stimulated. This form of perception is 'kinaesthetic', perception through the nerves and muscles.

The word came into use at the end of the nineteenth century, in the context of new ways of looking at the relationship of body and mind. The most famous early use of the term in relation to performance comes in the writings of F. Mathias Alexander (1869–1955). Beginning with the attempt to correct his own voice's tendency to fail in a recitation, Alexander developed a technique for physical re-education of the body which focused principally on lengthening the spine. In 1908 he published his insights as 'Re-education of the Kinesthetic Systems Concerned with the Development of Robust Physical Well-being'. The physical re-education aimed to intervene in and change habitual behaviours and learnt movements. By producing good movement it also produced a formula for good living. Through his technique, Alexander said, subjects learnt 'a kinesthetic way of adapting ourselves to our environment' (in Maisel 1974: xxix).

So our narrative begins with a different definition of kinaesthesia from the one with which we opened. Rather than perception through the nerves and muscles, we are concerned here with the sensory appreciation of muscular movement. By developing the kinaesthetic sense as understood in the latter definition, people can combat the effects of 'civilisation'. In Alexander's view, this had 'contaminated man's biological and sensory equipment, with a resultant crippling in the responses of the whole organism' (in Maisel 1974: xxix). In this respect Alexander's technique of re-educating the body applied not only to performers but to all those who felt crippled by civilisation. Three decades or so later a very similar solution to the problems of civilisation was put by Moshe Feldenkrais (1904–84) in a series of lectures in 1943–4. He argued that human problems derived from people's adjustment to prevailing economic and marital conditions.

The adjustment is as much physical as psychic, and indeed these two are related in that someone with a 'low kinaesthetic sense' feels only 'extreme inefficiency' rather than ease and fluency in their movement and being (1949: 111). Thus a psychiatric cure of a patient will depend partly on 'Re-education of the kinaesthetic sense' (p. 155).

This re-education depends on a heightened perception of 'small differences in sensation', a sensitivity to the 'proprioceptive nerve endings' coordinated by the inner ear (p. 108). Learning this sensitivity cannot be done intellectually. Depending on observation and imitation, intellectual learning, suggests Feldenkrais, is incomplete. In the same way Alexander had concentrated on a course of physical exercises rather than verbal analysis. At an early stage Alexander's pupil is instructed to do nothing in response to a set of commands: to stand or sit, for example. By doing nothing the pupil becomes aware of how the muscles prepare, involuntarily, to carry out an instruction. Thus habitual, unconscious, behaviour can be revealed and then changed.

This notion of kinaesthetic training for self-fulfilment is, however, a long way from the idea with which we began, the audience that is involuntarily, but literally, moved by a performance. The shift in the application of the word is not, however, unanticipated in Alexander's work. The exercise of consciously refusing verbal instruction demonstrates how the muscles respond involuntarily to external verbal suggestion. By extension, a performance that instructs an audience to be alert to villainy or tender to victimisation, through mechanisms of suspense and identification for instance, is also working on their 'proprioceptive nerve endings', their muscular attentiveness. While kinaesthetic responses can be stimulated by sound (Walzer 1993), the crucial development comes from the realisation of the link between kinaesthetic response and sight.

The concept of kinaesthetic perception, not as an activity of performers but as a mode of reception of performance, was articulated in 1970 by Bernard Beckerman in *The Dynamics of Drama*:

> Although theater response seems to derive principally from visual and aural perception, in reality it relies upon a totality of perception that could be better termed kinesthetic. We are aware of a performance through varying degrees of concentration and relaxation within our bodies. From actual experience performers can sense whether or not a

"house" is with them, principally because the degree of muscular tension in the audience telegraphs, before any overt sign, its level of attention. We might very well say that an audience does not see with its eyes but with its lungs, does not hear with its ears but with its skin.

(p. 150)

Beckerman had developed this idea from a reading of contemporary psychologists and philosophers of perception, in particular Rudolph Arnheim (1904–) and Michael Polanyi (1891–1976); another drama specialist, J.L. Styan, had been similarly influenced (Styan 1971: 65–6). Arnheim's *Art and Visual Perception* appeared in 1956. In clarifying how visual perception operates the book develops further the explorations of the interconnectedness of body and brain. For Arnheim visual perception can be modelled on 'kinaesthetic perception', in which 'experiences of tension are inherent' (Arnheim 1956: 339). Thus, by analogy, an experience of 'visual tension' will mean that visual perception is accompanied, and reinforced, by kinaesthetic sensation. The argument here can be seen as a bridge between Alexander and Feldenkrais's understanding of kinaesthetics in relation to therapeutic development and Beckerman's application of it to spectators. The crucial shift comes when Arnheim says that kinaesthetic stimulations are 'a kind of sympathetic resonance, which arises sometimes, but not necessarily always, in the neighbouring medium of muscle sense' (p. 339). Alexander and Feldenkrais suggest that a person's perception can be changed by re-education of the muscles; Arnheim is here suggesting that the muscles change in relation to perception.

A more thorough integration of the body into the activity of perception was proposed by Michael Polanyi. His book, *The Tacit Dimension* (1967), was based on a series of lectures given in 1962. His interest in how experience is shaped in order to produce knowledge derives from Gestalt psychology. The argument of his first chapter is that 'by elucidating the way our bodily processes participate in our perceptions we will throw light on the bodily roots of all thought' (p. 15). The body may consciously respond to, say, a direct threat, but it may also unconsciously adjust itself to, say, the formal arrangements of a superior's office. In the second case, through 'tacit knowing' we incorporate the formality, through the control of our muscles, into our body – 'or extend our body to include it – so that we come to dwell in it' (p. 16). As soon as he has introduced this idea of knowing something by 'dwelling' in it, Polanyi is able to add a new dimension to the concept of kinaesthetics. This comes from German philosophy of the end of the nineteenth century (specifically Dilthey and Lipps) which 'postulated that indwelling, or empathy, is the proper means of knowing man and the humanities' (p. 16) (see Keyword: Empathy). Polanyi's 'indwelling', or kinaesthetic perception, is discovered not only as the basis for, but a more precise concept than, 'empathy'.

Polanyi's logic here influenced Beckerman, who insisted:

> Nor do we have to discriminate the dramatic signals mentally in order to react. Perception includes subception, bodily response to stimuli before we are focally aware of the stimuli. In theater, this means that our bodies are already reacting to the texture and structure of action before we recognize that they are doing so.
>
> (1970: 150–1)

This is a form of Polanyi's 'tacit knowing': while our conscious attention is likely to be focused on what the whole play is 'saying', the particular signals and stimuli whereby it locally works are already being incorporated into our bodies. Later on, Beckerman will re-emphasise that involvement through kinaesthetic perception will function even where there is an absence of understanding, and add that space, the presence of other people and time-span all also contribute to this involvement. When these elements are added, the closeness of the connection between theories of kinaesthetic and phenomenological response becomes clear (see Keyword: Semiotics and phenomenology). So too, in Beckerman's somewhat polemical phrasing, the distance is clearly established from semiotic responses – based on understanding and 'reading' systems of signs. Kinaesthetic response occurs prior to a semiotic one.

The activity of both the performing and watching body is at the heart of Beckerman's 1970 book. In this respect it might appear to be of its moment. Maisel's edition of Alexander appeared in 1969, reprinted in 1974; Wilfred Barlow's *The Alexander Principle* appeared in 1973; Clive Barker's *Theatre Games* in 1972. Yet this moment would quickly seem dated and marginal. The impact in the humanities of film criticism specifically and then more general applications of poststructuralism favoured approaches that more deliberately 'read' the performed text. The publication in 1975 of Laura Mulvey's 'Visual Pleasure and Narrative Cinema' established in wearisome dominance a fairly mechanical 'voyeur' theory. Then the publication in 1980 of Keir Elam's *Semiotics of Theatre and Drama*, in Methuen's basically literary series New Accents, drove bodily activity and awareness yet further away from drama studies. From being an effective vehicle for analysing spectator response, kinaesthetics dwindled back into the domain of performance training for lifestyle improvement. It does not even appear in the index to Susan Bennett's *Theatre Audiences* (1990).

Yet, if the word is new, the description of the bodily engaged audience is a regular feature of theatre commentary: as Ford (1995) notes, for Aristotle the response of women, foreigners and lower orders was more base than that of the educated male. In the mid-eighteenth century, by contrast, the cult of sensibility led to a mode of watching where spectators allowed their bodies to be overcome by sobs and hysteria. The physically labile audience of nineteenth-century melodrama was, in turn, regularly noted by genteel commentators, for whom the ill-governed physicality of the working class was a source of embarrassed worry.

Attitudes to the physically expressive audience body offer a frame to discussions of kinaesthetic stimulation. When the word emerged at the end of the nineteenth century with enquiries into the interconnectedness of body and mind, it remained within a discourse of training and control. Its movement into a theory of response – of involuntary, but acceptable, physical engagement – coincided with a historical moment unusual in the West for its cultural obsession with revolution made through liberation of the body.

MIMESIS

Mimesis is a Greek word. Its persistence as such within English-speaking cultures is significant. For it has no fixed, reliable or agreed English equivalent. You can find it associated with the following English words: imitation, representation, copy, similarity, fake. The attempt to translate it immediately becomes an act of interpretation, and hence of debate. Much of the writing about mimesis is debate as to its meaning.

This debate is present in commentaries on one of the earliest treatments of mimesis, the poetic theory of Aristotle. An authoritative translator and editor, Stephen Halliwell, renders the word as 'representation'. But this word is among those rejected by Paul Woodruff in his attempt to clarify Aristotle's use: 'Aristotelian mimesis is not the same as imitation or fiction or reproduction or representation or make-believe; it is not expression; and it is not even the making of images or likenesses' (1992: 89). He argues that the making of likenesses gets closest to Aristotle's use, but even that does not explain how music can be mimetic. From here he suggests a definition that fits music and dance as well as poetry: 'Mimesis is the art of arranging one thing to have an effect that properly belongs to another' (p. 91).

Within this uncertainty, however, what does seem clear is that Aristotle was attempting to revise the previous theory of Plato. In *Republic* books 3 and 10, Plato discusses the problematic effects of mimesis. In book 3 he focuses on dramatic mimesis, which includes the recitation and reading aloud of poetry. His argument, as Stephen Halliwell puts it, is that 'the reciter is drawn into, and thereby takes on, the mental and ethical cast of each speaker'. Where these reciters are young men being educated, the problem is that the mimetic acts play a part in character formation (the word mimesis being linked to 'imitative or emulatory behavior'); representational activity is psychologically assimilated. This then is the logic behind Plato's suggestion that the future Guardians of the city should not be exposed to indiscriminately mimetic poetry, which might represent something other than virtue: it has to be excluded from the well-governed city (Halliwell 2002: 53, 54). In book 10 mimesis is extended to apply to all representation in poetry and visual arts. Here too there is more focus on the audience, rather than the actors/reciters. Socrates describes the audience's 'sympathetic' response as, in Halliwell's words, 'a sort of pleasurable emotional yielding or surrender' (pp. 77–8). The concern here, and throughout, is 'not the intrinsic nature of mimetic images but the use made of them' (p. 59).

In book 7 Plato tells a story to illustrate the relationship between Idea and appearance. One spin-off from this is a suggestion that mimesis can amount to a form of deliberate copying intended to deceive. The general association between mimesis and deception works in two main ways. The simplest has to do with making false copies: mimetic drama in performance is dangerous because it threatens an audience's ability to distinguish reality from illusion. Where mimesis is more dangerous, however, is in its impact on social interactions and social order. It can produce deception, as Woodruff puts it, 'concerning the identity of the speaker'. A speaker or image-maker can be credited with authority or knowledge that they do not possess.

In Aristotle's argument in *Poetics* 4 mimesis is used, says Halliwell, as: 'discernment of likeness . . . an active and interpretative process of cognition . . . a perspicacious discovery of significances in the world' (Halliwell 2002: 189). By this account the response to mimesis is far from being passive. To recognise likenesses is to make connections and to interpret. If we accept Halliwell's gloss, then Aristotle's view of the operation of mimesis takes us to the opposite pole from Plato. Far from encouraging us to be taken in by a false claim to authority and knowledge, mimesis enables us to gain a better understanding of what reality might be (by making connections and interpreting). The two opposed positions here seem to persist through all the subsequent discussions of mimesis. Both positions are engaged with the effort truly to know what reality is, but the difference between them, put crudely, goes like this: one is concerned to separate copy from reality, so as to avoid being taken in by illusion; the other wants to use copies as a way of understanding reality better.

The suspicion of mimetic illusion impinges most famously on the study of performance in two main areas. The first is one that students of Theatre Studies A level in Britain have drummed into them when they encounter Brecht in senior school. Brecht, they learn, was opposed to any form of theatre that encouraged the audience to submit to illusion: instead they were to watch the action of the stage as if at a sporting event, commenting and criticising even as they are taken up by the excitement. The actor must make 'an act of imitation which is at the same time a process of the mind' (Brecht 1964: 196). Pure imitation, a mere showing of what has been observed, is not enough: the point is to reflect on it.

Mimetic illusion has also been deliberately and knowingly exploited, however, as a technique of both negotiation and protection. This strategy has appealed to feminists who see women as caught up into a system of representation which is controlled by men, where the woman finds it difficult to escape from an image that is thrust upon her. Within the image she has no identity of her own and is simply assimilated to male representations. But to challenge it can mean speaking as a man, in masculine terms, and thereby still not inhabiting her difference as a woman.

This resistance to a male system of representation, allowing survival in it, has several versions, among them 'masquerade' and 'mimeticism'. The latter word is a coinage by the French feminist philosopher and psychoanalyst Luce Irigaray. It has associations with the idea of 'camouflage' (Whitford 1991: 72). But mimeticism, or, as she also calls it, mimicry, has an affirmative side: 'One must assume the feminine role deliberately. Which means already to convert a form of subordination into an affirmation, and thus to begin to thwart it.' The woman resubmits herself to masculine ideas about her 'but so as to make "visible", by an effect of playful repetition, what was supposed to remain invisible: the cover-up of a possible operation of the feminine in language'. At the same time, says Irigaray, because women are good mimics they are not totally absorbed by it: '*They also remain elsewhere*' (Irigaray 1994: 124). For feminist performance practitioners this strategy opened the way for explorations in staging mimesis, where it can be inhabited yet playful, and always refuse to confirm the assumptions of the male system of representation. In challenging the mechanisms of theatrical mimesis, feminist theatre intervenes in mimetic practice in general, and thereby takes forward the political struggle around control of representation and difference.

To see mimesis as a feminist strategy for dealing with, and perhaps re-making, reality is to enter into a new section of our survey of the word. Here we look more fully at an approach to mimesis which is governed by the relationship between adaptation to that which is outside the self and imposition of control over it.

The process of adaptation connects with the labour which transforms nature to facilitate human life. Copies need to be made in order to enable human beings to survive: a 'mimetic dance' originates as part of 'the actual techniques of production'. In George Thomson's 1941 account of the origins of Attic drama, *Aeschylus and Athens*, he begins with the ceremonies of food-gatherers in relation to their staple food. These ceremonies dramatically represent the habits of an animal. Their original function was presumably to give 'practice in the behaviour of the species, whose habits had to be studied before it could be caught' (Thomson 1973: 96, 11). In the same way, perhaps, Irigaray's concept of mimetism invites women to learn about phallic mimesis in order to combat it.

As we discuss elsewhere, Thomson locates the origins of drama, poetry and dancing in the mimetic rite. For our purposes here it is enough to note that mimesis is productive, in that it enables hunters to know more about the real animals they hunt. But the mimetic rite was also productive in distracting from reality; in the rite 'each performer withdrew, under the hypnotic effect of rhythm, from the consciousness of reality', only to return charged with new strength (Thomson 1973: 59). This attribution of artistic origins to basic processes of production was an analysis Thomson shared with other Marxists of his generation, among whom Christopher Caudwell, for example, traced the rhythms of poetry to the synchronisation of effort in the work group. But mimesis here is about more than learning a physical discipline, more than a means to an end. The hunter tries to be like an animal s/he hunts in order to know it and so capture it. The very production of likeness, between one being and another, is thus part of the productive process. This making of likenesses between things is the work of what Walter Benjamin calls the 'mimetic faculty', and he presumably has the same practices in mind as Thomson does when he speaks about 'the gift of producing similarities – for example, in dances, whose oldest function this was'. Mimesis may be said to be a productive act, then, not simply in enabling the hunter to hunt but in establishing similarities between things. But Benjamin takes it further: to the gift of producing similarities he adds 'the gift of recognising them' (1978: 333).

The recognition of similarities is something more than the attention to the accuracy of a copy. In his essay on the 'Mimetic Faculty' Benjamin presupposes an ancient world governed by 'magical correspondences and analogies'. Mimetic activity brings out the hidden similarities, the deep correspondences between things. In recognising these similarities a person may thus gain a deeper understanding of the interconnectedness of the world, and the ability to exist productively within it.

This is in an ancient world, however. The status of mimesis seemed to be very different in modern times. As Adorno and Horkheimer put it in 1944, in its earliest form humanity adapted to nature: mimesis was an imitation of the environment, to which the 'inner world' has to learn to conform. From here, 'Civilization has replaced the organic adaptation to others . . . by organized control of mimesis'; and thereafter by 'rational practice, by work' (1999: 180). This led to prohibitions on images and actors. It also led to the inverted mimesis which is anti-semitism, a projection of the inner onto the outer and a blurring of the two.

Neither Benjamin's nor Adorno and Horkheimer's is the most famous account of mimesis from this period, however. More familiar is Erich Auerbach's (1892–1957) *Mimesis*, written 1942–5. This text is principally an account of literary representations of reality, from Homer to Woolf. As such it is a long way distant from the wider social and political concerns we have been encountering. Mimesis here has to do with copying in a fairly narrow sense. For students of drama, theatre and performance therefore Auerbach's book is perhaps less useful than the tradition of work we have been discussing.

That tradition was re-emphasised in the early 1990s in a book that became significant for performance studies. Putting Benjamin together with Adorno and Horkheimer, in *Mimesis and Alterity* Michael Taussig reflected on mimesis in relation to colonialism and 'primitivism'. In particular he looks at the shaman as a transitional point between adaptation or 'yielding' to the other and the 'organisation of mimesis'. Sympathetic magic works not by making a visually accurate copy of the other but by developing a representation which 'shares in or acquires the properties of the represented' (1993: 47–8). While the shaman is seeking for control, the process involves an entry into the image, as it were a loss of self into the other. Mimesis is not simply a faculty of imitation but the 'deployment of that faculty in sensuous knowing, sensuous Othering' (p. 68). Alongside this deployment, mimesis has been organised so as to keep the other in place. Developing Adorno and Horkheimer's argument about anti-semitism, Taussig notes how colonisers asserted their power by imitating savages. And, further, he notes how skills in mimesis and knowledge of its power to access the spirit world can be organisationally confined to men, thereby disprivileging women and children.

The opposition of sensuous knowing to 'organised' mimesis is that between adaptation and imposition of control. Our next step from here is to see how this opposition relates to the concept of mimesis as mere copying, often of a deceptive sort. We can put these aspects together by using an observation by Elin Diamond. She notes that there is always a tension in the word mimesis because it can refer to both the 'activity of representing and the result of it': 'activity' has overtones of productive work, adaptation to and transformation of reality; 'result' is conceived as an inert copy of reality. In fact many uses of 'mimesis' tend to belong with one approach or another, rather than both at once. But for Diamond this slipperiness in the term is a useful starting point for her attempt to define what feminist mimesis might be.

In a deft overview of the major theories, she reiterates the regular argument that from Plato's point of view women are 'mimetic' creatures in that they are both readily subjugated to illusion and likely to deceive others. To engage in mimetic activity will thus make a man more womanly. Even while mimesis supposes itself to be making a copy of a reality the process of doing mimesis has effects: it feminises. Rather than celebrate a capacity for transformation, from the earliest days mimesis was opposed, in all its slipperiness, notes Diamond, by men. Plato's assault is followed by Aristotle. He, she says, 'will soon get rid of this interest in resemblances and improvisation' (Diamond 1997: x).

That word improvisation pops up more or less out of nowhere in Diamond's account. Where it comes from, we suggest, is not so much the performance activity Aristotle had in mind – a highly hieratic activity – but instead a theoretical binary which has men and fixedness on one side and women and productive slipperiness on the other (if that is not to put it too biologically). For Diamond is heading eventually towards a neat formulation: 'A feminist mimesis, if there is such a thing, would take the relation to the real as productive, not referential, geared to change, not to reproducing the same' (p. xvi).

Now this formulation may recall those approaches to mimesis as 'production'. Indeed Diamond invokes one of them when she puts Benjamin alongside Irigaray to argue, later in her book, for a radical conception of mimesis which is based on a '*nonidentical* similarity to the other' (p. 174). The problem is that this idea of mimesis is the one that Taussig attributes to fairly regular shamanic practices. So the arrival at a mimesis that may be described as either feminist or radical finds us somewhere where we have been before, which was both male and traditional.

In one respect, however, Diamond's argument can take our account of mimesis a stage further. For Diamond, one of the strengths of a feminist mimesis is that it would involve 'mimetically embodying/interpreting the other' (p. x). This idea of embodying the 'other' is one that we want to pause over. At this point mimesis starts to dissolve into something else. For hitherto we have looked at mimesis within two sets of terms: first, copy and deception; second, productive adaptation and control. Within each set of terms what has been foregrounded is human agency, whether in the work of distinguishing true from false or in creating images in order to survive and control. Now, however, we are looking at mimesis as a process in which a person enters into, submits to or is taken over by a copy, embodies the 'other'. The process is very similar to that of empathy (see Keyword).

Loss of self is seen negatively or positively in different societies. For Plato mimetic activity had a harmful effect on its agent, effeminising. For a shaman possession by the spirit world gave access to power. Alongside these examples we should now place Roger Caillois's essay on 'Mimicry and Legendary Psychasthenia' (1935). Caillois discusses camouflage among insects and animals, which he concludes is principally a '*luxury* and even a dangerous luxury' (1984: 25), for some camouflage makes an insect more liable to be eaten. He suggests that the end goal of the search for the similar 'would appear to be *assimilation to the surroundings*'. The relationship between subject and space then changes, bringing with it an alteration in subjectivity: 'The feeling of personality, considered as the organism's feeling of distinction from its surroundings, of the connection between consciousness and a particular point in space, cannot fail under these conditions to be seriously undermined' (pp. 27–8). He describes the process as '*depersonalization by assimilation to space*'. This is accompanied by 'decline in the feeling of personality and life' (p. 30, original emphases).

Underneath Caillois's reflections on animal camouflage there is an idea about humanity: 'there remains in the "primitive" an overwhelming tendency to imitation, combined with a belief in the efficacy of this imitation, a tendency still quite strong in civilized man, since in him it continues to be one of the two conditions for the progress of his untrammeled thought' (p. 27). While he concedes George Thomson's model of the productive mimetic rite, Caillois locates this within something larger – a human tendency to imitate (which may be compared with René Girard's view that mimesis is an underlying principle of both desire and competition: Girard 1996). That tendency to imitate can lead into the process of depersonalisation. This is perhaps more akin to the concept of a death drive than productive ritual. As such it suggests that one of the attractions of mimesis is not to do with claims to knowledge and control but precisely with their opposite, with the abandonment of human agency and personality, indeed with empathy and yielding.

PERFORMATIVITY

Performance Studies derives one major sense of 'performativity' from speech act theory. In a 1955 lecture series published in 1962 as *How to do Things with Words*, linguistic philosopher J.L. Austin distinguished between two kinds of utterance: 'constantives', or statements; and 'performatives' like 'I bless you', that perform an act in their being said. He also suggested that for linguistics, the success, or 'felicity', of utterances was more significant than their supposed truth or falsity. Having set up the constantive/performative binary, Austin then deconstructed it, in two basic moves. First, he identified 'implicit' performatives where, say, the command 'Take off your shoes!' is made with an implied but not spoken performative verb ('I command that . . . '). Second, he pointed out that all constantives might themselves be considered implicit performatives, since they are truth claims: 'I assert that . . . '.

Austin identified three possible aspects of an utterance. Beyond the 'locution': adherence to linguistic norms in order to make basic sense, were the 'illocution': what might *directly* be done in the act of utterance; and the 'perlocution': what might less directly be done through it. His pupil J.R. Searle insisted that since even a simple statement makes reference to objects and concepts and draws the interlocutor into that field of reference, almost all utterances are perforce both illocutionary and perlocutionary. The locutionary can no longer be regarded as neutral ground. As Carlson remarks, Searle shifts the focus from abstract concerns of structure to the concrete event of the utterance: its intention, context and effect. Carlson cites Searle: 'A theory of language is part of a theory of action' understood as 'a rule-governed form of behaviour' (in Carlson 1996: 61).

Further critical appropriations followed, outside the disciplinary frame of linguistics. Austin had confined speech acts to direct speech. Literary and theatrical forms were 'parasitic': their utterances are mere acts of citation, having a mimetic relationship to 'real' speech acts. But Derrida countered that citation was the universal condition for success of all performative utterances: 'the general condition of language is iteration' (Derrida 1977: 172–97). In order to be felicitous, they must be formulated according to pre-existing norms. Derrida's intervention is in the same spirit as his deconstruction of the hierarchised speech/writing binary: no utterance is originary, in the sense of issuing from a free autonomous subject. This might imply pessimism. But Derrida also argued that citation is never exact, because the context of utterance is always new. And since utterances are performative, they themselves create potentially limitless new contexts.

In a series of publications in the early 1990s, rhetorician Judith Butler built upon both Derrida's intervention and aspects of Performance Studies to illuminate gender as a performative act. As did Schechner, Butler adapts Turner's observations on ritual events and liminality in traditional cultures to address aspects of industrialised society. But while Schechner used the model of liminality to stress transformative and resistant practices, Butler uses the idea of ritual in the modern everyday to stress normative processes (see p. 121). And this is the link with Derrida. Butler understands gender as a set of constantly reiterated performances by which individuals are socialised according to compulsory systems of difference. The gendered body is a sedimentation of these repeated citations, whose constitutive role meanwhile goes unnoticed, precisely because they are not framed as performances. In fact the result of compulsory ritualised performance, gender thus appears as natural, foundational.

This does not, however, make the gender system unassailable. As does Derrida, Butler identifies the structural break between one citation and the next as the locus for transformation. Citations are never precise, and can be wilfully imprecise. While always already contained within the compulsory frame of gender difference understood as a language, playful utterances of the body can at least locally shift that contextual frame. If individual agency is, then, to be found in variations upon compulsory repetition, this too can have a sedimentary effect. Ultimately, Butler suggests, 'a radical proliferation of gender' within the frame of enforced repetition might '*displace* the very gender norms that enable the repetition itself' (Butler 1990: 148). As Janelle Reinelt puts it, 'the law itself is dependent on being cited' (Reinelt in Kennedy 2003: 1024).

McKenzie draws attention to the 'corrective' that Butler felt obliged to make to many readers of her first book, *Gender Trouble* (1990). Drawing on Foucault, Butler had presented the model of an enforced regime with structural weaknesses that provided opportunities for acts of resistance on a micro-scale. But elements of the intersecting Performance Studies community and radical queer movement, especially in the US, were quick to draw the implication that gender was a willed performance and hence more easily resisted than she had intended to imply. McKenzie attributes this to what he calls the 'liminal-norm' (McKenzie 2001: 49–53).

Butler now re-emphasised her distinction between social and aesthetic drama, by clarifying a distinction between performance and performativity. The performativity of gender was to be distinguished from the 'bounded act' subject to the will of the performer that constitutes a performance. The drag king's theatrical disruption of gender norms does not cancel the performer's gendered subjectivity: performativity 'consists in a reiteration of norms which precede, constrain, and exceed the performer' (Butler 1993: 234). As Reinelt again summarises, repeated successful iterations lead to a 'sedimentation that makes transformation difficult, even extraordinary' (Reinelt in Kennedy 2003: 1024).

McKenzie cites Butler within the frame of his wider argument, which here also turns on the idea of the performative. If the discourse of the liminal-norm obscured Butler's articulation of gender performativity as a 'punitive form of power', then the liminal-norm itself is best understood as 'an effect of performative power'. The ritual repetition of tropes of transgression within and about Performance Studies has provided it with an identity which obscures its relationship to technological and commercial performance. Against this, 'the disciplinary seals separating the paradigms are eroding under the pressure of certain citational forces' (McKenzie 2001: 166).

While the force of McKenzie's argument makes him stress 'misreadings' of Butler, she admitted in a 1993 essay that she has in fact changed her *own* position from a more utopian one (see Butler 1993: ix–xii). What is in process here is the tracing back and forth of a dialectic, albeit one dominated by one of its terms. Thus, even while sedimented iterations make transformation difficult, and gender parody restates the law it flouts, willed theatricalisations such as the drag king's can nudge both public and psychic contexts so as to interfere with citation and help performativity drift into new directions, new spaces. The parody makes the space for change, not the change itself.

A similar dialectic informs Elin Diamond's arguments around the terms 'performativity', 'performance' and 'theatre' in her editorial introduction to *Performance and Cultural Politics* (1996). Here she notes that Roach argues that the 'present' (the present time) both nominates and disguises 'the continuous reenactment of a deep cultural performance'. While this might suggest a fatalism, critique reminds us that these performances are 'unstable improvisations'. In Butlerian terms, Roach is talking about performativity. And, as Diamond stresses, an important cultural and political function of staged performance is as 'the site in which concealed or dissimulated conventions might be investigated.' Thus, 'as soon as performativity comes to rest on *a* performance, questions of embodiment, of social relations, of ideological interpellations, of emotional and political effects, all become discussable'. It is in this sense that Performance discovers 'theatre' as its 'repressed': aesthetic performance, whether theatre or live art, interrupts and frames the flow of the present and our immersion in its performativities (Diamond 1996: 2–5, original emphasis).

We have seen how the words 'performance' and 'performative' are relatively conflated or distinguished in the pursuit of various arguments. Following Austin and especially Searle, we might say that we have been tracking the performativity of these words in different contexts: their utterance does something, is efficacious. So in addition to the Butlerian sense of performativity as enforced reiteration, we have the more general sense of performativity as getting something done. There is also a very general metaphoric usage, especially in other disciplines, of 'performative' in the sense of 'like a performance', or to index the consideration of something in terms of performance – the 'performative aspects of dentistry', perhaps. We have also seen how 'a variety of theorists whose critique of Enlightenment cogito as fully self-present cause them to view their own critical acts as performative' (Diamond 1996: 2).

Jill Dolan's 1993 essay 'Geographies of learning' looks forwards to Theatre Studies becoming 'a site at which cultural problems, performed by cultural actors, are studied and investigated through critical theatrical production'. The performance events it staged would be 'always already critical, political and marked by difference, standing in oppositional relation to the academy and the profession'. Essential is the active participation of 'historically marginalised identities', people for whom the 'performativity' of identity is foregrounded by their being unrepresented in the still dominant humanist discourses about subjectivity; but who might politically need and want to claim a fixed identity in political struggle. Performative identities engage together in a theatre closely allied to the postmodern notion of the performative, to efficacious – performative – ends. The 'performative' here shifts productively between meanings (Dolan 1993: 417–21).

PRESENCE AND REPRESENTATION

Representation and presence

The word *representation* can carry overtones not simply of accurate imitation but of illusion and lying. The actor accurately copies an emotion he does not feel. And, according to the great French theorist of theatre Denis Diderot (1713–84), that is correct, for actually to feel the emotion he copied would make him a poor actor. Diderot's concept of the human body was, in Joseph Roach's words, of 'a virtually soulless machine possessing vital drives but no will' (1993: 130). From here flows Diderot's definition of the actor's talent, which 'consists, not in leaving everything to his sensibility as you suppose, but in imitating the exterior signs of emotion so perfectly that you can't tell the difference: his cries of anguish are marked in his memory, his gestures of despair have been prepared in advance; he knows the precise cue to start his tears flowing' (in Roach 1993: 133).

Actors, in Diderot's view, were morally neutral entities, 'fit to play all characters because they have none' (Diderot 1883: 65). Their art is simply an extension of the art practised by others who produce illusions in order to sustain a livelihood: the beggar, the seducer, the prostitute and the unbelieving priest. They feign, or represent, the feeling by appropriately organising voice, face and body. What distinguishes actors, as with other sorts of genius, is a capacity for reflection, a turning out from the self, away from personal feeling, in order objectively to observe and study, and thus understand, the truths of nature. Through a three-stage process of observation, reflection and experiment the actor creates a blueprint which will guide and control all muscular and vocal activity. 'A great actor is also a most ingenious puppet' (p. 62). Nothing is left to spontaneity or momentary inspiration. Thus, again and again, the actor may weep, touchingly, and always on cue.

Diderot's views in the posthumously published *Paradoxe* enraged a number of actors. He was specifically attacked by that craftsman of melodramatic emotion, Henry Irving. But not just him. As Roach points out, many of the experiments in theatre and Performance of the 1960s and 1970s onwards may be seen as attempts to cast off Diderot's picture of the mechanised actor, socially equivalent to someone who sells fakes or commodifies their body. The experiments of the 1960s avant garde sought to free the actor from subservience to text. The obligation to be constrained within a playwright's text curbs an actor's spontaneity. So too, the need to discipline the body through a process of rehearsal amounted to an alienation from one's own bodily potential.

Joseph Chaikin was an actor and director making experimental work in the late 1960s. In his book, *The Presence of the Actor* (1972), he writes that *presence* is 'a quality given to some and absent from others' (1972: 20). This is how it is commonly regarded, as some indefinable biological extra: some people just 'have it' and many don't.

As Chaikin goes on, however, it becomes clearer that 'presence' also results from the particular behaviour of the actor. While Chaikin may be seen as part of the avant garde of that period, this involves dispositions with regard not only to the audience but also to the text:

> He offers his voice and body to the material which has been fully understood and given meaning: that is, before he embarks on his task as an actor he has come into a meaningful agreement with the main intentions of the text. It is this balancing act of abandonment and control, of intelligence and innocence, which makes his performance remarkable.
>
> (1972: 21)

Although the actor 'offers' himself, it is not completely an act of surrender since the text has already been fully understood. The language Chaikin uses to describe the relationship between actor and text is that of partnership. His language for the relationship with an audience is more explicitly sensual: 'It's a kind of deep libidinal surrender which the performer reserves for his anonymous audience' (p. 20).

Some features here mark Chaikin's description as typical of the late 1960s. First the performer is valued over and above other elements of the work. The performer is not simply a vehicle for the author's text or under the control of someone else's vision: a 'meaningful agreement' has been achieved. Second the performer demonstrates a physical way of being that is itself liberated, in line with counter-cultural efforts to free the body from learnt discipline. Chaikin comments, 'I have a notion that what attracts people to the theater is a kind of discomfort with the limitations of life as it is lived, so we try to alter it through a model form' (p. 22); and cites Herbert Marcuse, the great contemporary guru who wrote about the sexually and emotionally repressive effects of capitalism.

Artaud and Derrida

Chaikin is not fully within the 'Artaudian' aesthetic, which was a major posthumous influence on experimental theatre and Performance in the late 1960s. Artaud's call in *The Theatre and Its Double* ([1938] 1970) for a 'Theatre of Cruelty' demanded an immediacy between performer, stage and audience. Any words would be treated purely as sounds rather than as sign-vehicles. To the generation of 1968 and the anti-Vietnam War movement, Artaud held out a promise of liberation from the constraints, impositions and misrepresentations of authority. The direct presence of the performer was a form of guarantee against the falsity of representations.

In treating presence and representation as opposed terms, and calling for a theatre of pure presence to defeat representation, Artaud is constructing what Derrida would later call a *hierarchised binary*. Derrida's critical technique of *deconstruction* is designed to collapse this. He, too, has a political project in hand, not dissimilar to that of Artaud and radical experimental theatre. Like them, he has in his sights less the direct manifestations of capitalism than what underpins it, the Western order itself. But he comes to a radically different conclusion. Let us see what he does with Artaud.

'The Theatre of Cruelty and the closure of representation' (Derrida [1966] 1978) falls into three main parts. Derrida celebrates Artaud for his recognition of what is at the very heart of theatre, and presents Artaud's argument; then speculates on what it implies in its own terms; and finally suggests another frame within which to think about its contents. It is a complex essay, made the more difficult because Derrida slips between his own voice and that of Artaud; he is unsettling terms, turning Artaud's argument against itself, while still celebrating Artaud.

First, Derrida summarises Artaud. Artaud rejects both Man and God as the antithesis of Life: in separating himself from Life by God, Man pollutes the divinity of the divine. God is associated with the principles of repetition and representation: 'as soon as there is repetition, God is there, the present holds on to itself and reserves itself, that is to say, eludes itself'. The *present* – the principle of immediacy – is aligned with Life. Representation kills the present. When it comes to theatre, '(t)he stage is theological so long as it is dominated by . . . a will to speech, by the layout of a primary logos which does not belong to the theatrical site and governs it from a distance'. The 'founding freedom' of the true stage must be regained, freed from 'the text and the author-god' (Derrida 1978: 234–46). The word 'repetition' has a particular poignancy in French, covering both '*repetition*' and 'rehearsal'. To rehearse is both to repeat in the rehearsal room, and to repeat the words of the author–god. It is, to deploy another pun, to be dictated to. The target is not speech as much as being spoken for:

> The stage is theological for as long as its structure, following the entirety of tradition, comports the following elements: an author-creator who, absent and from afar, is armed with a text and keeps watch over, assembles, regulates the time or the meaning of representation, letting this latter *represent* him as concerns what is called the content of his thoughts, his intentions, his ideas. He lets representation represent him through representatives, directors or actors, enslaved interpreters who represent characters.
>
> (Derrida 1978: 235)

In this much-quoted passage, Derrida seems to slip between his critical account of Artaud, and his own implied position. It is often taken as Derrida's direct opinion.

Second, Derrida asks how all theatres that have existed shape up to Artaud's demands. There follows a scathing critique in which all forms of Western theatre, including oppositional forms, are found to be lacking because they are ultimately 'theological'. They depend on the authority of something outside themselves and so defer the instantaneousness of Life. Derrida comments: 'In thus enumerating the themes of infidelity, one comes to understand quickly that fidelity is impossible.' So, if Artaud is in fact asking the impossible, 'under what conditions could an authentic "theatre of cruelty" "begin to exist?"'. Artaud's presence is at root pure *present-ness*. As Derrida glosses him: 'nonrepresentation' or 'original representation' is 'the unfolding of a volume . . . an experience which produces its own space . . . that is to say, the production of a space that no speech could condense or comprehend' (Derrida 1978: 237–47).

Now, third, Derrida thinks closely about the 'present'. The present's very 'present-ness' entails a sort of existing-for-itself. There is an 'interior fold' or duplication which 'steals simple presence of its present act'. And that governs not only theatre, but the whole of life. Artaud is indeed asking for the impossible. The 'profound essence' of Artaud's project was '*to erase repetition in general*'. Artaud's brilliance was to recognise a boundary and to play up against it. But the weapon he chose to cross it with, the notion of pure presence, was paradoxically at the very heart of the field of Western metaphysics since Plato. Intuitively, Artaud recognised the theatre as the principal apparatus for experiencing this 'irrepressible movement' of 'primitive repetition'. Tragedy is proper to the Western stage, 'not as the representation of fate, but of the fate of representation'. To put it another way, 'original repetition' might be thought of as 'the origin of tragedy as the absence of a simple origin'. Western culture's deep striving for present-ness to self makes the stage its most authentic apparatus. To be rid of theatre entails first the end of the Western metaphysics of presence itself (Derrida 1978: 245–50, original emphasis).

Just a year after Derrida's deconstruction of Artaud's search for presence, Michael Fried championed the 'present-ness' or 'instantaneousness' of modernist art against the mere 'presence' or 'temporality' of what was later to be regarded as postmodern works. A true work of art was 'wholly manifest' in an instant, achieved 'a continuous and entire *presentness* amounting, as it were, to the perpetual creation of itself'. The work of art was 'to defeat theatre' in order to attain such presence. And this struggle has in fact been most sharp in theatre itself. He names two practitioner-theorists who have worked towards excising the theatrical from theatre. One is Brecht, and the other is Artaud (see also chapter 9). Fried further reflects that of all art forms, it is the movie that manages to escape theatricality entirely. A phenomenology of cinema might celebrate that the actors are not 'physically present' and the screen not experienced as an object in itself 'existing . . . in specific physical relation to us' (Fried 1967: 136–40).

Toronto 1980

Derrida's essay was not translated into English until 1978, as part of the poststructuralist 'theory' wave that swept West from France. Derrida's influence, along with that of other leading theorists, was felt at a theatre colloquium at the University of Toronto in 1980. In a piece that was to become influential, Josette Féral argued there that one of the defining features of Performance was its antipathy to 'representation'. Performance achieves a 'continuous present' in which the performer becomes 'the point of passage for energy flows' that do not congeal into meaning or representation. The performer is returned to the level of the construction of subjectivity, and the audience receive this as a 'knowledge'. Performance thus 'demystifies the subject on stage' (Féral 1982: 173–8).

For Féral, Performance is 'theatricality in slow motion'. It occupies 'the limits of theatre' and so reveals its 'hidden face'. She adopts Lacan's distinction between the Imaginary and the Symbolic to identify two parts to theatricality. First are the *realities of the imaginary*, which originate in the subject and allow 'the flows of his desire to speak'. Second is a set of *specific symbolic structures* that fix the subject in the symbolic order. While both Performance and theatre deal with the Imaginary, theatre freezes its objects because it is tied to the symbolic order, whereas Performance sets them into play. And this lays bare theatricality, an endless play of positions and desire. Performance undoes the 'competencies' of theatre, to access the primary processes of the subject (Féral 1982: 171–9).

Féral observes that contemporary Performance 'paradoxically' resembles Artaud's prescriptions for a reborn stage. Later, to specify the 'infrasymbolic zone' of Performance, she invokes Derrida's notion of the 'margin'. This designates a conceptual or experiential 'frame' which is at once the 'most hidden', but thereby also the 'most important' aspect of the subject (Féral 1982: 174–8). We met this Derridean figure in his essay on Artaud, although Féral does not mention it. So things are not all that paradoxical after all. In his own essay, Derrida 'stages' Artaud as a subject torn to pieces, working at the very margin of Western metaphysics. So we need to rephrase a little. Contemporary performance as theorised by Féral is not very far from what *Derrida read out of* Artaud.

In investigating theatricality, the Toronto conference consciously took North American Performance as one of its key concerns and contemporary 'theory' as one of its chief means. But the theory itself comes loaded with some limited preconceptions about theatre. For instance, the Lacanian register of Féral's phrase, 'alienated in a figure of fixation like characters in the classical theatre' (1982: 177) carries an assumption about 'classical' theatre which would be questioned by, say, Bentley's or Beckerman's models of character as unfixed, as process (see Keyword: Character, mask, person).

Chantal Pontbriand's contribution to the Toronto conference also became influential in discussions of representation and presence. She argues that contemporary Performance manifests a different kind of presence than theatre, a 'neo-presence'. Her starting point is similar to Féral's: Performance 'unfolds in a real time and a real place without any imaginary or transcendental space-time a piori'; 'it presents; it does not re-present' (Pontbriand 1982: 155). Pontbriand's argument slips between the two discourses of presence that we have discussed in relation to the emergence of Performance, to circulate between three points: the 'present-ness' championed by formalists like Greenberg and Fried; the *ersatz* presence of theatricality posited by Fried; and Artaud's search for a 'presence' denied by 'theological' theatre, which Derrida claimed was unattainable.

Drawing on Walter Benjamin's 'The Work of Art in the Age of Mechanical Production' ([1936] 1973b), Pontbriand suggests that Performance, as did printing, democratically cancels the 'aura' of the artwork and simultaneously activates it in the beholder's 'particular situation'. The move from representation in theatre to presentation in Performance is a move from aura to 'simple actuality'. Performance, based in process and presenting non-related fragments, achieves 'radical presence' by refusing the metaphysics of wholeness. She dates the formalist drive, by which the various art genres sought their own specificity, from the advent of mechanical reproduction; and suggests that it also heralded entirely new genres, like cinema and Performance (Pontbriand 1982: 156–7).

Pontbriand considers the use of technical mediation in Performance. While some suspect that it implies a 'theological' distant origin, Pontbriand mobilises McLuhan to suggest that mediation is merely bodily extension, a 'displacement of energy'. Benjamin celebrated cinema because it brought reality closer by framing and cutting. For Pontbriand,

Performance does the same. There is nowhere for their attention to rest. Pontbriand's point of arrival is Richard Foreman. The shocking mobility of frames, cuts and deferrals in his theatre is designed, in his words, to 'evoke the source'. He says, 'the desire to write a certain kind of sentence (gesture) is akin to the desire to live'. The proper function of art is to 'awaken a hunger for immersion in being-conscious-of-process' (in Pontbriand 1982: 157–60).

In making a good evocation of Foreman's theatre, Pontbriand meanwhile establishes Performance as an exclusionary genre: contemporary 'shamanistic' performances are excluded, for being mystificatory. This generic specification of Performance depends upon a slipperiness around the two discourses on 'presence' which she mobilises. Performance engenders 'shock' and foregrounds actual circumstances in contrast to the 'contemplation' of modernist formalism. But it achieves *coherence* as an artform through the operational principle of energy.

Pontbriand and Fried both seek the specification of genres, and both find cinema a paradigmatic form, though for at least ostensibly different reasons. For Fried it keeps the body at bay; for Pontbriand it brings the preconscious apprehension of life closer. Pontbriand's 'neo-presence', that hovers at the gates of ungraspable reality, is in the present-ness of the present, and embodies the desire for life, sounds very much like the Artaud that Derrida finds intuitively specifying the very borders of Western metaphysics. Foreman sits on the same cusp. But, thanks to neo-presence, we can now specify it as proper Art. Pontbriand's 'neo-presence' of Performance turns out to be a neat collision between Fried's 'present-ness' and the dance around that different 'presentness' that Derrida stages for Artaud . And the *ersatz* presence of obtrusive objects and real bodies showing off is nowhere to be seen (Pontbriand 1982: 157–60; and see Auslander 1997: 54–7).

The absorption of Derrida

In his astute overview of the period Michael Vanden Heuvel suggests that there is a relationship between the presence established by the performer and the sense of something larger and more abstract, an ideal of Presence (which is possibly what attracted Chaikin's audience). The 'potency' of Presence as an ideal lay in the performer's ability to capture and enact spontaneously the totality of reality and to make it available to the spectator. By seeming to comprehend one's deepest intuitive levels of being and therefore create and express one's genuine grasp of reality, the performer became the paradigm of the ideal authentic self.

(Vanden Heuvel 1991: 44).

This 'ability' of the performer rests on a combination of physical technique and the illusion it generates: 'the disciplined performing body is exhibited as the empowered source whose physical aura can capture and guarantee Presence and once again recuperate reality in all its spatial, temporal, and psychic fullness' (p. 45).

Vanden Heuvel's book appeared in 1991. Close on the heels of the theory decade, his analysis deliberately identifies what had become, by then, the usual suspects – 'guarantee', 'fullness', 'authentic' and of course 'self'. Chaikin's late-1960s innocence has been laid bare, in Vanden Heuvel's text, by the arrival of poststructuralism in the intervening period, under the leadership mainly of Derrida.

The absorption of the Derridean critique into accounts of acting can be tracked across the 1980s. For example Philip Auslander's essay '"Just be your self": *logocentrism* and *différance* in performance theory' begins by summarising Derrida's ideas of difference and *différance*, and then quotes the concept of the 'theological stage' with its absent author-creator who regulates the representation of his thoughts. But as Derrida's ideas were absorbed into writing on theatre/Performance they tended to be modified by already-existing concepts.

For instance Chaikin and the other performance makers of the late 1960s wanted a stage free of domination by an 'author-creator'. This was one element of the context within which developed an understanding of what Derrida was saying. For Derrida the logos can be present to itself, eventually being like godhead. His account of the 'text' of the theological theatre relates properly to this: 'a verbal fabric, a logos which *is said* in the beginning' (1978: 236). But the 1960s performance context, and the mindset that followed, understood Derrida's logos in a more narrow, and literal, way, as authors and texts. In the early 1980s Auslander went beyond this, but still in a fairly literal way. He suggested that the authorising *logos* of the performance, its assumed point of origin and source of value, could be the director's concept and indeed the actor's self. From here he goes on to explore the concept of the actor's self, and the presence of that self, in the theories of Stanislavsky, Brecht and Grotowski.

Auslander returned to the topic in 1992 in *Presence and Resistance*, where in one of his overview chapters he traced the change from 1960s experimental performance, with its 'politics of ecstasy' (Timothy Leary's phrase, borrowed by Schechner), to the postmodern practices of the late 1980s. He summarises the political value placed on presence: 'because the presence of the actor as one living human being before others is spiritually and psychologically liberating in itself, pure presentation of performer to audience is the best means available to the theater to make a radical spiritual/political statement' (Auslander 1994: 37). Postmodern theatre makes a presentation, not a representation.

The use of the word presence in the theory decade tended to imply a mistaken belief in the 'unified subject'. Old-style theatre talks about a star having presence, as a sort of natural quality, an extension of their self. Auslander would say that this sense we have of a performer's self is actually a product, an effect of micro-relationships with respect to space, time, gesture, sound, etc. (1997: 36). There are, then, two elements to this idea of 'presence'. One is ethical/political: to encourage the illusion of 'presence' is unhealthy because it encourages an illusion that the subject is unified, whole. The other element is historical/aesthetic: old theatre is characterised by its production of this illusion, its 'classical presence'. New Performance does not allow this illusion, it knows and shows that 'presence' is an effect.

There is a deep problem with these assumptions, and it goes all the way back to Derrida's overstatement of the case with respect to a 'theological theatre'. Only for a very short period could theatre be described as attempting to lock an audience into 'passive' uncritical viewing. Many historical audiences consciously watched the techniques as they produced 'presence'. This is also the case for Oriental theatre. In his analysis of the techniques of Oriental theatre, theatre anthropologist Eugenio Barba identified a set of physical micro-techniques, learnt muscular disciplines, which together constitute what he calls the 'pre-expressive'. It is the way the performer stands, occupies space, physically 'is'. The overall discipline of the body comes from training which can produce the sensation of 'presence'. The techniques are what an audience watches.

It is, then, difficult to demonstrate that old-style theatre is simply perpetuating the ethically dubious idea of 'presence'. What we have to be interested in is the growth of the assumption that it does so. This has to do with the operation of assumptions that combine the ethical and historical. So too it has to do perhaps with the shift from the focus on the performer's work to that of the theorist.

In his attempt to capture the problematic of postmodernism in 1977, Benamou drew the conclusion that we must not choose between Presence and Absence; we are in the realm of an undecidability between categories and their deconstruction (Benamou 1977: 5). Meanwhile, it is a common observation that theatre enacts a circulation between the presence of the actor and the absence of the person represented; and the absence of the person of the actor under the role. And this can be a fetish of presence, its deconstruction, or a circulation between both (and see Phelan 1997: 3–4).

SEMIOTICS AND PHENOMENOLOGY

Semiotics is concerned with the ways in which meaning is made and exchanged in society. It is a description and analysis of the various processes of signification and communication. Semiotics, in the short-hand definition, is the study and understanding, the science, of signs.

This science emerged from the work of the linguist Ferdinand de Saussure, developed in lectures given to his students in Geneva 1906–11, and the philosopher C.S. Peirce (1839–1914), working in America (see Hawkes 1978). Its value for the analysis of performed work comes largely from its capacity to deal with objects, images, non-verbal sound alongside that which is verbal, for all constitute signs in differing and complex relations to what they represent. Its first application to the theatre was made by the so-called Prague School structuralists working in the 1930s and 1940s. Their work, according to Keir Elam, changed dramatic poetics for the first time since Aristotle. The key year was 1931, which saw publication of Otakar Zich's *Aesthetics of the Art of Drama* and Jan Mukarovsky's 'An Attempted Structural Analysis of the Phenomenon of the Actor'. Their work, together with that of their peers, is well described by Elam (1980). He identifies as the primary insight of the Prague School the idea that (in Bogatyrev's words) 'on the stage things that play the part of theatrical signs . . . acquire special features, qualities and atributes, that they do not have in real life' (Elam 1980: 7). A table on stage may be exactly the table that has been used to dump coats and bags on in the rehearsal room, but once on stage in performance it acquires quotation marks, representing not itself but the whole category of tables (p. 8). Similarly every twitch of an actor, even an unintentional reflex, is seen as a quotation, received as a sign.

This basic principle of the Prague School was re-stated in 1968 by the Polish semiotician Tadeusz Kowzan (Elam 1980: 20). Enlarged into a book which came out in 1975, it heralds the second wave of theatre semiotics. The driving-force was partly Parisian (post)structuralism and partly Italian semiotics. Patrice Pavis's *Problèmes de sémiologie théâtrale* appeared in 1976, and Anne Ubersfeld's *Lire de théâtre* in 1977. The English speaking world had an introduction to Kowzan in the pages of *The Drama Review*, to be followed an issue later by 'Semiotics of Theatrical

Performance' (1977) by Umberto Eco, who worked at Bologna. Eco attempted for the first time a definition of theatre semiotics. It was based on Peirce's approach combined with insights from the Prague School. To this he added Erving Goffman's 'frame analysis' (where the contextual frame within which we see something affects the meaning we put on it).

For Eco the 'elementary mechanisms of human interaction and the elementary mechanisms of dramatic fiction are the same'. That observation eased the passage from narrow semiotic analyses to cultural, or more particularly ideological, analyses. Thus Eco notes Kowzan's insistence that the object of study is not the literary text but the 'performance, or the *mise-en-scène*' – the physical arrangements which articulate and set a frame to the activity within them. From here, near the end of his article, he observes that the mise en scène works as ideological statement, and a semiotic analysis of it is also an analysis of 'the production of ideologies' (Eco 1977: 107–17 *passim*).

What tends to fade from view is that alternative to mise en scène, the performance. Mise en scène was a more attractive object partly because it still could be made to behave like written text: while Keir Elam's *The Semiotics of Theatre and Drama* notionally attends in part to action and the dramatic world it is underpinned by minute verbal analysis. But perhaps a more substantial reason for the focus on mise en scène was its contemporary popularity within film theory where semiotic approaches were proliferating. Film studies was an emerging discipline; through the journal *Screen* it was connected into the newest European thinking; its analysis and theorising had none of the conservative baggage over which English departments had to do battle in the late 1970s. As it established itself as a university discipline film studies contrasted with another relatively young discipline. Drama hovered between text analysis, practical work and history. Above all it did not have an aggressively articulate theoretical apparatus. As Patrice Pavis (2000) notes, semiotics had the charisma of hard science in its promise to be able to analyse any sort of dramatic event. And to university drama and then senior-school classes it gave a model of analysis that attended with as much rigour to the non-verbal as to the verbal. It had a set of protocols, and a foundation in what by then was known as 'Theory', which guaranteed that it was not ephemeral. These protocols, the identification of the signifier, the definition of its relationship to the signified, offered a package that could be taught and learned.

Even while one version of semiotics was entering the textbooks, some of its proponents were, however, shifting ground. The mise en scène in film is different from that in theatre in that nothing is actually physically present. The filmed body cannot change its behaviour in relation to it. Readings of mise en scène remain readings, and they tend to bracket off the social situation in which the performance happens – in the presence of an audience. An audience brings with it attitudes, preconceptions, knowledges which establish a cognitive framework within which they 'read' the performance. So for semioticians the topic of the audience became important. Elam devotes short sections to the way it makes meaning from the play. Borrowing from Goffman, like Eco, the idea of the 'frame', he suggests 'Every spectator's interpretation of the text is in effect a new *construction* of it according to the cultural and ideological disposition of the subject' (Elam 1980: 87, 95). To this he adds 'horizon of expectations' (p. 94) from the 'reception theory' of Hans Robert Jauss. This suggests the spectator brings to the event knowledge of text, critics' and friends' opinions, and measures the event against them.

Something is missing, however. In her book *L'école du spectateur* (1981) Anne Ubersfeld gives the final chapters to 'Le travail du spectateur' and 'Le plaisir du spectateur'. The feeling of pleasure by actual minds and bodies: with this notion we are in rather different territory from 'reading' the mise en scène, and discovering its ideological signification. We are instead in the territory of the experiential, the felt – where objects are not signs, but simply objects. The audience is not simply a collection of psyches 'reading' the mise en scène; it is a set of bodies in relationship to one another and to the space they are in, a set of eyes moving in their sockets. The 'I' also has an 'eye'.

That quotation is from a theorist of phenomenology, Stanton Garner, Jr. In his incisive book *Bodied Spaces* (1994) he defines the general aims of phenomenology:

> to redirect attention from the world as it is conceived by the abstracting "scientific" gaze (the objective world) to the world as it appears or discloses itself to the perceiving subject (the phenomenal world); to

> pursue the thing as it is given to consciousness in direct experience; to
> return perception to the fullness of its encounter with its environment.
>
> (p. 2)

Phenomenology's roots go back to the early twentieth-century philosopher Edmund Husserl and then, more recently, Maurice Merleau-Ponty. Merleau-Ponty's significant contribution was a theorisation of seeing and experience based on the actual physical body, a fleshly entity which practised in the world; not simply done to, but doing. That necessary insistence on the biological and emotional realities of the body that performs and the body that watches was affirmed, in the theatrical setting, by Herbert Blau, who pointed out that the performer on stage 'can die there in front of your eyes; is in fact doing so. Of all the performing arts, the theater stinks most of mortality' (Blau 1982: 83).

By the early 1990s phenomenology had become the target of post-structuralists. Its interest in the experiential and the felt was seen as not only outmoded but anti-analytical. In focusing on the lived reality of the physical situation it is blind to historical circumstance and, in particular, the contradictions of historical process. In the field of drama the dominance of semiotics, with its poststructuralist affiliation, produced a hostile environment in which to explore the usefulness of phenomenology. Few did it before Garner, but among those few was Bert States.

As States sees it, phenomenology is more able to articulate the contradictory nature of theatre than semiotics is: 'the phenomenological critic strives to show how theater becomes theater – that is, how theater throws up the pretense that it is another kind of reality than the one constituting the ground on which its pretense is based'. For the phenomenologist objects in theatre have a double quality: they are signs, but they are 'self-given'. While semiotics takes 'cultural units' as data, phenomenology deals with the conditions of their formation (States 1992: 372, 374). From here Garner argues that, by addressing the material realities of the performance situation, phenomenology offers the means to resist the anti-theatricality of poststructuralism.

Stepping back from the debates, we can see the two approaches as opposed but necessarily interconnected. The experiential provides the conditions for signification; in trying to write about what is ungraspable phenomenology needs signification. Each theoretical discourse has been productive in different ways for the discipline, and has produced the discipline as different. Theatre semiotics was, relatively late, imported by theorists of drama and theatre, within a culture of Theory and 'reading'. Theatre phenomenology seems to have been embraced as much by makers as by analysts of performance (if that distinction is allowable). It has come to importance not simply in making sense of a theatre of physical images that abjure meaning, but also in making it.

BIBLIOGRAPHY

Adorno, Theodor and Horkheimer, Max (1999) *Dialectic of Enlightenment*, London: Verso.

Agnew, Jean-Christophe (1986) *Worlds Apart: The Market and the Theater in Anglo-American Thought, 1550–1750*, Cambridge: Cambridge University Press.

Anderson, Perry (1998) *The Origins of Postmodernity*, London: Verso.

Arnheim, Rudolph (1956) *Art and Visual Perception: A Psychology of the Creative Eye*, London: Faber & Faber.

Artaud, Antonin (1970) *The Theatre and Its Double*, trans. Victor Corti, London: Calder & Boyars.

Ashcroft, Bill, Griffiths, Gareth and Tiffin, Helen (eds) (1995) *The Post-Colonial Studies Reader*, London: Routledge.

Aston, Elaine (1995) *An Introduction to Feminism and Theatre*, London: Routledge.

Attali, Jacques (1985) *Noise: The Political Economy of Music*, trans. Brian Massumi, Minneapolis: University of Minnesota Press.

Auerbach, Erich (1974) *Mimesis: The Representation of Reality in Western Literature*, trans. Willard R. Trask, Princeton: Princeton University Press.

Auslander, Philip (1994) *Presence and Resistance: Postmodernism and Cultural Politics in Contemporary American Performance*, Ann Arbor: University of Michigan Press.

Auslander, Philip (1997) *From Acting to Performance: Essays in Modernism and Postmodernism*, London & New York: Routledge.

Auslander, Philip (ed.) (2003) *Performance: Critical Concepts in Literary and Cultural Studies*, London: Routledge.

Austin, Gayle (1990) *Feminist Theories for Dramatic Criticism*, Ann Arbor: University of Michigan Press.

Austin, J.L. (1962) *How to do Things with Words: The William James Lectures Delivered at Harvard University in 1955*, ed. James O. Urmson, London: Clarendon Press.

Banes, Sally (1998) *Subversive Expectations: Performance Art and Paratheater in New York 1976–85*, Ann Arbor: University of Michigan Press.

Barba, Eugenio (1986) *Beyond the Floating Islands*, trans. Judy Barba *et al.*, New York: PAJ Publications.

Barba, Eugenio (1995) *The Paper Canoe: A Guide to Theatre Anthropology*, trans. Richard Fowler, London: Routledge.

Barba, Eugenio and Saverese, Nicola (1991) *A Dictionary of Theatre Anthropology: The Secret Art of the Performer*, London: Routledge.

Barber, C.L. (1959) *Shakespeare's Festive Comedy: A Study of Dramatic Form and its Relation to Social Custom*, Princeton: Princeton University Press.

Barish, Jonas (1981) *The Anti-theatrical Prejudice*, Berkeley: University of California Press.

Barker, Clive (1977) *Theatre Games: A New Approach to Drama Training* London: Eyre Methuen.

Barlow, Wilfred (1973) *The Alexander Principle*, London: Victor Gollancz.

Barroll, J. Leeds (1974) *Artificial Persons: The Formation of Characters in the Tragedies of Shakespeare*, Columbia: University of South Carolina Press.

Barthes, Roland (1977) 'From Work to Text', in *Image-Music-Text*, London: Fontana/Collins.

Bassnett, Susan (1989) 'Struggling with the Past: Women's Theatre in Search of a History', *New Theatre Quarterly* **18** (5): 107–12.

Bastian, H.C. (1880) *The Brain the Organ of the Mind*, International Scientific Series 29, London: Kegan Paul & Co.

Bateson, Gregory (1972) 'A Theory of Play and Fantasy', in *Steps to an Ecology of Mind: Collected Essays in Anthropology, Psychiatry, Evolution and Epistemology*, London: Intertext Books.

Battcock, Gregory (ed.) (1968) *Minimal Art: A Critical Anthology*, New York: Dutton.

Battcock, Gregory and Nickas, Robert (eds) (1984) *The Art of Performance: A Critical Anthology*, New York: E.P. Dutton.

de Beauvoir, Simone (1997) *The Second Sex*, trans. and ed. H.M. Parshley, London: Vintage.

Beckerman, Bernard (1970) *Dynamics of Drama: Theory and Method of Analysis*, New York: Alfred A. Knopf.

Bell, Catherine (1992) *Ritual Theory, Ritual Practice*, Oxford: Oxford University Press.

Benamou, Michel (1977) 'Presence and Play', in Michel Benamou and Charles Caramello (eds) *Performance in Postmodern Culture*, Madison, WI: Coda Press, pp. 3–7.

Benamou, Michel and Caramello, Charles (eds) (1977) *Performance in Postmodern Culture: Theories of Contemporary Culture*, volume 1, Madison, WI: Coda Press.

Benjamin, Walter (1973a) 'What is Epic Theatre?', in *Understanding Brecht*, trans. Anna Bostock, London: Verso.

Benjamin, Walter (1973b) 'The Work of Art in the Age of Mechanical Production', in Hannah Arendt (ed.) *Illuminations*, trans. Harry Zohn, London: Collins/Fontana.

Benjamin, Walter (1978) 'On the Mimetic Faculty', in Peter Demetz (ed.) *Reflections: Essays, Aphorisms, Autobiographical Writings*, New York: Schocken Books.

Bennett, Susan (1990) *Theatre Audiences: A Theory of Production and Reception*, London: Routledge.

Bentley, Eric (1948) *The Modern Theatre*, London: Robert Hale.

Bentley, Eric (1965) *The Life of the Drama*, London: Methuen & Co.

Bentley, Eric (1967) *The Theatre of Commitment and Other Essays on Drama in our Society*, London: Methuen & Co.

Berne, Eric (1968) *Games People Play: The Psychology of Human Relationships*, Harmondsworth: Penguin

Bharucha, Rustom (1993) *Theatre and the World: Performance and the Politics of Culture*, London: Routledge.

Bharucha, Rustom (2000) *The Politics of Cultural Practice: Thinking through Theatre in an Age of Globalization*, London: The Athlone Press.

Birringer, Johannes (1993) *Theatre, Theory, Postmodernism*, Bloomington and Indianapolis: Indiana University Press.

Blau, Herbert (1982) *Take up the Bodies: Theater at the Vanishing Point*, Urbana: University of Illinois Press.

Boal, Augusto (1979) *Theatre of the Oppressed*, London: Pluto Press.

Bourdieu, Pierre (1998) *Outline of a Theory of Practice*, trans. Richard Nice, Cambridge: Cambridge University Press.

Bradley, A.C. (1911) 'Hegel's Theory of Tragedy', in *Oxford Lectures on Poetry*, London: Macmillan.

Bradley, A.C. (1983) *Shakespearean Tragedy*, London: Macmillan.

Bratton, Jacky (2003) *New Readings in Theatre History*, Cambridge: Cambridge University Press.

Brecht, Bertolt (1964) *Brecht on Theatre: The Development of an Aesthetic*, ed. and trans. John Willett, New York: Hill & Wang.

Brook, Peter (1996) 'The Culture of Links' in Patrice Pavis (ed.) *The Intercultural Performance Reader*, London: Routledge.

Brooks, Cleanth and Heilman, Robert B. (1966) *Understanding Drama*, New York: Holt, Rinehart & Winston.

Burke, Kenneth (1945) *A Grammar of Motives*, New York: Prentice-Hall.

Burke, Kenneth (1966) *Language as Symbolic Action: Essays on Life, Literature, and Method*, Berkeley and Los Angeles: University of California Press.

Burns, Elizabeth (1972) *Theatricality: A Study of Convention in the Theatre and in Social Life*, London: Longman.

Burns, Elizabeth and Burns, Tom (eds) (1973) *The Sociology of Literature and Drama*, Harmondsworth: Penguin.

Butler, Judith (1990) *Gender Trouble: Feminism and the Subversion of Identity*, London: Routledge.

Butler, Judith (1993) 'Critically Queer', in *Bodies That Matter: On the Discursive Limits of 'Sex'*, London: Routledge, pp. 223–42.

Caillois, Roger (1961) *Man, Play and Games*, trans. M. Barash, New York: Free Press of Glencoe.

Caillois, Roger (1984) 'Mimicry and Legendary Psychasthenia', trans. John Shepley, *October* **31** (Winter): 17–32.

Carlson, Marvin (1994) *Theories of the Theatre: A Historical and Critical Survey, from the Greeks to the Present* (expanded edition), Ithaca, NY and London: Cornell University Press.

Carlson, Marvin (1996) *Performance: A Critical Introduction*, London: Routledge.

Carroll, Nöel (1986) 'Performance', *Formations* **3**: 62–82.

Case, Sue-Ellen (1988) *Feminism and Theatre*, Basingstoke: Macmillan.

Case, Sue-Ellen (ed.) (1990) 'Introduction' *Performing Feminisms: Feminist Critical Theory and Theatre*, Baltimore: Johns Hopkins University Press, pp.1–13.

Case, Sue-Ellen (ed.) (1996) *Split Britches: Lesbian Practice / Feminist Performance*, London: Routledge.

Caudwell, Christopher (1937) *Illusion and Reality: A Study of the Sources of Poetry*, London: Macmillan & Co.

Chaikin, Joseph (1972) *The Presence of the Actor: Notes on the Open Theater, Disguises, Acting, and Representation*, New York: Athenaum.

Chambers, E.K. (1903) *The Medieval Stage*, Oxford: Clarendon Press.

Coleridge, S.T. (1930) *Coleridge's Shakespeare Criticism*, ed. T.M. Raysor, London: Constable & Co.

Coleridge, S.T. (1985) *The Major Works*, ed. H.J. Jackson, Oxford: Oxford University Press.

Counsell, Colin (1996) *Signs of Performance: An Introduction to Twentieth-century Theatre*, London: Routledge.

Csikszentmihalyi, Mihaly (1975) *Beyond Boredom and Anxiety: The Experience of Play in Work and Games*, San Francisco: Jossey-Bass.

Csikszentmihalyi, Mihaly (1979) 'The Concept of Flow', in Brian Sutton-Smith (ed.) *Play and Learning*, New York: Gardiner Press.

Davidson, Clifford (ed.) (1993) *A Tretise of Miraclis Pleyinge*, Kalamazoo, MI: Medieval Institute Publications, Western Michigan University.

Davis, Tracy C. (1989) 'A Feminist Methodology in Theatre History', in Thomas Postlewait and Bruce A. McConachie (eds) *Interpreting the Theatrical Past: Essays in the Historiography of Performance*, Iowa City: University of Iowa Press.

Debord, Guy (1994) *Society of the Spectacle*, New York: Zone.

Deleuze, Gilles and Guattari, Félix (1984) *Anti-Oedipus: Capitalism and Schizophrenia*, trans. Robert Hurley, Mark Seem and Helen R. Lane, London: The Athlone Press.

Deleuze, Gilles and Guattari, Félix (1988) *A Thousand Plateaus: Capitalism and Schizophrenia*, trans. Brian Massumi, London: The Athlone Press.

Derrida, Jacques (1977) 'Signature, Event, Context', *Glyph* 1.

Derrida, Jacques (1978) *Writing and Difference*, trans. Alan Bass, London: Routledge & Kegan Paul.

Diamond, Elin (1989) 'Mimesis, Mimicry and the "True-real"', *Modern Drama* **32**: 58–72.

Diamond, Elin (1992) 'The Violence of "We": Politicizing Identification', in Janelle G. Reinelt and Joseph R. Roach (eds) *Critical Theory and Performance*, Ann Arbor: University of Michigan Press, pp. 390–9.

Diamond, Elin (1993) 'Rethinking Identification: Kennedy, Freud, Brecht', *Kenyon Review* **15** (2): 86–99.

Diamond, Elin (1996) 'Introduction', in Elin Diamond (ed.) *Performance and Cultural Politics*, London: Routledge, pp. 1–11.

Diamond, Elin (1997) *Unmaking Mimesis: Essays on Mimesis and Theater*, London: Routledge.

Dibdin, Charles, Jr. (1826) *History and Illustrations of the London Theatres*, London.

Dibdin, Charles, Sr. (1797–1800) *A Complete History of the Stage*, London: printed for the author, five volumes.

Diderot, Denis (1883) *The Paradox of Acting*, trans. W.H. Pollock, London: Chatto & Windus.

Dolan, Jill (1993) 'Geographies of Learning: Theatre Studies, Performance, and the "Performative"' *Theatre Journal* **45**: 417–41.

Dolan, Jill (1995) 'Response to W.B. Worthen', *The Drama Review* **39** (1): 28–34.

Dolan, Jill (1996) 'Fathom languages: Feminist Performance Theory, Pedagogy, and Practice', in Carol Martin (ed.) *A Sourcebook of Feminist Theory and Performance: On and Beyond the Stage*, London: Routledge, pp. 1–20.

Douglas, Mary (1996) *Natural Symbols*, London: Routledge.

Dryden, John (1968) *Of Dramatic Poesy and Other Critical Essays*, ed George Watson, London: Dent, two volumes.

Eco, Umberto (1977) 'Semiotics of Theatrical Performance', *The Drama Review* **21** (1).

Elam, Keir (1980) *The Semiotics of Theatre and Drama*, London: Methuen.

Elias, Norbert (2000) *The Civilizing Process: Sociogenetic and Psychogenetic Investigations*, trans. Edmund Jephcott, Oxford: Blackwell.

Eliot, T.S. (1999) *Selected Essays*, London: Faber & Faber.

Esslin, Martin (1976) *An Anatomy of Drama*, London: Temple Smith.

Esslin, Martin (1987) *The Field of Drama*, London: Methuen Drama.

Feldenkrais, Moshe (1949) *Body and Mature Behaviour: A Study of Anxiety, Sex, Gravitation and Learning*, London: Routledge & Kegan Paul.

Féral, Josette (1982) 'Performance and Theatricality: The Subject Demystified', trans. Terese Lyons, *Modern Drama* **25** (1): 170–81.

Féral, Josette (1992) 'What is Left of Performance Art? Autopsy of a Function, Birth of a Genre', *Discourse* **14**: 148–9.

Fergusson, Francis (1953) *The Idea of a Theater*, New York: Doubleday Anchor Books.

Ford, Andrew (1995) 'Katharsis: The Ancient Problem', in Andrew Parker and Eve Kosofsky Sedgwick (eds) *Performativity and Performance*, London: Routledge.

Foucault, Michel (1979a) *Discipline and Punish: The Birth of the Prison*, trans. Alan Sheridan, Harmondsworth: Penguin.

Foucault, Michel (1979b) 'What is an Author', in Josué V. Harari (ed.) *Textual Strategies*, Ithaca: Cornell University Press, pp. 141–60.

Foucault, Michel (1981) *The History of Sexuality*, trans. Robert Hurley, Harmondsworth: Penguin.

Fried, Michael (1967) 'Art and Objecthood', reprinted from *Artforum*, in G. Battcock (ed.) *Minimal Art: A Critical Anthology*, New York: Dutton, 1968, pp. 116–47.

Frye, Northrop (1973) *Anatomy of Criticism: Four Essays*, Princeton: Princeton University Press.

Fuss, Diane (1995) *Identification Papers*, New York and London: Routledge.

Garner, Stanton B. Jr. (1994) *Bodied Spaces: Phenomenology and Performance in Contemporary Drama*, Ithaca, NY: Cornell University Press.

Geertz, Clifford (1975) *The Interpretation of Cultures*, London: Hutchinson.

Gilbert, Helen and Tompkins, Joanne (1996) *Post-colonial Drama: Theory, Practice, Politics*, London: Routledge.

Giles, Steve (1981) *The Problem of Action in Modern European Drama*, Stuttgart: Akademischer Verlag Hans-Dieter Heinz.

Girard, René (1996) *The Girard Reader*, ed. James G. Williams, New York: The Crossroad Publishing Company.

Goffman, Erving (1956) *The Presentation of Self in Everyday Life*, Edinburgh: University of Edinburgh Social Sciences Research Centre.

Goldberg, Roselee (1979) *Performance: Live Art 1909 to the Present*, London: Thames & Hudson.

Goldberg, Roselee (1988) *Performance Art: From Futurism to the Present*, London: Thames & Hudson.

Goldmann, Lucien (1964) *The Hidden God: A Study of Tragic Vision in the Pensées of Pascal and the Tragedies of Racine*, trans. Philip Thody, London: Routledge & Kegan Paul.

Goldmann, Lucien (1973) '"Genetic Structuralism" in the Sociology of Literature', in Elizabeth Burns and Tom Burns (eds) *The Sociology of Literature and Drama*, Harmondsworth: Penguin.

Goldmann, Lucien (1981) *Racine*, trans. Alastair Hamilton, introduction by Raymond Williams, London: Writers and Readers.

Goldthorpe, Rhiannon (1984) *Sartre: Literature and Theory*, Cambridge: Cambridge University Press.

Goreau, Angeline (1980) *Reconstructing Aphra: A Social Biography of Aphra Behn*, New York: Dial.

Gosson, Stephen (1582) *Playes Confuted in Five Actions*, London.

Graver, David (1995) *The Aesthetics of Disturbance: Anti-art in Avant-garde Drama*, Ann Arbor: University of Michigan.

Green, André (1979) *The Tragic Effect: The Oedipus Complex in Tragedy*, trans. Alan Sheridan, Cambridge: Cambridge University Press.

Gurr, Andrew (1970) *The Shakespearean Stage 1574–1642*, Cambridge: Cambridge University Press.

Halliwell, Stephen (trans and commentary) (1987) *The Poetics of Aristotle*, London: Duckworth.

Halliwell, Stephen (2002) *The Aesthetics of Mimesis: Ancient Texts and Modern Problems*, Princeton: Princeton University Press.

Harris, Geraldine (1999) *Staging Femininities: Performance and Performativity*, Manchester: Manchester University Press.

Hawkes, Terence (1978) *Structuralism and Semiotics*, London: Methuen & Co.

Hays, Michael (1983) Introduction 'The Sociology of Theater', *Theater* 15 (1): Winter.

Hazlitt, William (1991) *Selected Writings*, ed. and introduced by Jon Cook, Oxford: Oxford University Press.

Hobbes, Thomas (1976) *Leviathan*, ed. C.B.Macpherson, Harmondsworth: Penguin.

Home, Stewart (1991) *The Assault on Culture: Utopian Currents from Leftism to Class War*, Stirling: A.K. Press.

Huizinga, Johann (1949) *Homo Ludens: A Study in the Play-Element in Culture*, London: Routledge & Kegan Paul.

Hunt, Albert (1976) *Hopes for Great Happenings: Alternatives in Education and Theatre*, London: Eyre Methuen.

Hutcheon, Linda (1988) *A Poetics of Postmodernism: History, Theory, Fiction*, London: Routledge.

Irigaray, Luce (1985) *Speculum of the Other Woman*, trans. Gillian C. Gill, Ithaca, NY: Cornell University Press.

Irigaray, Luce (1994) 'The Power of Discourse and the Subordination of the Feminine', in Margaret Whitford (ed.) *The Irigaray Reader*, Oxford: Blackwell.

Jackson, Shannon (2004) *Professing Performance: Theatre in the Academy from Philology to Performativity*, Cambridge: Cambridge University Press.

James, D.G. (ed.) (1952) *The Universities and the Theatre*, London: George Allen & Unwin.

James, Mervyn (1983) 'Ritual, Drama and the Social Body in the Late Medieval Town', *Past & Present* **98** (February): 3–29.

Jameson, Fredric (1981) *The Political Unconscious: Narrative as a Socially Symbolic Act*, London: Methuen.

Jeyifo, Biodum (1996) 'The Reinvention of Theatrical Tradition', in Patrice Pavis (ed.) *The Intercultural Performance Reader*, London: Routledge.

Jencks, Charles (1987) *Post-modernism: The New Classicism in Art and Architecture*, New York: Rizzoli.

Johnson, Samuel (1969) *Dr Johnson on Shakespeare*, ed. W.K. Wimsatt Harmondswoth: Penguin.

Johnson, Samuel (1971) *The Complete English Poems*, ed. J.D. Fleeman, Harmondsworth: Penguin.

Jones, Amelia (1998) *Body Art/Performing the Subject*, Minneapolis: University of Minnesota Press.

Jones, Amelia (2000) Survey, in Tracey Warr (ed.) *The Artist's Body*, London: Phaidon.

Jones, Amelia and Stephenson, Andrew (eds) (1999) *Performing the Body: Performing the Text*, London: Routledge.

Jones, Ernest (1949) *Hamlet and Oedipus*, London: Victor Gollancz.

Kane, Nina (nd) 'Humani Nil Alienum: A Post-War History of Theatre at Leeds University', unpublished dissertation.

Kaprow, Allan (1966) *Assemblages, Environments & Happenings*, New York: Harry N. Abrams.

Kaye, Nick (1994a) 'British Live Art' in *Performance Art: Into the 90s*, London: Art and Design Magazine, pp. 87–91.

Kaye, Nick (1994b) *Postmodernism and Performance*, Basingstoke: Macmillan.

Kennedy, Dennis (ed.) (2003) *The Oxford Encyclopedia of Theatre and Performance*, Oxford: Oxford University Press, two vols.

Kershaw, Baz (1999) *The Radical in Performance: Between Brecht and Baudrillard*, London and New York: Routledge.

Kirby, Michael (1985) 'Happenings: An Introduction', in Mariellen R. Sandford (ed.) *Happenings and Other Acts*, London: Routledge.

Knights, L.C. (1946) 'How Many Children Had Lady Macbeth?', in *Explorations*, London: Chatto & Windus.

Knights, L.C. (1962) *Drama and Society in the Age of Jonson*, London: Chatto & Windus.

Kostelanetz, Richard (1968) *Theatre of Mixed Means*, New York: Dial Press.

Kott, Jan (1998) 'The Eating of the Gods, or *The Bacchae*', in John Drakakis and Naomi Conn Liebler (eds) *Tragedy*, Harlow: Addison Wesley Longman.

Lacan, Jacques (1977) 'Desire and the Interpretation of Desire in *Hamlet*', *Yale French Studies*, **55** (6): 11–52.

Lamb, Charles (1903) 'On the Tragedies of Shakespeare Considered with Reference to their Fitness for Stage Representation', in E.V. Lucas (ed.) *The Works of Charles and Mary Lamb*, Vol. 1, London: Methuen, pp. 97–111.

de Landa, Manuel (1998) *War in the Age of Intelligent Machines*, New York: Zone Books.

Lane, Richard J. (2000) *Jean Baudrillard*, London: Routledge Critical Thinkers.

Langbaine, Gerard (1971) *An Account of the English Dramatick Poets*, ed. John Loftis, Los Angeles: William Andrews Clark Memorial Library.

Langer, Suzanne (1953) *Feeling and Form: A Theory of Art Developed from Philosophy in a New Key*, London: Routledge & Kegan Paul.

Laplanche, J. and Pontalis, J.-B. (1983) *The Language of Psycho-Analysis*, trans. Donald Nicholson-Smith, London: The Hogarth Press.

Larrain, Jorge (1979) *The Concept of Performance*, London: Hutchinson.

de Lauretis, Teresa (1987) *Technologies of Gender: Essays on Theory, Film and Fiction*, Basingstoke: Macmillan.

Leacroft, Helen and Leacroft, Richard (1958) *The Theatre*, London: Methuen & Co.

Leacroft, Helen and Leacroft, Richard (1984) *Theatre and Playhouse: An Illustrated Survey of Theatre Building from Ancient Greece to the Present Day*, London: Methuen.

Leacroft, Richard (1988) *The Development of the English Playhouse: An Illustrated Survey of Theatre Building in England from Medieval to Modern Times*, London: Methuen.

Lear, Jonathan (1992) 'Katharsis', in A.O. Rorty (ed.) *Essays on Aristotle's* Poetics, Princeton: Princeton University Press.

Ley, Graham (1999) *From Mimesis to Interculturalism: Readings of Theatrical Theory Before and After 'Modernism'*, Exeter: University of Exeter Press.

Lukács, Georg (1969) *The Historical Novel*, trans. H. and S. Mitchell, Harmondsworth: Penguin.

Lukács, Georg (1971) *History and Class Consciousness: Studies in Marxist Dialectics*, trans. Rodney Livingstone, London: Merlin Press.

Lyotard, Jean-Francois (1989) *The Postmodern Condition: A Report on Knowledge*, trans. Geoff Bennington and Brian Massumi, foreword Fredric Jameson, Manchester: Manchester University Press.

MacAloon, John J. (1984) *Rite, Drama, Festival, Spectacle: Rehearsals toward a Theory of Cultural Performance*, Philadelphia: Institute for the Study of Human Issues.

McGann, Jerome (1991) *The Textual Condition*, Princeton: Princeton University Press.

McHale, Brian (1987) *Postmodernist Fiction*, London: Methuen.

McKenzie, Jon (2001) *Perform or Else: From Discipline to Performance*, London and New York: Routledge.

Macherey, Pierre (1978) *A Theory of Literary Production*, trans. G. Wall, London: Routledge & Kegan Paul.

Maisel, Edward (ed.) (1974) *The Alexander Technique: The Essential Writings of F. Matthias Alexander*, London: Thames & Hudson.

Malone, Edmond (1790) 'An Historical Account of the English Stage', in Vol. 1, pt 2 of *The Plays and Poems of William Shakespeare*, ten volumes, London: H. Baldwin.

de Marinis, Marco (1983) 'Theatrical Comprehension', trans. Giovanna Levi, *Theater* **15** (1: Winter).

Marranca, Bonnie (ed.) (1996) *The Theatre of Images*, Baltimore: Johns Hopkins University Press.

Martin, Randy (ed.) (1998) *Chalk Lines: The Politics of Work in the Managed University*, Durham, NC: Duke University Press.

Massumi, Brian (1992) *A User's Guide to Capitalism and Schizophrenia: Deviations from Deleuze and Guattari* Cambridge, MA: MIT.

Mauss, Marcel (1992) 'Techniques of the Body', in Jonathan Crary and Sandford Kwinter (eds) *Incorporations*, New York: Zone.

Millett, Kate (1972) *Sexual Politics*, London: Abacus

Milling, Jane and Ley, Graham (2001) *Modern Theories of Performance: From Stanislavsky to Brecht*, Basingstoke: Palgrave.

Mills, C. Wright (1999) *The Sociological Imagination*, New York: Oxford University Press.

Mitter, Shomit (1992) *Systems of Rehearsal: Stanislavsky, Brecht, Grotowski and Brook*, London: Routledge.

Moore, Honor (ed.) (1977) *The New Women's Theatre*, New York: Vintage.

Mulvey, Laura (1975) 'Visual Pleasure and Narrative Cinema', *Screen* **16** (3: Autumn).

Nagler, A.M. (1959) *A Source Book in Theatrical History*, New York: Dover Publications.

Nietzsche, Friedrich (2000) *The Birth of Tragedy*, trans. Douglas Smith, Oxford: Oxford University Press.

Omotoso, Kole (1982) *The Theatrical into Theatre: A Study of the Drama and Theatre of the English-speaking Caribbean*, London, Port of Spain: New Beacon Books.

Orgel, Stephen (1995) 'The Play of Conscience', in Andrew Parker and Eve Kosofsky Sedgwick (eds) *Performativity and Performance*, London: Routledge.

Pater, Walter (1889) 'Style', in *Appreciations: With an Essay on Style*, London: Macmillan, pp. 1–36.

Pavis, Patrice (1983) 'Socio-Criticism', trans. Helen Knode, *Theater* **15** (1: Winter).

Pavis, Patrice (1992) *Theatre at the Crossroads of Culture*, trans. Loren Kruger, London: Routledge.

Pavis, Patrice (ed.) (1996) *The Intercultural Performance Reader*, London: Routledge.

Pavis, Patrice (2000) 'Theory and Practice in Theatre Studies in the University', *Studies in Theatre and Performance* **20** (2): 68–86.

Percy, Thomas (1765) *Reliques of Ancient English Poetry*, three volumes, London.

Pfister, Manfred (1993) *The Theory and Analysis of Drama*, trans. John Halliday, Cambridge: Cambridge University Press.

Phelan, Peggy (1993) *Unmarked: The Politics of Performance*, London: Routledge.

Phelan, Peggy (1997) *Mourning Sex: Performing Public Memories*, London: Routledge.

Pitkin, H.F. (1967) *The Concept of Representation*, Berkeley: University of California Press.

Plant, Sadie (1992) *Most Radical Gesture: Situationist International in a Postmodern Age*, London: Routledge.

Polanyi, Michael (1967) *The Tacit Dimension*, London: Routledge & Kegan Paul.

Pollock, Griselda (1987) 'Feminism and Modernism', in Rozsika Parker and Griselda Pollock (eds) *Framing Feminism: Art and the Women's Movement 1970–1985*, London: Pandora, pp. 79–122.

Pontbriand, Chantal (1982) 'The Eye Finds no Fixed Point on Which to Rest . . . ', trans. C.R. Parsons, *Modern Drama* **25** (1): 154–62.

Postlewait, Thomas and McConachie, Bruce A. (eds) (1989) *Interpreting the Theatrical Past: Essays in the Historiography of Performance*, Iowa City: University of Iowa Press.

Puchner, Martin (2002) *Stage Fright: Modernism, Anti-Theatricality, and Drama*, Baltimore: Johns Hopkins University Press.

Redfield, Robert (1962) 'Civilizations as Cultural Structures', in Margaret Park Redfield (ed.) *Human Nature and the Study of Society*, Chicago: University of Chicago Press.

Reinelt, Janelle G. (1992) 'Introduction: Feminisms', in Janelle G. Reinelt and Joseph Roach (eds) *Critical Theory and Performance*, Ann Arbor: University of Michigan Press.

Reinelt, Janelle G. and Roach, Joseph R. (eds) (1992) *Critical Theory and Performance*, Ann Arbor: University of Michigan Press.

Reinhardt, Nancy S. (1981) 'New Directions for Feminist Criticism in Theatre and the Related Arts', in Elizabeth Langland and Walter Gove (eds) *A Feminist Perspective in the Academy: The Difference it Makes*, Chicago: University of Chicago Press.

Rich, Adrienne (1980) 'Toward a Woman-centered University' (1973–4), in *On Lies, Secrets and Silence*, London: Virago.

Roach, Joseph R. (1993) *The Player's Passion: Studies in the Science of Acting*, Ann Arbor: University of Michigan Press.

Rose, Martial (1979) *The Development of Drama in Higher Education, 1946–1979*, Winchester: Winchester Research Papers in the Humanities.

Rozik, Eli (2002) *The Roots of Theatre: Rethinking Ritual and other Theories of Origin*, Iowa City: University of Iowa Press.

Sandford, Mariellen R. (ed.) (1995) *Happenings and Other Acts*, London: Routledge.

Savage, George (1959) 'American Colleges and Universities and the Professional Theatre', *New Theatre Magazine: The Quarterly Magazine of Repertory and University Drama* 1 (October): 8–12.

Savran, David (1988) *Breaking the Rules: The Wooster Group*, New York: Theatre Communications Group.

Sayre, Henry M. (1989) *The Object of Performance: The American Avant-Garde Since 1970*, London: University of Chicago Press.

Schechner, Richard (1988) *Performance Theory*, London: Routledge.

Schechner, Richard (1992) 'A New Paradigm for Theatre in the Academy', *The Drama Review* **36** (4): 7–10.

Schechner, Richard (1996) interviewed by Patrice Pavis, 'Interculturalism and the Culture of Choice', in Patrice Pavis (ed.) *The Intercultural Performance Reader*, London: Routledge.

Schechner, Richard (2002) *Performance Studies: An Introduction*, London: Routledge.

Schiller, Friedrich (1989) *On the Aesthetic Education of Man in a Series of Letters*, trans. Reginald Snell, New York: Continuum.

Schneider, Rebecca (1997) *The Explicit Body in Performance*, London: Routledge.

Servos, Norbert (1984) *Pina Bausch-Wuppertal Dance Theater, or, The Art of Training a Goldfish*, Cologne: Ballett Bühnen Verlag.

Shepherd, Simon and Womack, Peter (1996) *English Drama: A Cultural History*, Oxford: Blackwell.

Sidney, Philip (1975) *A Defence of Poetry*, ed. J.A. Van Druten, Oxford: Oxford University Press.

Singer, Milton (ed.) (1959) *Traditional India: Structure and Change*, Philadelphia: The American Folklore Society.

Singer, Milton (1972) *When a Great Tradition Modernizes: An Anthropological Approach to Indian Civilization*, London: Pall Mall Press.

Smith, A.C.H. (1972) *Orghast at Persepolis: An Account of the Experiment in Theatre Directed by Peter Brook and Written by Ted Hughes*, London: Eyre Methuen.

Smith, Owen (1998) 'Developing a Fluxable Forum: Early Performance and Publishing', in Ken Friedman (ed.) *The Fluxus Reader*, Chichester: Academy Editions.

Southern, Richard (1948) *The Georgian Playhouse*, London: Pleiades Books.

Soyinka, Wole (1988) 'The Fourth Stage: Through the Mysteries of Ogun to the Origin of Yoruba Tragedy', in *Art, Dialogue and Outrage: Essays on Literature and Culture*, Ibadan: New Horn Press.

Spolin, Viola (1963) *Improvisation for the Theatre: A Handbook of Teaching and Directing Technique*, London: Pitman Publishing.

Spurgeon, Caroline (1935) *Shakespeare's Imagery and What it Tells Us*, Cambridge: Cambridge University Press.

Stanislavsky, Konstantin (1936) *An Actor Prepares*, trans. E.R. Hapgood, London: Geoffrey Bles.

Stanislavsky, Konstantin (1951) *Building a Character*, trans. E.R. Hapgood, London: Reinhardt & Evans.

Stanislavsky, Konstantin (1963) *Creating a Role*, trans. E.R. Hapgood, London: Geoffrey Bles.

States, Bert O. (1992) 'The Phenomenological Attitude', in Janelle G. Reinelt and Joseph R. Roach (eds) *Critical Theory and Performance*, Ann Arbor: University of Michigan Press.

Stiles, Kristine (1990) 'Performance and its Objects', *Arts Magazine* **65** (3: November): 35–47.

Stiles, Kristine (ed.) (1998) *Out of Actions: Between Performance and the Object 1949–79*, curated by Paul Schimmel, London: Thames & Hudson.

Styan, J.L. (1971) *Drama, Stage and Audience*, Cambridge: Cambridge University Press.

Sutton-Smith, Brian (1979) 'Epilogue: Play as Performance', in Brian Sutton-Smith (ed.) *Play and Learning*, New York: Gardiner Press.

Suvin, Darko (1970) 'Reflections on Happenings', *The Drama Review*, **14** (3): 125–44.

Taussig, Michael (1993) *Mimesis and Alterity: A Particular History of the Senses*, London: Routledge.

Thomson, George (1973) *Aeschylus and Athens*, London: Lawrence & Wishart.

Turnbull, Colin (1990) 'Liminality: A Synthesis of Subjective and Objective Experience' in Richard Schechner and Willa Appel (eds) *By Means of Performance: Intercultural Studies of Theatre and Ritual*, Cambridge: Cambridge University Press.

Turner, Victor (1975) *Drama, Fields, and Metaphors: Symbolic Action in Human Society*, Ithaca, NY and London: Cornell University Press.

Turner, Victor (1982) *From Ritual to Theatre: The Human Seriousness of Play*, New York: PAJ Publications.

Turner, Victor (1992) *The Anthropology of Performance*, New York: PAJ Publications.

Turner, Victor (1995) *The Ritual Process: Structure and Anti-Structure*, New York: Aldine de Gruyter.

Ubersfeld, Anne (1981) *L'école du spectateur*, Paris: Editions Sociales.

Vanden Heuvel, Michael (1991) *Performing Drama/Dramatizing Performance: Alternative Theater and the Dramatic Text*, Ann Arbor: University of Michigan Press.

Vernant, Jean-Pierre and Vidal-Naquet, Pierre (1990) *Myth and Tragedy in Ancient Greece*, trans. Janet Lloyd, New York: Zone Books.

Vince, R.W. (1989) 'Theatre History as an Academic Discipline', in Thomas Postlewait and Bruce McConachie (eds) *Interpreting the Theatrical Past: Essays in the Historiography of Performance*, Iowa City: University of Iowa Press.

Walzer, Robert (1993) *Running with the Devil: Power, Gender, and Madness in Heavy Metal Music*, Hanover, NH: University Press of New England.

Warton, Thomas (1774–81) *History of English Poetry*, three volumes, London.

Webber, M., Stephens, C. and Laughlin, C.D (1983) 'Masks: A Re-examination, or "Masks? You mean they affect the brain?"', in N.R. Crumrine and M. Halpin (eds) *The Power of Symbols: Masks and Masquerade in the Americas*, Vancouver: University of British Columbia Press.

Whitford, Margaret (1991) *Luce Irigaray: Philosophy in the Feminine*, London and New York: Routledge.

Whitford, Margaret (ed.) (1994) *The Irigaray Reader*, Oxford: Blackwell.

Wickham, Glynne (1962) *Drama in a World of Science and Three Other Lectures*, London: Routledge & Kegan Paul.

Wiles, Timothy J. (1980) *The Theater Event: Modern Theories of Performance*, Chicago: University of Chicago Press.

Willett, John (1977) *The Theatre of Bertolt Brecht*, London: Eyre Methuen.

Williams, David (1996) 'Remembering the Others that Are Us: Transculturalism and Myth in the Theatre of Peter Brook', in Patrice Pavis (ed.) *The Intercultural Performance Reader*, London: Routledge.

Williams, Raymond (1966) *Modern Tragedy*, London: Chatto & Windus.

Williams, Raymond (1973) *Drama from Ibsen to Brecht*, Harmondsworth: Penguin.

Williams, Raymond (1981) *Culture*, London: Fontana.

Williams, Raymond (1983) *Writing in Society*, London: Verso.

Wilson. F.P. and Wilson, John Dover (1956) *Sir Edmund Kerchever Chambers 1866–1954*, Proceedings of the British Academy, Vol. 42, London: Oxford University Press.

Wollen, Peter (1993) *Raiding the Icebox: Reflections on Twentieth-Century Culture*, London: Verso.

Woodruff, Paul (1992) 'Aristotle on *Mimesis*', in A.O. Rorty (ed.) *Essays on Aristotle's Poetics*, Princeton: Princeton University Press.

Wooler, T.J. (ed.) (1814–16) *The Stage*, London.

Wooler, T.J. (ed.) (1817–24) *The Black Dwarf*, London.

Worthen, W.B. (1995) 'Disciplines of the Text/Sites of Performance', *The Drama Review* **39** (1): 13–28.

Elizabeth Wright (1989) *Postmodern Brecht: A Re-presentation*, London: Routledge.

Wyndham, H.S. (1906) *The Annals of Covent Garden Theatre from 1732 to 1897*, two volumes, London: Chatto & Windus.

Zarrilli, Phillip B. (1986) 'Towards a Definition of Performance Studies', Parts 1 and 2, *Theatre Journal* (October): 372–6; (November): 493–6.

Zurbrugg, Nicholas (1998) 'A spirit of large goals: Fluxus, Dada and Postmodern Cultural Theory at Two Speeds', in Ken Friedman (ed.) *The Fluxus Reader*, Chichester: Academy Editions.

INDEX